**PERGAMON GENERAL PSYCHOLOGY SERIES**
EDITORS
Arnold P. Goldstein, *Syracuse University*
Leonard Krasner, *SUNY at Stony Brook*

# Child Behavior Analysis and Therapy
## Second Edition

## Donna M. Gelfand
## Donald P. Hartmann
*University of Utah*

**PERGAMON PRESS**
New York    Oxford    Toronto    Sydney    Paris    Frankfurt

Pergamon Press Offices:

**U.S.A.**        Pergamon Press Inc., Maxwell House, Fairview Park,
Elmsford, New York 10523, U.S.A.

**U.K.**         Pergamon Press Ltd., Headington Hill Hall,
Oxford OX3 0BW, England

**CANADA**        Pergamon Press Canada Ltd., Suite 104, 150 Consumers Road,
Willowdale, Ontario M2J 1P9, Canada

**AUSTRALIA**      Pergamon Press (Aust.) Pty. Ltd., P.O. Box 544,
Potts Point, NSW 2011, Australia

**FRANCE**        Pergamon Press SARL, 24 rue des Ecoles,
75240 Paris, Cedex 05, France

**FEDERAL REPUBLIC**   Pergamon Press GmbH, Hammerweg 6,
**OF GERMANY**     D-6242 Kronberg-Taunus, Federal Republic of Germany

**Copyright © 1984 Pergamon Press, Inc.**

**Library of Congress Cataloging in Publication Data**

Gelfand, Donna M., 1937-

Child behavior analysis and therapy.

Bibliography: p.
Includes indexes.
1. Behavior therapy. 2. Child psychotherapy.
3. Behavioral assessment in children. I. Hartmann,
Donald P. II. Title. [DNLM: 1. Behavior therapy--In
infancy and childhood. WS 350.6 G316c]
RJ505.B4G44      1984      618.92'8914      83-24356
ISBN 0-08-028054-4
ISBN 0-08-028053-6 (pbk.)

Cover photo: John Telford

*Printed in the United States of America*

PERGAMON INTERNATIONAL LIBRA
of Science, Technology, Engineering and Social Studies

*The 1000-volume original paperback library in aid of educa
industrial training and the enjoyment of leisure*

Publisher: Robert Maxwell, M.C.

recommended for adoption for class use an
of 12 or more copies the inspection copy m
The Publishers will be pleased to receive su
titles to be published in this important inter

# Pergamon Titles of Related Interest

**Cartledge/Milburn** TEACHING SOCIAL SKILLS TO CHILDREN:
Innovative Approaches, Second Edition

**Karoly/Steffen/O'Grady** CHILD HEALTH PSYCHOLOGY: Concepts
and Issues

**Morris/Kratochwill** THE PRACTICE OF CHILD THERAPY

**Morris/Kratochwill** TREATING CHILDREN'S FEARS AND PHOBIAS:
A Behavioral Approach

**Ollendick/Hersen** CHILD BEHAVIORAL ASSESSMENT: Principles
and Procedures

**Schwartz/Johnson** PSYCHOPATHOLOGY OF CHILDHOOD: A
Clinical-Experimental Approach, Second Edition

**Varni** CLINICAL BEHAVIORAL PEDIATRICS: An Interdisciplinary
Bio-behavioral Approach

# Related Journals*

ANALYSIS AND INTERVENTION IN DEVELOPMENTAL DISABILITIES
APPLIED RESEARCH IN MENTAL RETARDATION
BEHAVIORAL ASSESSMENT
JOURNAL OF CHILD PSYCHOLOGY AND PSYCHIATRY

**\*Free specimen copies available upon request.**

# Contents

# PREFACE

Like its predecessor, this edition of *Child Behavior Analysis and Therapy* is designed to help students complete nearly every aspect of a child behavior therapy project, from obtaining consent to work with a particular child to the final step of writing a paper describing the project and its outcome. The intended audience for this book consists of graduate and undergraduate students and includes practicing professionals who may not have worked with children or used behavior therapy techniques. It would help, but is not strictly necessary, to have completed some previous coursework on social learning or behavioral principles and behavior therapy techniques. The book is meant to be used as a text in classes or in individually supervised practica in child behavior therapy or special education. This is not a how-to-do-it manual for solo use without clinical supervision, but is designed to be used as an aid in supervised instruction. Perhaps more than other educational endeavors, learning clinical and counseling practice requires continuous sensitive and informed supervision. Therapeutic errors are costly and must be avoided because some portion of the client's welfare may be at stake.

However, with appropriate supervision, this book can be used to assist the student in:

- recruiting the help of child clients and their caretakers

- conducting behavioral assessments

- developing data collection methods

- checking observational reliability

- collecting data bearing on treatment success

- increasing the frequency or intensity of desirable behaviors

- decreasing the frequency or intensity of undesirable behaviors

- increasing the generalization and durability of treatment effects

- demonstrating experimental control of the target behavior

- graphing or otherwise analyzing the data

- phasing out and concluding the therapy program

- preparing a written report of the program and its results

Students need not be intimidated by this lengthy list of behavioral objectives. No one intervention program is likely to touch upon all of the contents of this book. The child's problem and circumstances will determine the particular assessment, therapy, and data analysis methods to be employed. The book aims to be complete, so we have included the various intervention tactics most commonly used at the present time. Also, we have indicated tactics to be avoided by novices because of their difficulty in design and application or because there are insufficient data on their effectiveness.

Thus the constituent parts of behavioral assessment and therapy receive extensive consideration, including both the scientific aspects and the informal skills useful in building and maintaining rapport with the child and the child's parents and teachers. The latter valuable but usually informally taught clinical skills can determine the outcome of a therapy attempt. Above all, we hope to assist the student in appropriately involving the therapy participants — the child and caretakers — in as many aspects of the intervention as possible. If treatment efforts are to be successful and the effects enduring, the therapist cannot be the major source of influence, because usually the therapist will be available only for a limited time. In the longer term, the child and her associates must be helped to become the regulators. As the book will explain, we know little as yet about enhancing the generality and durability of treatment effects. However, we do know that every effort must be made to do so if therapeutic gains are to be meaningful.

Much has changed since the first edition of this book was published in 1975. The traditional ties to the animal learning area have weakened somewhat as behavior therapists have come to better understand and use children's remarkable cognitive and linguistic abilities. Older research reports typically utilized nonverbal prompting and shaping procedures as well as tangible reinforcers in programs resembling those of the animal learning experiments. These procedures were of demonstrated utility, but mainly with the severely developmentally delayed, who were only minimally responsive to verbal cues. In time the clientele changed and diversified so that more children of normal or near-normal intelligence and language abilities participated in behavior therapy or special education programs. It is unnecessarily slow and awkward to work with these children mainly through nonverbal means. Consequently, the animal learning-derived theoretical models and training procedures were less helpful, and more cognitive ones assumed new importance. Times and practices have changed; this edition emphasizes the utility of taking advantage of typically human abilities and devising effective verbal methods of intervention. The increasing emphasis on verbal interchanges in child assessment and therapy reflects the field's greater reliance on contributions from developmental and cognitive psychology. Too, the child behavior therapy field has become generally more eclectic. The basic commitment to objective evaluation continues, but now assessment and treatment methods might be drawn from nearly any aspect of psychology and education, and not from just learning or clinical practice.

Another new feature of the revised edition is the extended consideration of the ethics of various types of child interventions. In the past decade, professional organizations, legislatures, and the judiciary have codified the ethical use of clinical and educational procedures. This book features these ethical guidelines, since they apply regardless of who — master therapist or beginner — is working with a child. It is especially important that novices learn the ethics of therapeutic practice, because of the danger that students are more aware of their immediate need to perform well and obtain a good grade or evaluation than of the nature of their clients' needs. In contrast, experienced practitioners experience less evaluation pressure in their clinical work.

We believe that more is to be learned from administering a treatment intervention directly than from instructing caretakers in doing so, particularly for inexperienced child therapists. The therapist who lacks first-hand experience may find it difficult to devise feasible and effective interventions for others' use. Accordingly, this book is directed toward training readers in the direct administration of treatment programs. However, those who wish to guide others in program administration will find useful information here as well.

In accordance with our preference for behavioral specificity in clinical work, we have provided guideposts for determining students' mastery of the material. Behavioral objectives precede each section and inform readers of what they should know after reading that chapter section. Immediately following each section is a list of probe questions to test the student's mastery of the information. The probe questions can be used by students as tests of their knowledge, or can be used in a similar fashion by instructors in conducting individual student interviews or in written examinations. A project checklist is also provided to remind the student to complete each required step in the behavior modification project. Typical student-designed projects are ambitious in scope and the academic term is usually too brief to complete them. Therefore, students are advised to design projects with modest goals, and instructors might find it useful to ask students for midterm progress reports so that plans can be revised as necessary.

Features new to this second edition include a lengthier presentation of therapy techniques that have grown in popularity in the interim such as response reduction methods positive practice and restitutional overcorrection, verbal criticism, and response cost. New and more varied reinforcement tactics receive extended consideration, as does the importance of assessing a therapy program's social validity or consumer acceptability. New developments in the experimental design and analysis field are reflected in the more extensive consideration given the simultaneous and the changing criterion designs.

Finally, we have adopted a new writing style designed to minimize sexist language. Rather than invariably referring to hypothesized individuals in the masculine gender, we have interspersed masculine and feminine pronouns. This may not entirely solve the problem, however, because one sharp-eyed student noted our intended solution, and complained that we had a negative bias toward girls. The student felt that rather than using the traditional masculine gender in describing children with psychotic, retarded, or hyperactive behavior, we referred to some of the children as "she." (Actually the student incorrectly perceived us as exclusively using feminine pronouns.) We are at a loss to know how to pacify everyone, but hope that readers will accept our solution in the egalitarian spirit in which it was intended.

As a glance at the References section will indicate, many different researchers have participated in the development and evaluation of behavioral assessment and therapy techniques that are covered in this book. We are indebted to all of them. We are grateful to our teachers, particularly to Albert Bandura who had a profound influence on our professional and oenological interests. Quinn McNemar's influence is reflected in the methodology and analysis chapters of this book. Many of our associates and students offered help in various forms. The following reviewers' suggestions were most useful in the preparation of the second edition: Billy A. Barrios, University of Mississippi; John P. Foreyt, Baylor College of Medicine, Houston, Texas; James H. Johnson, University of Florida; Robert J. McMahon, University of British Columbia; and William Pfohl, Western Kentucky University. We are grateful to John Hodge, Carol Shigetomi, and Lynne Zarbatany for their helpful suggestions; to Paul Vinciguerra for his work in locating references and in critiquing several chapters; and to Andrea Stavros for superb typing and editing. Hilde Varah and Kathleen Luker also were invaluable typists and assistants. Pergamon Senior Editor Jerome Frank helped us by being at once marvelously patient and appropriately demanding. His expertise made this second edition possible. Grant Number HD 06914 from the National Institute of Child Health and Human Development supported some of the research described in these pages. Finally, we appreciate our families' willingness to wait while we wrote just one more page. Over many repetitions this produced the number of pages in this book. Sid Gelfand and Barbara Hartmann: We couldn't have done it without you.

D.M.G.
D.P.H.

# Chapter 1
# INTRODUCTION

## Behavioral Objectives for Chapter 1, Section 1

*Study of Section 1 will allow you to:*

1. *Distinguish between child behavior therapy and other treatment approaches.*

2. *Enumerate the types of skills and knowledge required of a competent child behavior therapist.*

3. *Recognize and respond effectively to misguided conceptions of behavior therapy.*

## SECTION 1. INTRODUCTION

This book presents a description of contemporary behavior therapy and applied behavior analysis procedures for use in treating children's behavior problems. That is an ambitious aim, to be sure, because the past 20 years have seen the development of a great many behavior analysis and behavior change techniques. In fact, there are so many different approaches to child behavior therapy that the field might best be considered an aggregate of various intervention strategies, all sharing a few key features. Perhaps the most central defining characteristic of the behavioral approach is a commitment to continuing empirical evaluation of treatment effectiveness. In theory, an evaluative orientation could be compatible with almost any type of psychotherapy; but in practice, behavior therapists are particularly noted for their strong allegiance to objective treatment evaluation.

A second defining feature of behavior therapy is its basis in knowledge derived from psychological research (Ross, 1978). Initially, behavior therapists insisted that their techniques were drawn nearly totally from learning principles and from procedures developed in laboratory research on learning, especially from carefully controlled studies conducted with animal subjects. For example, Eysenck (1959) claimed that behavior modification represented an advance over earlier, less effective psychodynamic formulations in that behavior modification had an empirical and scientific base stemming from "modern learning theory." However, in recent years contributions to behavior therapy have come from new areas of research which are far afield from learning theory. For example, the study of causal attributions, the properties of social systems, and new developments in cognitive psychology in general all have been fruitfully incorporated into behavior therapy programs. Over the years the scope of the field has considerably broadened and diversified, a trend which probably will continue for some time (O'Leary & Carr, 1982).

It would be incorrect to conclude that nearly any intervention approach could legitimately wear the behavioral banner, however. Despite their apparent contrasts, most types of behavior therapy share the following common features (Kazdin, 1978):

1. A focus on contemporary determinants of behavior rather than a search for early life events which might affect current behavior patterns.

2. A belief that overt behavior change is the most important criterion for use in treatment evaluation. Other changes may be important as well (e.g., the client's feelings of satisfaction with the outcome), but no other criterion outweighs observable changes in the client's behavior.

3. Specification of treatment techniques to the point that replication by other therapists is possible. This may require the use of videotaped or filmed demonstrations, but, no matter what the presentation medium, the therapist's techniques should be clearly described and communicated.

4. Basing treatment philosophy and techniques on controlled psychological research, rather than on clinical folklore or unverified theories.

5. Having precision and specificity in defining and measuring, as well as in treating the behaviors which are the targets of the therapeutic intervention.

Treatment approaches which fail to meet most of the preceding criteria are best described as something other than behavior modification or behavior therapy. However, failure to meet *all* of the criteria does not disbar a treatment from being labeled behavior therapy.

Like any popular field of inquiry, behavior therapy is a dynamic one, growing and changing as a result of its own particular successes and failures. Along with the trend toward incorporation of diverse aspects of psychological knowledge has come an increasing appreciation for the subtlety and complexity of the therapeutic endeavor. Early enthusiasts proclaimed the apparent simplicity of the behavior modification process and were delighted with its clear conceptual basis and straightforward techniques which lent themselves to use by parents, teachers, and others who ordinarily are responsible for socializing and educating children (Gelfand & Hartmann, 1975). In comparison, traditional approaches to psychotherapy were seen as indirect and relatively ineffective, relying on highly trained professional therapists and requiring extended treatment periods. Behavioral therapists shunned the elaborate conceptual and procedural trappings of the psychodynamic approach.

Although those points of contrast still hold true, present-day behavior therapists recognize that changing isolated problem behaviors in particular settings may leave major sources of difficulty untouched. For example, it may be possible to reduce the frequency of a child's temper tantrums at home without rendering his parents less hostile and demanding, his teacher more supportive, his homework more adequate, or his social interactions with schoolmates more skillful. Although in some cases successfully treating a single inappropriate behavior adequately addresses the child's problem, in others one must recognize the contributions of factors such as the mother's social isolation (Wahler, 1980), the maladaptive family social system (Alexander, Barton, Schievo, & Parsons, 1976), the family's resistance to change (Patterson, 1982), their and the community's beliefs concerning the advisability of change, and the appropriateness of the means by which the change is effected (Wolf, 1978). Moreover, it may be necessary to teach children complex and subtle skills such as what to say to agemates and how to say it. At present, behaviorally oriented clinicians are concerning themselves with all of the preceding factors, which are recognized as important determinants of the therapeutic process.

Student therapists may be somewhat disappointed to learn that it can prove difficult to choose the target behaviors for therapeutic change and to identify the best treatment methods to produce that change. Children's behavioral patterns are complex, and may differ markedly in various social contexts and over time. Consequently, it can be a challenge to decide which behavior to select for change, how to modify it, and in which context to do so. Recent research by Wilson and Evans (1983) has suggested a considerable degree of disagreement among behavior therapists regarding the selection of the target behavior for initial modification. Perhaps we should not be too surprised to find a diversity of opinion regarding just which behaviors therapists should select for modification. Whether to and how to exert social influence to alter another person's behavior is a complex social and ethical issue. As we shall argue in Chapter 2, many different people have a legitimate role in determining the aim and the nature of the therapeutic enterprise. The result is that the therapist's task often proves more formidable than a cursory reading of the literature would suggest.

In addition, therapists encounter conflicting claims for efficacy by proponents of different treatment approaches. For example, some writers advise limiting ourselves to the study of overt, observable behaviors (Baer, Wolf, & Risley, 1968; Skinner, 1953b). Others believe that individuals' behavior problems are based on their thinking processes and perceptions, and that the faulty thought processes must be altered in order to change behavior patterns (Beck, 1974; Meichenbaum, 1977). These two conceptual approaches hardly could be more diverse, yet both qualify as legitimate variants of contemporary behavior therapy. The existence of such extreme alternatives can thoroughly confuse novice therapists. For example, to treat fearful and avoidant behavior, one might embark on a program of systematic desensitization, implosion or flooding, relaxation, assertion, modeling either with or without guided participation, or self-instructional talk (see Chapters 5, 6, and 7 for descriptions of these techniques). Choosing intelligently among these alternatives requires an up-to-date knowledge of the relevant treatment evaluation research literature. This book aims to help students make such choices from among the better established and evaluated interventions by summarizing the information available on each technique's efficacy, and by offering interested readers suggestions regarding sources of information on techniques of special interest to them.

Behavior therapists must be familiar with many aspects of psychology. As Kalish (1981) has pointed out, behavior therapy is not a collection of standard techniques, but, instead, requires some acquaintance with behavior principles (and, one might add, with cognitive processes as well). The therapist must draw on many bodies of knowledge in order to formulate the treatment plan with the greatest chance of success. This means translating information about the nature of the child's problem and circumstances and about psychological processes and methods into a concrete plan of action to counteract the problem. There is nothing cut-and-dried about such a problem-solving effort — conducting child behavior therapy is not easy, but it can be immensely rewarding.

As previously suggested, choosing a target behavior and an intervention technique are only part of the process. In addition, the therapist must conduct a careful functional analysis of the effects of the treatment intervention. Here again some specialized knowledge is required. What type of experimental design and what, if any, statistical data analysis are appropriate? Fully half of the chapters of this book are dedicated to the task of teaching student therapists what they will need to know in order to evaluate the effectiveness of their work. This heavy emphasis on evaluation faithfully reflects the empirical bias of the behavioral approach. We evaluate what we do.

To summarize the preceding discussion, the behavioral approach to therapy is characterized by a foundation in an increasingly broad range of psychological theory and empirical research, and an abiding commitment to specificity, precision, and continuous evaluation of the treatment process. The treatment's effectiveness must constantly be examined in an objective, systematic fashion, taking into account not only the degree of behavior change accomplished, but the change's impact on the client and affected others.

## *Misconceptions About Behavior Therapy*

Perhaps undeservedly, behavior therapists face a certain degree of public hostility to their theories and practices. Although it can be argued legitimately that behavioral techniques are merely tools which can be used either constructively or punitively (Redd & Sleator, 1978), some critics charge that behavioral techniques rob clients of self-determination, and deny them their rights to privacy, comfortable surroundings, recreation, and considerate treatment. In fact, some treatment programs have been legislatively and judicially directed to cease withholding amenities such as access to television sets, adequate meals delivered on time, comfortable furniture, privacy, etc., even though making such attractive items contingent upon improved behavior has proved to be an effective treatment technique (see the judicial ruling in *Wyatt v. Stickney*). At present, the legal prerogatives of those who serve as treatment agents and clients are being increasingly specified, and later we shall describe the current guidelines and requirements for the treatment of clients by therapists as we discuss each individual intervention technique. In general, however, we advocate that therapists make every effort to treat their child clients with consideration, respecting their autonomy and dignity, and permitting them as much determination in the nature and goals of the therapy intervention as is consistent with their level of understanding. Table 1-1 presents a suggested "Bill of Rights" for children receiving psychological treatment. The list of rights is based more on the consideration of children's feelings in the matter of treatment than on any body of laws.

**Table 1-1.** A "Bill of Rights" for Children in Psychotherapy

1. *The Right To Be Told the Truth.* Children should be informed of events that affect them and should never be lied to by the therapist. As Ross (1980) has stated, "When children are old enough to be talked to, they are old enough to be told the truth" (p. 68).

2. *The Right To Be Treated as a Person.* This implies that the child's right to privacy and confidentiality should be respected and the therapist should not divulge information shared by the child in treatment sessions nor should sessions be recorded or observed without the child's knowledge or permission.

3. *The Right To Be Taken Seriously.* The therapist, in particular, should listen carefully to the child and neither dismiss nor make light of the child's observations, opinions, or feelings.

4. *The Right To Participate in Decision Making.* Like adults, children should be allowed to express their opinions in matters involving their lives, and their opinions should carry some weight. Too often adults make the important decisions involving children and only later inform the children. Therapists surely should not behave in this cavalier fashion toward children.

Reproduced from Gelfand, Jenson, and Drew, 1982, p. 455.

It is advisable for behavior therapists to inform themselves about the existence and nature of prejudices against behavioral approaches. Otherwise, they run the risk of alarming or antagonizing potential clients and others who could support the therapy program. There is now a small, but growing research literature concerning perceptions of behavioral treatment programs. The research findings indicate that college undergraduate students, at least, do show some antipathy toward the terminology and conceptual basis of behavior modification. The students tend to consider interventions more acceptable when they are described in the language of personal growth and humanism than when exactly the same interventions are described more mechanistically in terms of reinforcement contingency management (Kazdin & Cole, 1981; Woolfolk & Woolfolk, 1979; Woolfolk, Woolfolk, & Wilson, 1977). In general, the less coercive treatment techniques find wider acceptance than the harsher ones, which appear to leave little choice or independence to the client (Kazdin, 1981b). Since behavior modification techniques are generally perceived as coercive in nature, it is hardly surprising that they lack popular appeal.

Suggested remedies to allay suspicion regarding behavioral treatments have ranged from relabeling the procedures in more acceptable terms to strictly limiting the use of the more obtrusive techniques. Saunders and Reppucci (1978) have advised replacing labels such as behavior modification with less negatively perceived ones, and Wilson and Evans (1978) suggested humanizing the language of behavior therapy, especially since there is some question concerning the utility of terminology borrowed from animal learning experiments as applied to human functioning. In addition, behavior therapists must make special efforts to be flexible, friendly, and supportive in dealing with clients and their families, teachers, and associates. Student therapists who lack professional status and are working under considerable time and evaluation pressure may find their situation somewhat uncomfortable at first. They can unknowingly create suspicion and resentment by appearing inflexible, cold, businesslike, and preoccupied with their own needs and performance and with the rate of progress of their therapy projects. The entire behavior therapy field, not just the individual therapist, suffers from such self-preoccupation and resulting negative reactions. Appropriate presentation of oneself, expressions of appropriate concern for the welfare of the client and others, and appreciation of legitimate, existing constraints on the availability of resources and cooperation from others all are vital to the successful conduct of a therapy program, and to the advancement of behavior therapy in general. Scientific method and concern for others go hand-in-hand in the behavior therapy endeavor.

# Probe Questions for Chapter 1, Section 1

1. *Dr. J. attempts to enhance her child therapy client's self-esteem by rewarding the boy with praise and points each time he says something positive about himself. Is this an example of behavior therapy? Explain the basis for your conclusion.*

2. *State the five features characteristic of behavior therapy.*

3. *What are some of the problems facing the behavior therapist who works with children?*

4. *What rights should child-clients have?*

5. *What suggestions would you give to someone who wished to increase the public acceptability of behavioral approaches to therapy?*

## Behavioral Objectives for Chapter 1, Section 2

*After reading Section 2, you should be able to:*

1. *Budget your time so that you can complete your project and submit a written report in the time available.*

2. *Identify likely sources of potential child-clients.*

3. *Consider the advantages and disadvantages of working with a partner.*

## SECTION 2. HOW TO USE THIS BOOK

How do you learn to conduct behavior therapy with children? The same way in which you learn any very complex skill, whether playing a musical instrument, eating with chopsticks, or learning a foreign language. The task seems insuperably difficult at first, because so many different things must be done at the same time. At nearly the same time, the therapist must enlist the cooperation of key people in an agency, school, or family in order to procure a child-client, become acquainted with the child, and select a target behavior for treatment. That is not all, because the therapist also must comb the literature for descriptions of treatment programs for that target behavior, select an experimental design for use in demonstrating treatment effectiveness, prepare a precise operational definition of the target behavior, construct a usable data collection procedure, and assess the reliability of observation of the target behavior. Finally, in the happy event that the student has survived the preceding hurdles, a detailed report of the entire process must be prepared and turned in to the instructor.

Perhaps the best way to get a feeling for what will be required is to skim the entire book quickly before beginning your child behavior change project. You should review the entire list of procedures so you can budget your time reasonably and plan your program accordingly. Then, as you approach each portion of the program (for instance, the gathering of baseline data), you can study the appropriate material in more depth.

A word of warning: This type of project will require amazing amounts of time and effort. Do not embark on a behavior change project unless you are prepared to make the commitment and to meet a demanding schedule.

Carrying out many tasks nearly simultaneously can prove confusing at times. To help you remember the component steps of a behavior change project and the approximate order of their completion, we provide a project checklist (see Table 1-2). Each step in this checklist is accompanied by a notation indicating the chapters and sections relevant to that task.

**Table 1-2.** Checklist for Behavior Modification Project

| Place check here when completed | |
|---|---|
| _____ | 1. Choose target behavior and perform preliminary cost-benefit analysis (see Chapter 2). |
| _____ | 2. Obtain your supervisor's permission to treat this target behavior in this setting. |
| _____ | 3. Obtain school administrator's and/or parent's permission to observe the child (Chapter 2). |
| _____ | 4. Interview caretakers to help determine the nature of the child's problem (Chapter 2). |
| _____ | 5. Observe the child's behavior (Chapter 2). |
| _____ | 6. State your preliminary functional hypothesis and evaluate your hypothesis with further behavior observations, if necessary (Chapter 2). |
| _____ | 7. Define the target behavior (Chapters 2 and 3). |
| _____ | 8. Choose a design for demonstration of experimental control (Chapter 4). |
| _____ | 9. Make baseline observations and graph them (Chapters 3 and 9). |
| _____ | 10. Assess the reliability of your data (Chapter 8). |
| _____ | 11. Specify the treatment program to be used; write a script (Chapters 5, 6, and 7). |
| _____ | 12. Obtain consent from caretakers, supervisor, and child (if appropriate) to carry out this program (Chapters 2 and 5). |
| _____ | 13. Conduct the treatment program, keeping daily records of the child's behavior (Chapter 9). |
| _____ | 14. Demonstrate experimental control over the target behavior (Chapter 4). |
| _____ | 15. Continue to assess the reliability of your data (Chapter 8). |
| _____ | 16. Phase out program and, if possible, include procedures for increasing the durability and generalizability of treatment effects (Chapter 7). |
| _____ | 17. If possible, observe the child periodically after the termination of treatment to assess the rate of the target behavior (Chapter 9). |
| _____ | 18. Thank caretakers and child for their cooperation (Chapter 10, Section 3). |
| _____ | 19. Remove and restore any equipment you may have used. Clear up if necessary (Chapter 10, Section 3). |
| _____ | 20. Summarize your data on the effects of the treatment program (Chapter 10). |
| _____ | 21. Submit a report describing your program to supervisor and host school or agency (Chapter 10). |

Refer to the checklist throughout your project; this information should help you remember to complete each step and allow you to find the needed instructions easily. Consult your instructor before omitting any of the steps listed. When you have completed each portion of your project, place a check mark beside that item. This may not seem like a fantastic reinforcer, but it's better than nothing.

## Student Pairs

We recommend that students work in pairs in conducting their child behavior change projects. This working arrangement has several advantages over solo attempts. One of the most important considerations is that the child gets double the amount of treatment time, and thus probably can improve much faster than if there were only one therapist. The student therapists profit from having a partner as well. The two students can learn specific skills from each other and can conveniently check the reliability with which each conducts the sessions and observes and records the child's behavior. Since each student in a pair can serve as an independent observer, it is not necessary to arrange for some other person to come to the therapy session to serve as a reliability checker. Sometimes it is very difficult to talk someone else into traveling to the child's treatment agency, school, or home in order to help you check your reliability as an observer. And, since observers' accuracy can change over time, more than one reliability check will be required. Accurate, objective behavior recording is a vital element of child behavior analysis, so reliability checks are absolutely necessary. This is most easily accomplished by working in pairs, both members of which are available at the same time to check on the adequacy with which the therapeutic program is delivered as well as on the accuracy of behavior recording.

But partnership can have disadvantages also. The joint effort is somewhat like having a roommate. Partners who do not do their share in arranging for, in conducting, and in writing a report of the therapy process are much resented by their more careful, dependable, and compulsive co-workers. If you find yourself paired with someone who is not doing an appropriate amount of the work and leaving it to you, make alternate arrangements as soon as possible. Sometimes it is better to do a project alone.

## Obtaining Child Subjects

Now, the first of the challenges — where can one contact a child to serve as a behavior change client? In most instances, instructors ask the administrators of child treatment institutions, special education classes in public schools, and other such facilities for permission to allow students to work with the children there. The range of possible student therapist placements is very broad, including, but not limited to, daycare centers, nursery schools, and institutions serving the developmentally retarded, the physically handicapped, and the delinquent. Because their specific mission is to improve their child-clients' behavior, treatment institutions are likely to agree to participate.

They are especially pleased if they receive copies of the papers describing the students' projects and detailed instructions regarding each project so that the institution's staff can assume responsibility for conducting the interventions after the students' projects are terminated. It is both stimulating and bothersome to treatment staff to have students working in their institutions. Being unfamiliar with the agency's procedures and new to the treatment enterprise, student therapists can get in the way. This means that students and instructors must take particular care not to upset agencies' routines or devise intervention tactics that are at odds with the child's customary program.

Sometimes a student's schedule makes it nearly impossible to conduct a project at a school or agency. A project still can be completed, especially if there are children in the student's family or neighborhood who might profit from some behavioral improvement (and who could not?). In such cases, remember that parental permission is required before a child can be treated (see Chapter 2 for a description of how to go about obtaining parents' informed consent). Also, whenever feasible, the children themselves should freely agree to participate.

## The Interview Method

This book is designed for, but not limited to, use in an interview format. Individual interviews of students on assigned readings have two distinct advantages over the customary written forms of instruction: First, the students gain confidence in their ability to speak, and not merely to write, about the material. Somehow, writing mastery does not translate into proficiency in speaking about the work, but it is perfectly possible to do both through the combined use of the interview method and the traditional assignments such as exams and papers. A second advantage of the interview format is that students keep up with the reading assignments. There is no alternative; either one has read the material and is prepared for an interview, or it is embarrassingly obvious that this is not the case. Rather than being embarrassed, students generally complete reading assignments promptly. Since it seems clear that there are distinct advantages to the interview method, let us now present the ingredients of that instructional approach.

The interview method was inspired by the work of Keller (1966, 1968), and requires that the student satisfactorily demonstrate knowledge of each portion of the text in a recitation session with an interviewer. The beauty of this method is that the interviewer need not be the course instructor or a teaching assistant. Any class member who already has mastered the material to be covered in the interview is qualified to become an interviewer. This means that after having successfully been interviewed, each class member is prepared to serve as interviewer of other students. Students become instructors for their classmates, and they learn a lot in the process.

*How to carry out an interview.* The interview procedures devised by Ferster and Perrott (1968) yield impressive results in terms of students' mastery of the material, so it is basically their method that we present here. Those authors offer the following guidelines: The interview should be brief, no more than ten minutes per chapter section or brief chapter. Students who are thoroughly familiar with the material can summarize it readily in a few minutes. If the student becomes confused or introduces irrelevant material, the interview should be terminated and not resumed until the student has restudied the pertinent sections.

It is helpful to provide each student with a 3 × 5-inch index card bearing the student's name and listing each chapter and section for which he or she has successfully completed an interview. After each interview is completed the interviewer takes the card and notes the material covered, an act that gives the student some reinforcing feedback and provides a record of his or her progress. These records also allow instructors to monitor the rate of class members' progress so they can adjust the length of reading assignments if necessary.

Students: Do not be apprehensive about the interview process! It will seem strange and somewhat intimidating at first, but it will give you a gratifying grasp of the material, and you can impress others with more facts about the readings than they may want to know. And the function of the interview is instructional, not evaluative. If you cannot correctly summarize the chapter or answer a particular probe question, nothing tragic will happen. You simply will be asked to prepare further, and then request another interview on the same reading matter. The following examples should reassuringly illustrate correct and incorrect interviewer responses to a student's error in answering a question:

*Correct Interviewer Response:* "Can you think of any other guidelines for using an overcorrection program? If not let's have you read Section 3 again, and I'll interview you on it either today if we have time or next time for sure."

*Incorrect Interviewer Response:* "No, you shouldn't use overcorrection unless you have tried other, less aversive procedures, things like criticism and response cost. That's because of the general principle that you should use the least coercive, least intrusive procedures first." (This person is a true professor, but not a good interviewer.)

When you are serving as an interviewer, take special care not to appear distressed or punitive when students are unable to answer all the questions. A simple, matter-of-fact comment that the student should reread the section will suffice. Be careful not to give an interviewee credit for a questionable answer in order to spare his feelings. This is not a favor to him since he gets a false sense of mastery, which is soon dispelled in later interviews or in examinations.

Things are more pleasant when the student demonstrates mastery of the assignment. Then you can show appropriate enthusiasm for a good performance, and compliment the student on a fine job. He has worked hard and deserves some recognition for it.

Ferster and Perrott (1968) recommend that interviewers be businesslike and unobtrusive. An interviewer's function is to assess whether the student knows the material, not to chat or lecture. To achieve this goal, Ferster and Perrott instruct the interviewer to speak only on three occasions: (a) at the beginning of the interview or intermittently throughout to inform the student of the specific task (e.g., "Let's look at the probe questions for this part. Question 3 asks you what response cost is and when to use it."); (b) at the close of the student's answer to indicate topics omitted, or to ask that the student elaborate certain points (e.g., "What else can you tell me about setting up a favorable training environment?") or to inform him briefly about points he has misunderstood (e g., "You didn't get the part about the self-instructional training quite right. Let's cover that again next time."); and (c) at the close of the interview to recommend study methods or to suggest a faster or slower pace of progress, or to make some general remark.

The interview assessment is open book. During a recitation session, the interviewer asks the student to explain a graph, summarize a section, or answer selected probe questions. The student then turns to the relevant passages in the textbook and uses the book or his notes in responding to the interviewer's question. There is no need to memorize the text, but the student should be able to talk knowledgeably about it in a brief interview. Students should not engage in false heroism, such as refusing to refer to the book during the interview. This practice is needlessly stressful, and nothing is to be gained by it.

*Classroom interview procedures.* As mentioned previously, anyone who is thoroughly familiar with the subject matter can serve as an interviewer, whether instructor or class member. With larger classes, the instructor can interview several students before the beginning of the class period. Then those students who satisfactorily complete their own interviews can proceed to interview the other members of the class. There might be several interviews going on simultaneously in the classroom, and the instructor could sit in on some of the interviews to ensure that they are conducted properly and that the standards of acceptability do not vary too much among interviewers. This is seldom a problem, however, since interviewers tend to imitate their own interviewers in the questions they pose and the answers they accept.

We have found that the interview method lends itself well to a variety of instructional formats, thus providing the instructor many options. For example, interviews can cover all or only a portion of the assigned reading.

And interview sessions can constitute any segment of the class time that the instructor desires — a half hour, some other portion, or all of the scheduled class sessions. Moreover, students can be asked to study the reading assignments either during or outside of the scheduled class meeting times. Flexibility in grading procedures is also accommodated within the interview format. Passing the interviews can constitute a part of the class grade, in combination with written exams and a paper, and other grading arrangements are possible. Students who fail to complete interviews on all of the assigned readings could be penalized, or the interviews could just provide preparation for written exams. Many options are open. The interview method is extremely flexible and can be employed in a wide variety of contexts as determined by the instructor and the nature of the class.

## Overview

The field of child behavior therapy is an active and expanding one, and many different types of procedures sport the behavior therapy banner. Perhaps the single most defining feature is a commitment to objective evaluation of therapeutic procedures and to accountability. Child behavior therapy is no simple panacea for children's problems. In addition to modifying a single target behavior, it may be necessary to consider features of the family and the community which affect the child's behavior in order to treat the child effectively. Student therapists will need the help of professional educators or clinicians in selecting a target behavior and treatment program appropriate to the child's circumstances. However, with adequate supervision, the student who carefully follows this book's instructions should be able to succeed in completing a child behavior change program. It is not the success or failure of the intervention that is most important; rather, your ability to cope with difficulties should be the determining factor in your satisfaction with your work.

## Probe Questions for Chapter 1, Section 2

1. *Why is it important to skim through the book at this point?*

2. *What are the advantages and disadvantages of students working in pairs?*

3. *Where can child clients be located in your community?*

4. *Describe the interview method and the types of errors which can be made by interviewers.*

# Chapter 2
# HOW TO SELECT A TARGET BEHAVIOR

## Behavioral Objectives for Chapter 2, Section 1

*After studying this section, you should be able to perform the following tasks:*

1. *Identify and resolve ethical issues in child behavior therapy.*

2. *Interview the child's caretakers to obtain* specific *information about the problem behavior — its type, rate, antecedents, and social consequences — and the nature and outcome of previous treatment attempts.*

## SECTION 1. ETHICAL CONSIDERATIONS AND PRELIMINARY INFORMATION GATHERING

### *Consider Ethical Issues*

Influence attempts are pervasive in social interactions. People try to influence each other's behavior every day. Consider the parent, teacher, physician, psychologist, advertiser, and even the friend. Each attempts to modify the behavior of the child. Each is, in a way, a behavior modifier, and each must implicitly or explicitly make a judgment concerning the ethics of the intended behavior manipulation. This is not to say, however, that the pervasiveness of the issue implies that behavior therapists can evade or escape the question of the ethics of the therapy enterprise. Every therapist has a professional and legal mandate to follow the most rigorous ethical codes possible in assessing and treating clients.

Behavior therapists have long been concerned about the ethical issues necessarily involved in any attempt to influence the behavior of another person (see Kanfer, 1965; Krasner, 1964; Rogers & Skinner, 1956). Ethical questions become more important and immediate as the means to modify behavior become more potent. Greater power entails greater responsibility. Since many behavior therapy techniques have been shown to be highly effective, there has been intense concern about their use. The essential issues concern (a) who shall decide which behaviors are desirable and which should be changed, and (b) which techniques shall be used to bring about change. In many cases, the law provides the answer to the former question. Children are the wards of their parents, and under ordinary circumstances the decisions concerning modification of a child's behavior are made by the parents or by others acting for them — for example, by state agencies charged with the protection of children, or by hospital or public school officials. These individuals or agencies have the authority to grant permission to clinicians to assess and treat children.

The matter is not always this simple, however. There are some unwise or unfit parents or guardians who fail to act in the child's interests, for example, by punishing the child cruelly for minor instances of disobedience that are well within normal bounds. Parents, teachers, or guardians, therefore, cannot and should not carry the entire burden of deciding which child behavior is changeworthy and how the change should be accomplished. Even student therapists who are working under supervision must be aware of the ethics involved in child therapy. The therapist is not merely an agent of the parents, of the school, or even of the child, but must determine how best to serve all concerned. Therapists cannot respond automatically to requests to change a child's behavior but must independently assess their own ethical and legal responsibility in the matter. Unfortunately, there is no easy, automatic way to deal with these important and basic issues. Supervisors and other experienced clinicians should always be consulted prior to the student's initiating any type of contact with potential clients, and again when planning the behavioral assessment and treatment strategies. They will have faced and resolved many such issues in the course of their careers. The selection of the means by which to improve the child's behavior must be approached cautiously. The child's caretakers have the right to decide on the acceptability of treatment procedures advised by the therapist, and the therapists must inform them of all of the treatment options available to them from others as well as from the therapist.

In many treatment settings, such as public schools, the parents must be encouraged to attend a conference at which any special educational programs for their children are discussed by school administrators, teachers, therapists, and anyone else involved in the treatment program. Moreover, Public Law 94-142 requires that the conference be held at a time when it is possible for working parents to attend, such as late afternoon or evening. For unusual educational procedures, such as those involving punishment of any type, parents must be completely informed about and give their written consent to have the treatment implemented. Since they are not themselves expert in the field, caretakers do not ordinarily propose the intervention program. But they can veto any procedure suggested to them. They must be fully informed regarding treatment plans so that they can in fact exercise this right. Further, they must be informed of their right to withdraw their consent at *any* time.

Similarly, insofar as possible, the child should be informed of the nature of the treatment, and should give his consent if he is competent to make such a decision. Children who are very young, severely retarded, psychotic, or nonverbal are often unable to make treatment decisions for themselves, so their parents and other guardians assume that responsibility. Normally the child also has the right to decide not to participate in the program if his parents agree or if he is competent to do so.

## Preliminary Data Gathering

There are many alternative methods for obtaining information concerning a child's behavior. These methods differ in their utility, trustworthiness, and in the time and expense they require. Methods in common use include interviews with caretakers and child, psychological testing, and behavior observations. Some form of interview is perhaps the most frequently used assessment technique (Swan & MacDonald, 1978; Wade, Baker, & Hartmann, 1979), particularly during the early phases of assessment (Hawkins, 1979). The clinician usually asks the child's parents, teacher, and others who know her well for their interpretations of her behavior. The teacher's impression of the child is often invaluable, since the teacher can assess how customary or rare the child's behavior is for those in the relevant age group (Hartmann, Roper, & Bradford, 1979). Teachers see many children over many hours, and so often have a better grasp of the norms for child behavior than therapists do. These accounts are then checked for accuracy against other sources, such as school or medical records, test results, and the records of trained observers. Caretakers' reports and school and clinic records can give helpful data also, but are susceptible to biases such as halo effects resulting from the informant's general feeling about the child. Thus, these accounts may be of invaluable help at times, but may prove misleading at others. Similarly, psychological tests may prove revealing to the experienced clinician, although not to the novice who lacks the knowledge and skills to interpret them. For this reason, the records and test results may be of limited use for student therapists.

Direct, objective behavior observation is the second most common form of assessment used by behavior therapists (interviews are first according to Wade, Baker, & Hartmann, 1979). A specific behavior is identified as representing some adjustment problem, and that behavior is modified directly in the treatment. For this type of intervention, actual observation of the target behavior's rate and of the circumstances surrounding its occurrence often provides the most useful assessment information. Other assessment techniques such as child self-reports and self-monitoring, parent reports, academic grades, and achievement test scores add supporting information. This information may include descriptions of (a) the child's assets — e.g., social skills, compliance with instructions, and memory; (b) stimuli and activities that can be used to reinforce appropriate responding, and (c) the likelihood of cooperation from important individuals in the child's environment (Kanfer & Saslow, 1969; Tharp & Wetzel, 1969). While these sources of assessment information may aid in constructing an effective intervention program, to date none of them has matched direct observation in general utility.

Although careful and objective observations of the child's actual behavior are perhaps the most likely of all sources to provide useful information, observational techniques are hardly free from flaws. Even trained observers can be biased, and can report seeing what they expect to see (e.g., improved behavior while the treatment is in effect), rather than what the child actually does (Hartmann & Wood, 1982). Moreover, the observer's presence can distract, inhibit, or upset the child, causing him to behave atypically. In the chapters to follow, we describe methods for counteracting observer bias and the reactive effects on the child's and caretakers' behavior of an observer's presence. There is as yet no really effective method for reducing the high cost of extensive behavior observations. Since they are very time consuming, such data collection techniques are fairly expensive. Nevertheless, they are not as costly as are invalid ones regardless of their comparative speed or ease of administration. See Wiggins (1973, Chapter 8) and Fiske (1978) for a discussion of the relative merits of the various assessment techniques; for discussions of specific techniques, see the journals, *Behavioral Assessment* and *Journal of Behavioral Assessment*. On this faintly optimistic note, we proceed to the discussion of selecting and measuring one or more specific behaviors or classes of behavior to serve as the target for intervention.

Generally speaking, the child has the right to receive the least intrusive treatment procedures possible. That is, the courts have indicated that when the government mandated treatment, the treatment should be done so as to curtail the individual's freedom to the least extent possible. What does intrusiveness mean? Reese (1982) has defined intrusiveness in terms of three dimensions: (1) the public acceptability of the treatment for the behavior being changed (see Kazdin, 1980; Wolf, 1978; and Chapter 6, Section 1 for a discussion of the acceptability of various treatment interventions); (2) the amount of discomfort and stress the treatment procedure produces; and (3) the degree of restriction of liberty necessitated by the treatment. But intrusiveness must be weighed against effectiveness. Very unobtrusive treatments that are also very ineffective subject the client to continued pain and suffering, and so are unacceptable if better alternatives exist. The therapist and the caretakers must become informed about the treatment's probable effectiveness, based upon published evaluation data if possible (Association for Advancement of Behavior Therapy, 1977), and must be told the anticipated length of treatment time required, and the known or conjectured positive and negative side effects of the procedure. If an aversive training procedure also produces anger, resentment, defiance of caretakers, or avoidance of them, it is best shunned, if alternatives exist. However, if the target behavior is dangerous to others or to the client himself, and if positive training techniques have failed, then aversive procedures might be acceptable, even required, despite their negative side effects. For example, it is clearly more desirable that a child receive several painful electric shocks in an aversive treatment procedure than that he go blind as a result of persistent head-banging (Tate & Baroff, 1966) or risk falling from a perilous height (Risley, 1968). However, if the same behavioral goal probably could be accomplished through less intrusive techniques such as overcorrection (see Chapter 6, Section 5), then the latter, less aversive intervention should be used.

Some ethical quandries are less straightforward, however. Should a child be fined for moving around the classroom when her teacher has instructed her to remain at her desk? Should young pupils be prohibited from talking to one another for the teacher's convenience? Should children be reinforced for quietly following instructions even when the instructions appear foolish or arbitrary (see O'Leary, 1972 and Winett & Winkler, 1972 for a discussion of these questions). Should a girl be placed in isolation timeout for refusing to obey requests from her parents? Should her persistent cruelty toward animals be punished or be allowed to continue if nonpunitive control methods prove ineffective? These are not simple questions, and we can offer no simple solutions. No technique can be applied routinely without consideration of the rights and the responsibilities of parents, institutions, the child, and society at large. Therapists must weigh the respective merits of the arguments for and against intervention and must reach an informed decision.

To help you in this task, we have prepared a list of suggested guidelines (see Table 2-1). Since treatment ethics regarding the rights of clients and students are in a state of transition, this list may not be definitive and may even prove incorrect in some respects. It represents our own opinions as well as federal regulations, court opinions on constitutional rights, and professional codes of ethics (see *Ethical Principles for Psychologists*, and *Specialty Guidelines for Delivery of Services by Clinical Psychologists, American Psychologist*, 1981, and the pamphlet entitled, *Ethical Issues for Human Services*, which is available from the Association for Advancement of Behavior Therapy, 15 West 36 Street, New York, NY 10018). Perhaps the best therapists can do is to ensure that their efforts do comply with state and federal requirements, that the rights of the child, guardians, and associates are protected, and that the child receives the most effective treatment available under existing circumstances.

**Table 2-1.** Ethical Consideration in Child Behavior Modification

---

To protect the rights and welfare of the child-client and his caretakers, the therapist should be able to answer each of the following questions affirmatively.

1. *Caretaker Permission.* Did you obtain the appropriate care agent's fully informed consent to carry out the proposed modification program? Did the caretakers understand that they could withdraw the child's participation at any time, and that other community programs are available? Did they extend written permission if requested?

2. *School or Treatment Agency Permission.* If the program is to be carried out under the auspices of a school or institution, did the responsible officials give their fully informed consent?

3. *Child Consent.* If appropriate in terms of his age and abilities, did the child-client also give his fully informed consent? Does he understand that he may withdraw at any time?

4. *Consensus.* Is there agreement among those responsible for the child's welfare that the anticipated behavior change is desirable?

5. *Treatment Methods.* Will positive methods be used to modify the target behavior (i.e., those involving shaping, positively reinforcing incompatible behavior, modeling, positive instructions)?

6. *Aversive Procedures.* Are aversive procedures (e.g., criticism, deprivation of privileges, time-out, response cost) to be used *only* after positive methods were thoroughly tried and failed? Will you use the least restrictive methods? Are aversive procedures accompanied by positive consequation of desired behaviors? Does the potential benefit to the child clearly outweigh any discomfort he might experience? (See Chapter 6 for a more complete discussion of ethical issues in aversive control.)

7. *Protection of Rights.* Are the child's basic rights protected? (These include his legal and constitutionally guaranteed rights as interpreted by judicial decisions; see Wexler, 1973.) Does the child have access to an adequate diet, comfortable and safe surroundings, exercise, education, recreation, and privacy?

8. *Right to Effective Treatment.* Is the child receiving the most effective treatment currently available for his particular behavioral problem? This may be one of the client's most important moral rights, and one that is not often adequately considered.

---

# Probe Questions for Chapter 2, Section 1

*1. Why must behavior therapists be particularly sensitive to ethical issues?*

*2. Can parents be depended upon to protect their child's interests as regards treatment? Explain.*

*3. Under what circumstances are children unable to give consent for their own treatment?*

*4. What types of assessment procedures do behavior therapists find to be most useful, and why?*

## Behavioral Objectives for Chapter 2, Section 2

*After studying this section, you should be able to perform the following tasks:*

1. *Recognize the criteria for the selection of target behaviors.*

2. *Define a behavioral deficit. Judge the suitability of a particular low-rate behavior as a target for modification.*

3. *Define behavioral excesses. Judge the suitability of a specified high-rate behavior as a target for modification.*

4. *Give examples of behavior under inappropriate stimulus control. State the conditions under which such a behavior would be a suitable modification target.*

5. *Perform a cost-benefit analysis for treatment of a specific target behavior.*

### SECTION 2.
### CRITERIA FOR TARGET BEHAVIOR AND
### INFORMAL COST-BENEFIT ANALYSIS

### *Apply Criteria*

Now let's consider the criteria by which to judge the suitability of a potential target behavior. Somewhat different rules apply in the treatment of behavioral excesses, behavioral deficits, and inappropriate stimulus control (the latter produces perfectly good behavior, but in the wrong setting). However, whatever the type of problem, it is important to *socially validate* your choice of target behaviors, that is, the target behavior should be important to the child's social or academic adjustment (Baer, Wolf, & Risley, 1968), and should be so viewed by the child's family and associates (Kazdin, 1977b; Wolf, 1978). Also, as suggested by Mash and Terdal (1981), target behaviors for treatment should have at least some of the following features:

1. The behavior is a critical component for successful performance in the home, on the playground, or in school. For example, such behaviors include attending to school tasks, positive social responses to others, and imitating a therapist demonstrating speech sounds or movements.

2. The behavior provides entry into the natural reinforcement contingencies operating in the child's social milieu, and thus will be maintained following treatment termination.

3. The target behavior is positive, and specifies what a child should do rather than what the child does wrong. This avoids labeling.

4. The behavior is essential to normal development, e.g., spoken and written language, toileting, physical self care such as toothbrushing, motor skills, and academic skills.

Advanced students and professionals who are experienced in treating children's problem behaviors can employ somewhat different criteria from those presented here. Their experience should permit them to deal successfully with the more serious behavioral problems that novices are best advised to avoid. More detailed coverage of criteria for use in selecting specific target behaviors is offered in Mash and Terdal (1976, 1981), and in *Behavioral Assessment* and the *Journal of Behavioral Assessment*.

*Behavioral deficits.* Sometimes a child fails to engage in some behavior pattern generally considered normal and desirable for a child of his age and circumstances. The appropriate behavior fails to occur (a) sufficiently frequently, (b) with adequate intensity, (c) in appropriate form, e.g., baby talk in a 5-year-old, or (d) under socially appropriate conditions, e.g., not speaking to teachers (Kanfer & Saslow, 1965). For example, an 8-year-old child may fail to comply with most of his parents' requests (a social deficit), and may not do his homework (an academic deficit). The therapist's job is to devise interventions to address the child's most problematic behavioral deficits.

Many students prefer to work with a behavioral deficit problem for their initial modification project because this provides them with the opportunity to learn modeling, shaping, and verbal instructional skills. Furthermore, children are likely to consider therapists who reinforce them to be attractive and desirable companions. The resulting pleasant relationship with the child is itself likely to be highly rewarding, certainly much more so than if the therapist must apply punitive intervention techniques. So there are many pleasant side effects in the use of positive treatments for behavioral deficits, and such techniques always should be considered initially in planning the therapeutic intervention.

The following list suggests some criteria to follow in the selection of a behavior to serve as the target of modification efforts.

1. You should be able to specify a response that will remedy the child's performance deficit, e.g., that the child should answer questions directed to her by adults, or that the child should play with other children rather than seeking out only the teacher.

2. The child's performance deficit should not be a monumental one, such as complete mutism or a school-aged child's failure ever to walk upright. A short-term behavior therapy program would probably fail to help such children to any meaningful degree, and might dissuade others from working with the child. A treatment failure also may make the child's caretakers more reluctant to seek similar help in the future, and the untreated behavior might persist or worsen. Treatment of these problems is best left to professionals.

3. The occurrence of the child's performance deficit should be in a setting and time at which you can be present to monitor the child's behavior. Don't rely on the possibly unreliable reports of others.

4. The child's behavior should not be under the exclusive control of situations or persons you cannot control. In illustration, if the reason for a child's failure to speak in the classroom is that the other children ridicule her for her speech impediment, you may be unable to encourage the child to speak to her classmates if you are unable to modify the classmates' behavior as well as improve the child's productive speech. Be sure that you can gain control of the functional environmental variables.

5. If you intend to work with a child at a school or treatment facility, make sure that the child has a good attendance record. The child's frequent absences would frustrate your attempt to work with her, or even make it impossible to do so in the time period you may have available. *In any case, it is always advisable to select a second child to serve as a substitute in case the first child you choose to work with becomes ill, transfers to another school, or declines to participate.* If you can identify another child with a similar behavioral deficit, replacing your first-place child is often easier than beginning again with an entirely new type of treatment program.

6. You should also make sure that you can get the proper space and equipment in the setting in which the project will be conducted. No matter how appealing it may sound, a project requiring elaborate equipment may prove impossible to carry out because of inadequate facilities. This is a particular problem in crowded clinics and schools.

7. Consult your instructor and the child's teachers or regular therapists about dealing with this problem in this setting. They may suggest a useful intervention method, one which they know has worked well with the child.

If the child and target behavior you are considering fail to meet any of these criteria, it might be wise to select another behavior or some other child to participate in your project. Advanced students and professional clinicians can successfully employ less restrictive guidelines should they wish to do so.

Our students have found that certain types of deficits are particularly attractive as target behaviors. Instruction in speech, reading, arithmetic, such as learning multiplication tables, and discrimination of colors, shapes, and objects are all relatively easy to carry out, and much can be achieved in relatively brief time periods. Other interesting target behaviors have been exercising, ball-throwing skills, and toothbrushing and other grooming responses. Moreover, few ethical problems arise with these types of target behaviors since these skills are virtually universally considered vital to normal development. In addition, since schools and treatment centers have a responsibility to teach such skills, it is often unnecessary to obtain special parental permission for the student therapist to conduct training programs unless highly unusual procedures are to be employed. Of course, parental permission should not be waived except with the permission of the appropriate school or agency officials. Also, you should consider educational and preventive training programs to teach children (and sometimes whole classrooms of them) useful skills such as how to identify emergency situations and make emergency telephone calls (Rosenbaum, Creedon, & Drabman, 1981), when and how to use automobile seat belts (Geller, Casali, & Johnson, 1980), how to identify and deal with potential child molesters (Pocke, Brower, & Swearingen, 1981), and how to respond to home emergency fire situations (Haney & Jones, 1982; Jones, Kazdin, & Haney, 1981). Those and other similar training programs can teach children helpful skills that they might not otherwise acquire until much later, if ever.

*Behavioral excesses.* Next we will consider the case in which the child exhibits a distinct, readily apparent, maladaptive behavior such as inappropriately monopolizing the teacher's attention, cursing, nail-biting, stealing, lying, or bed-wetting. The class of behaviors is excessive in terms of (a) frequency, (b) intensity, or (c) duration (Kanfer & Saslow, 1965). The following criteria will help you decide whether you should select this as the target behavior.

1. The undesired behavior should occur at a high rate, preferable several times an hour. Lower rate behaviors will be difficult for you to observe. If a child has a temper tantrum only three times a week, chances are that you could observe him for several weeks and never see the target behavior. If he is somehow reinforced for just one of his tantrums (which is likely to be the case if you are not present to administer consequences), your treatment attempt may fail.

2. The undesired behavior should be fairly consistent in rate from day to day. It is extremely difficult to establish a stable baseline on behaviors with highly variable frequencies. Unfortunately, many changeworthy behaviors are likely to vary considerably in daily frequency, e.g., tantrums, aggressive attacks, and failure to comply with instructions.

3. The caretakers, and preferably the child herself, should consider the behavior to be at least slightly undesirable, as in the case of frequent talking out-of-turn, wandering around the classroom bothering others, or eating with fingers rather than utensils.

4. The target behavior should *not* be extremely deviant or have serious consequences. Leave the control of arson, self-injurious behavior, or violent physical attacks on others to more experienced clinicians. Your instructor probably knows the community's treatment resources and can help you make appropriate referrals.

5. The behavior should occur at a time and place at which you can consistently observe it. If you can't observe it, you may be unable to obtain a reliable estimate of its rate, and consequently you might not be able to treat it. For example, the child may engage in hair-pulling and self-injurious behavior only after being put to bed each evening. Such a problem can be treated through parent training, but, again, parent training is best left to the

professionals. If you cannot arrange to observe the behavior, you may not be able to treat it effectively.

6. The behavior should not be under the exclusive control of events or persons you cannot control, e.g., negative child behavior toward parents resulting from frequent beatings from abusive parents.

7. Remember to make sure that the child has a good attendance record and that another child (preferably one with a similar problem) is available to serve as your client in case you must terminate your work with the child you select initially.

8. Obtain your instructor's agreement to your dealing with this particular set of client and caretakers and this target behavior in this particular setting.

You should probably select an alternative behavior to treat if the behavior you are considering for modification fails to meet one or more of the preceding criteria.

*Inappropriate stimulus control.* A problem can also occur because a behavior, while not inappropriate in itself nor of inappropriate rate, is under inappropriate stimulus control. A child may display cooperative behavior, but only in the presence of his antisocial friends, not while at home or at school. The goal here would be to transfer his cooperative behavior to the home and school settings (which would be a behavioral deficit problem in those locales), and to decelerate his cooperation in illegal and destructive endeavors (a behavioral excess problem). It often proves necessary to work simultaneously on the acceleration and deceleration aspects of the behavior at issue. Whenever this circumstance occurs, review the criteria for both behavioral excesses and deficits before deciding upon a target. Your responsibility as a therapist and educator is to use only positive, nonaversive training programs whenever possible.

## Begin a Cost-Benefit Analysis

If the behavior under consideration meets the preceding sets of guidelines, evaluate the desirability of changing that target behavior. What are the possible consequences of modifying the behavior?

## Evaluate the Consequences to the Caretakers

*Positive consequences or benefits.* The child's regular caretakers must be considered in planning the treatment effort. For example, a teacher might gain more time to devote to instruction rather than continuing to attempt to discipline the child. The teacher also might have increasingly positive interactions with the child, and suffer fewer headaches. Teaching becomes much more pleasant if occasions for nagging and threatening are reduced. But what if the other children, who are not receiving special treats or privileges, become jealous of the target child? Research findings indicate that you can put the caretaker's mind at rest about these types of negative side effects. If anything, the other children may become better behaved (Broden, Bruce, Mitchell, Carter, & Hall, 1970; Christy, 1975), although some studies have found no effect on non-treated classmates' behavior (Fantuzzo & Clement, 1981).

*Negative consequences or costs.* Perhaps the program will involve the teacher and will require recording the occurrences of the behavior and contingent administration of reinforcers. The program might disrupt classroom routines or, if the program is conducted in the home, family activities may be interfered with, inconveniencing other family members. Moreover, caretakers may resent their failure to remedy the problem while you, a smart-aleck student and outsider, may succeed. Try to protect their pride and dignity as much as possible.

What imposition on the teacher's or family members' or peers' time and other responsibilities or prerogatives will the program represent? How can you minimize these negative consequences?

## Evaluate the Consequences to the Child

*Anticipated positive consequences.* For example, the child may seem more acceptable to caretakers and other children, or have greater success in schoolwork, in social relationships with others, or in athletics. The child may acquire skills in self-regulation which are useful in many different endeavors.

*Possible negative consequences or costs.* Be careful not to label the child's problem in a negative way, for this may adversely affect the manner in which others perceive the child's potential for positive change (Gelfand, Jenson, & Drew, 1982, Chapter 5; Guskin, Bartel, & MacMillan, 1975). Even simply treating the child's undesirable behavior may be socially harmful and render the child less acceptable to teachers and classmates. The child may be embarrassed by being singled out as needing help. Being different from peers is a source of agony for many children whose classmates taunt them about their failings. You should also consider the impact on the child's academic work of being taken away from her classroom lessons to participate in the therapy program. This problem can be reduced by timing the therapy sessions so as not to conflict with important classroom instruction times. If the child is distressed by the program, she might opt not to participate.

## Evaluate the Consequences to Yourself

Since you will invest a considerable amount of time and effort in the treatment enterprise, you also should consider the consequences for yourself.

*Anticipated positive consequences.* You will undoubtedly feel relieved, pleased, and proud to have helped the child. And you will have acquired therapeutic skills which you can use to help others. This is why you will want to plan your approach as carefully as possible so as to maximize chances of success.

*Costs.* How time consuming will this project be? Do you have the necessary time, energy, equipment, and transportation to conduct the project? Do you have access to sufficient funds to purchase the necessary equipment and reinforcers? What scheduling problems might arise for you and your partner? How would you take it if the treatment efforts failed? Table 2-2 presents a form which you can use to remind you to consider as many as possible of the anticipated positive and negative consequences associated with the treatment plan.

**Table 2-2.** Preliminary Cost-Benefit Analysis

Child Target Behavior: _____

Treatment Program Goals: _____

Optional: Description of Proposed Treatment Program: _____

| *Anticipated Costs* | *How to Minimize Costs* (Aim for two procedures designed to minimize each anticipated cost.) |
|---|---|
| 1. To Caretakers: | 1. To Caretakers: |
| 2. To the Child: | 2. To the Child: |
| 3. To You, the Behavior Modification Agent: | 3. To You: |
| *Anticipated Benefits* | *Decision* _____ |
| *1. To Caretakers:* | _____ |
| *2. To the Child:* | _____ |
| *3. To You:* | _____ |

The preliminary analysis should be begun now and the final analysis can be completed at the conclusion of the collection of the baseline data. Then, if you can fairly and confidently conclude that the benefits clearly outweigh the costs of intervention, proceed to the therapy or training program proper.

## Probe Questions for Chapter 2, Section 2

1. *What seven criteria should be used to select a behavioral deficit for modification?*

2. *Why is it wise to select a behavioral deficit as the target for your first behavioral therapy project?*

3. *Describe the eight criteria to use in selecting a behavioral excess for modification.*

4. *What is inappropriate stimulus control?*

5. *Describe how to conduct a cost-benefit analysis.*

## Behavioral Objectives for Chapter 2, Section 3

*Study of this section should enable you to:*

1. *Make behavior observations appropriately and without bothering or upsetting the child or others in the situation.*

2. *Record your behavior observations in a three-column form, if appropriate.*

3. *Informally assess your accuracy as an observer, and identify sources of error.*

## SECTION 3.
## PRELIMINARY OBSERVATIONS AND
## FUNCTIONAL ANALYSIS

### *Make Preliminary Observations*

Making careful preliminary behavior observations accomplishes several objectives. First, it helps to acquaint you with the child and her behavior in the natural environment of her home or school. Second, it gives you practice in making objective, minimally interpretive observations of child behavior. These observations, in combination with careful recording of correlated environmental events, are crucial in performing a functional analysis of the child's behavior. In addition, the functional analysis frequently dictates the details of the modification program. When you know which stimuli are correlated with the occurrence of the target behavior, you can often tell how to arrange to change the child's behavior. Finally, your behavior observations provide some check on the accuracy of the caretaker's report regarding the child's behavior. The caretaker's report may not suffice, since it is subject to halo effects, memory failure or distortion, and the caretaker's conclusions may be based on unrepresentative or inadequate samples of the child's behavior, or on other misleading factors (Evans & Nelson, 1977; Hartmann & Wood, 1982; Wiggins, 1973; Yarrow, Campbell, & Burton, 1968). However, therapists usually start with the caretaker's descriptions to guide the initial phase of assessment.

### *Suggestions for Observers*

Some rules of conduct apply whenever you make behavioral observations of children. The following suggestions are based on Broden's (undated) recommendations and on our own experience.

1. Obtain the caretaker's permission to observe the child in his normal social environment or wherever the treatment project will take place. If this is to occur at a school, the principal's, the teacher's, and the parents' permission ordinarily will be required. Check with the school principal and the child's teachers to discover whose permission must be requested.

2. *For observations in the classroom*, the teacher may wish to introduce you to the class so the students will know who you are and why you are visiting them. Observers are more likely to be accepted by the class if the teacher offers a rationale for their presence (Hartmann & Wood, 1982). Teachers have their own favorite ways to introduce visitors, so discuss it with the one you are working with prior to your first entry into the classroom. The message you want to convey is that you will be visiting the class and might work with or teach some of the children. Do not announce or cause the teacher to announce that you are there to observe and work with Johnny, since this might possibly embarrass and frighten him. There is no way to become completely nonintrusive in the classroom, but one can only become less likely to cause the children to behave atypically (Lytton, 1971; Mash & Terdal, 1976, Part V). The following instructions will help you avoid attracting attention during observations, which might inspire giggling, staring, squirming, or misbehavior in the children.

3. Time your arrival and departure to coincide with a normal break in the classroom routine or at a time during which children are working on individual or small group projects. That way you won't attract much attention or risk disrupting the teacher's lesson presentation. If you must enter the room during an instructional time, say nothing and move unobtrusively to your vantage point for observing the child or children of particular interest. Do not move around the room unless it is absolutely necessary in order to see the child (see Hartmann & Wood, 1982).

4. Observers should blend into the background as much as possible, so don't dress or act in a conspicuous fashion. Don't chew gum or eat candy, and try to interact with the children as little as possible during observation periods. If you are conducting observations on the playground, wearing mirror-lensed dark glasses may help conceal which child you are observing, a great advantage since children older than about six years become uncomfortable when being observed. However, mirror-lensed glasses may make you appear somewhat sinister, so have a friend help you check the effect before using them in observation. Vary the apparent object of your gaze from time to time to prevent the target child from becoming too self-conscious.

5. Don't strike up long conversations with the children, although it might be tempting to do so. You want them to behave as normally as possible, just as though you were not there. If they talk to you, answer their specific questions as briefly as possible, then turn away and busy yourself with something else. Some observers simply ignore young children's approaches and con-

tinue writing until the children give up and leave them alone. Briefly but politely telling older children that you are busy will accomplish the same purpose.

6. Stay out of the traffic pattern. Sit at the back of the room in an inconspicuous place from which you can see but cannot easily be seen so that you won't interfere with the children's concentration on their work. A good observation vantage point is at the side or back of the room and in an unvarying location from day to day.

7. Wait until the children have become accustomed to your presence before you begin making systematic behavior observations so they will behave in their usual fashion. This may take varying periods of time, and is important early in the observation process when you are still a novelty to the children. You can, however, practice recording observations during the acquaintance period, and can refine your behavioral definitions and select the optimal time of day to make your observations throughout the project.

8. Make your observations at the same time each day. This regularity creates less classroom or home disturbance and guarantees that changes observed in the child's behavior are not due simply to variations in the time of day at which the observations took place.

9. Your project is an imposition on caretakers, so show them that you realize this and are grateful for their help. Let them know as early as possible what your schedule will be for working with the child, and solicit their advice before deciding when and where you will be conducting the project. Caretakers are usually, and rightfully, somewhat skeptical initially, but willing to cooperate if your project sounds reasonable.

10. *For observations in the home*, you might ask the child's parents to introduce you as a student who is interested in learning how to work with children and families. Make sure that the parents do not introduce you as some sort of police officer who has come to make the kids behave. In homes, as in schools, be as unobtrusive as possible, while not allowing participants to escape by staying on the phone, in the bathroom, or leaving the scene. A habituation period is just as, if not more, important in the home as at school.

## The Observation Record Format

Your next task will be to make your observations in a manner that will help you identify the situational determinants, if any, of the child's behavior. A number of antecedent and consequent events can affect behavior. Antecedents include *setting events* such as the child's state of deprivation or satiation for various consequences (Bijou & Baer, 1961; Kantor, 1958), as well as *discriminative stimuli* which signal the likelihood of particular responses being reinforced or punished. Consequences are those *neutral, rein-*

forcing, and *punishing events* that function, respectively, to extinguish, strengthen, or suppress the responses that they follow. For example, to understand why a physically normal child has temper tantrums between 5:00 and 7:00 p.m. nearly every day, it would be helpful to know that during this time period his dinner time is approaching, so he probably feels hungry and tired. His mother and father are usually preoccupied with preparing dinner and talking to each other, which deprives the child of their attention (all setting events which increase the probability of temper tantrums). In addition, his brothers and sisters may be surly, too, since they also are food-deprived, tired, and attention-deprived, thus modeling quarrelsome behavior (which could be considered a setting event, see Wahler & Fox, 1981), and punishing the child's interaction attempts. In such circumstances, the child in question may coerce attention, food, and enforced rest and isolation from his family by engaging in ill-tempered outbursts.

Remediation procedures might concentrate on setting events; for example, young children could be given an after-school snack and a nap to forestall trouble, or the family's dinner time could be changed to an earlier time. And the parents might be taught how to increase their children's desirable behavior so that evenings became quieter and pleasanter for the whole family. Such a program would involve manipulation of (a) setting events — namely, the food, rest, and attention deprivation, and the fact that the child had learned to act obnoxiously in this situation, (b) discriminative stimuli, such as parental behaviors signaling the potentiality of inadvertently attending to, and thus reinforcing misbehavior, and (c) consequent social events, e.g., reinforcing the children's cooperation in cleaning up, setting the table, and helping with kitchen tasks. The new regime would require the parents to state rules for their children's conduct, abide by those rules, reinforce desired behavior, and either ignore or punish quarrelsome behavior with response cost in the form of fines or deprivation of privileges or other penalties. All of these intervention procedures will be discussed at length in later portions of this book.

*Setting events.* Since setting events remain essentially unchanged throughout the usual observation session, you should preface your observation record with information and speculations regarding relevant setting events. For example, you should investigate and report the child's likely deprivation for the particular reinforcer you intend using (fortunately, it is difficult for most of us to become satiated on attention, praise, money, and other generalized reinforcers). You should also inquire about the child's current state of health and alertness and the instructions he has been given concerning you and your project. Other setting events could consist of the child's having experienced some unsettling experience, such as separation from friends or family members, parental separation or divorce, stressful medical or dental treatments, etc.

*Antecedent events (discriminative stimuli).* You should note carefully the stimulus events associated with each of the child's responses. For example, in interpreting the child's behavior of standing on his desk, it is important to know that the teacher's statement, "Everybody get to work, please. Everyone sit down," preceded the child's action. The teacher's instruction may well have served as a discriminative stimulus for the student's disruptive behavior.

*Child's behavior.* In addition, you will require a careful description of the child's behavior. Does he look at the teacher, does he smile or make a funny face, does he remain standing on the desk or sit down quickly? All these aspects of his behavior should be noted.

*Consequent social events.* What happened immediately after the child's response? What are the social consequences of his action? Does the teacher continue to pay attention to him or turn away? Again, you must record precisely what happened following the child's behavior.

This "three-term contingency" (Bijou, Peterson, Harris, Allen, & Johnston, 1969; Skinner, 1953a), which includes antecedent stimulus and setting events, the child's responses, and the consequent events, provides the information necessary to a functional analysis. In addition, you should be attentive to the behavioral models provided by the teacher and the students, even if somewhat removed in time from the child's misbehavior. Do the other students frequently defy the teacher? Does this consistently attract the teacher's attention? Events other than those immediately preceding or following the child's misbehavior may powerfully influence the child.

Table 2-3 presents an example of the three-column observation record that includes a description of the physical and behavioral setting, the antecedent stimulus and consequent social events as well as the responses emitted by the child who is the primary object of observation. A functional analysis of the determinants of the child's behavior based upon these observational data follows: This child's mother and, to a lesser extent, his teacher are intermittently reinforcing his crying and protesting by complying with his demands and attending to him when he misbehaves (events 19–25). More consistent use of the time-out procedure of placing him in a chair in an adjoining room (event 9) combined with adult attention and praise for socially appropriate behavior would probably effectively reduce his frequent complaints and demands. The treatment presently employed by the mother and teacher will probably eventually increase Jack's cooperative behavior, but only after considerable disruption of group activities, annoyance to the other children, and wear and tear on all involved. It appears that all participants would profit from the introduction of the suggested revised child management procedures. (*Note*: Helen Fishler recorded these observations as part of a child psychology class project.)

**Table 2-3.** Sample Three-Column Behavior Observation Format

Setting: A cooperative nursery school in which the children's mothers participate on a regularly scheduled basis. There are 14 children between the ages of 3½ and 4 years. Jack is a cute, chubby four-year-old boy whose mother is assisting the nursery schoolteacher this afternoon. A group of three children are making objects out of Play Dough while seated at a small table. Jack is standing by the table and also working with the Play Dough.

| Time | Antecedent Event | Response | Consequent Social Event |
|---|---|---|---|
| 1:30 pm | | 1. J says, "I need a knife." | 2. Children ignore him. |
| | 2. Children ignore him. | 2. J cries, screams, "That's mine" to girl using knife. | 3. Girl ignores him. Teacher: "Sit here." |
| | 3. √ | 4. J: "No. Knife." | 5. Teacher (T): "That's not the decision you made, remember?" |
| | 5. √ | 6. J throws dough back into the bucket. He begins to cry again. | 7. J's mother and T ignore him. |
| 1:35 | 7. √ | 8. J leaves room; returns two minutes later crying as loudly as before. | 9. T takes J to an adjoining room, and tells him: "You can sit here until you can stop crying." |
| | 9. √ | 10. J sits on chair, gradually stops crying, then gets up and returns to other room. | |
| 1:40 | 11. J's mother is operating a tape recorder. The children are recording statements of their favorite foods. Mother (M) asks each individually what his favorite food is. M: "J, what is your favorite food?" | 12. "Marshmallows." | 13. M: "O.K., now let's hear what Cathy's favorite is." (Continues until all have had a turn.) "Shall we listen to our tape now?" |

| | 13. √ | 14. J shouts "Yes" with other children. | 15. M replays tape. |
|---|---|---|---|
| 1:45 | 15. √ | 16. "That sounded like me, Mom, roll it back." J begins to thrash his arms and cry. | 17. M reverses tape to play J's voice again. |
| | 17. √ | 18. J stops crying. Then says, "What is your ickiest food?" | 19. Group ignores him. |
| | 19. √ | 20. J listens to tape, whines occasionally. Suddenly J begins jumping and crying, screams, "Turn it all back again." | 21. M reverses tape and plays it back again. |
| 1:52 | | | |
| | 22. After conclusion of tape, M asks the children where they want to go on summer vacations. | 23. J starts crying again | 24. T: "Your mother is talking." |
| 1:54 | 24. √ | 25. J cries louder | 26. M and T ignore him. |

Student therapists who wish to complete an extensive and formal behavioral analysis of this type can find more extensive instructions for doing so in Bijou et al. (1969). In many instances, the caretaker's report or referral provides sufficient information so that only a brief observation is required for verification. Sometimes it is possible to proceed directly to taking baseline data on the target behavior.

## Assess Observer Accuracy

If you are working with a fellow student, now is a good time to begin checking observer accuracy. Do you both agree on the nature of the child's problem, if any? Did you record only behavior you actually witnessed, or did one of you make unshared inferences? What suggestions can each of you make regarding possible treatment techniques? If the problem seems to stem from the teacher more than from the child, how can this tactfully be remedied? This is when you will begin to be glad that you aren't working all by yourself.

## *Perform a Preliminary Functional Analysis of the Determinants of the Target Behavior*

The most you can get from behavior observations alone is some indication of covariation of particular stimuli and the occurrence of the target behavior. For example, an antecedent stimulus of teasing by playmates may be reliably followed by the target child's crying. Probably the playmates' teasing produced the crying, but you can never be completely sure regarding cause and effect from observations alone. You cast your best guesses as a working hypothesis which helps determine your treatment plan. Even successful treatment outcomes do not provide unequivocal proof of the hypothesis. You may be successful for reasons you do not currently understand. Such is the nature of the clinical enterprise.

At this point you are ready to define the target behavior more precisely and speculate about its environmental controls. After that you begin gathering baseline data on its present rate of occurrence while you plan an intervention program.

## Probe Questions for Chapter 2, Section 3

1. How should observers behave in school and home settings?

2. When the teacher asks him to sit down, Jimmy usually remains standing, but when his teacher gets really angry and shouts at him, Jimmy sits down. What setting events, antecedents, and consequent social events might be involved in this case?

3. What are antecedent and setting events, and how are they used in treatment programs?

# Chapter 3
# DEVELOPING A PROCEDURE
# FOR COLLECTING DATA

## Behavioral Objectives for Chapter 3, Section 1

*After study of Section 1 of this chapter, you should be able to:*

1. *Describe the primary advantages and disadvantages of systematic data collection.*

2. *Distinguish between direct and indirect measures of a target behavior, and between topographic and functional response definitions.*

3. *Devise a target response definition that is meaningful and produces reliable data.*

## SECTION 1. RESPONSE DEFINITIONS

### Introduction

In the previous chapter we described interview and observational methods of providing data that you should find useful in (a) diagnosing problem behaviors and (b) identifying controlling variables to aid in designing an effective intervention. *Diagnosis* and *design* are two of the three functions of data collection that need to concern you. The third function of data collection, treatment *evaluation* (e.g., Mash & Terdal, 1976) will be the focus of this chapter, and much of Chapters 8 and 9. Of course, our discussion of procedures for obtaining data having an evaluation function will also be useful to you for collecting data having diagnostic and treatment design purposes.

Our emphasis on data collection and evaluation is consistent with major themes in this "age of accountability" (Bloom & Fischer, 1982). However, behavioral psychology, unlike more recent converts to this position, has always had an empirical orientation. Because of a popular disinclination to collect and scrutinize clinical data, today's principles and procedures too often become tomorrow's artifacts and clinical curiosities. It is to be hoped that a firm data base will lessen this faddism.

An argument commonly raised against data-oriented approaches to treatment is that they are unnecessary: "If you have changed behavior, parents and other caretakers will inform you of the change." Unfortunately, reports from parents and teachers are notoriously unreliable. Sometimes caretakers are honestly mistaken (e.g., Harris, Wolf, & Baer, 1964); at other times their glowing reports reflect factors quite irrelevant to treatment effectiveness such as their consideration for the feelings of the therapist (Hathaway, 1948; Kiesler, 1983). Social convention requires some expression of gratitude to a person who has attempted to help. Thus, the thanks, and perhaps reassurances, of caretakers may lead therapists to overestimate their own effectiveness. Assessment of treatment outcome is unlikely to succeed unless substantial attention is given to systematic and objective data collection.

## Advantages and Disadvantages of Data Collection

In addition to the advantages described above, other benefits accrue during the process of obtaining good data (Hawkins, 1979; Haynes, 1978, p. 31 ff). While taking baseline observations on the target behavior, you will become more familiar with the child's repertoire of behavior in a naturalistic situation; you will have a check on the accuracy of significant caretakers' verbal reports; you may discover important controlling variables for the target behavior that were previously overlooked; and you will receive practice in developing definitions and rating scales.

Regular data collection during the treatment phase of your program is perhaps even more beneficial. This continuous record should allow detection of ineffective treatment procedures at a time when a change in tactics is still possible. (This does not mean, however, that methods should be abandoned before they have had a reasonable chance to effect change!) Daily, or even momentary, fluctuations in the rate of the target behavior can alert you to changes in the effectiveness of your reinforcers, to misplaced or omitted sequences in your programming of materials, and even to mistakes in your interpersonal interactions with the child. In addition, a prominently displayed record of your daily progress with the child can also function as a powerful reinforcer for you, for the child, and for the child's caretakers.

The data-oriented approach to behavior change that we are suggesting also may prove disappointing: The data may indicate that your treatment techniques are unsuccessful or that any improvement that occurred was not due to your intervention. When reliable data are at hand, it is more difficult to delude yourself and to take credit for producing change when no credit is due. Perhaps, this explains the penchant traditional behavior change agents had for not gathering data or for gathering data that were sufficiently ambiguous to allow for face-saving interpretations. Furthermore, the extensive behavior observations we are recommending are expensive, time consuming, and in some cases *reactive*. (Reactive measures are those that influence the behavior they are intended to measure, such as TV cameras installed in areas of high risk for shoplifting; see Kazdin, 1979, and Webb, Campbell, Schwartz, & Sechrest, 1966.) We welcome the development of technologies that would allow us to make better use of our time. Unfortunately, the most promising non-reactive approaches — such as physical trace or permanent-product measures, archival records, and hidden sensors — sometimes raise sticky ethical issues or may not be readily available for student projects (Sechrest, 1979; Webb, Campbell, Schwartz, Sechrest, & Grove, 1981). While still other assessment technologies may be available, such as self-monitoring with older children, they too are not without fault (e.g., Nelson, 1977). However, the problems associated with various data collection technologies, like those associated with life, pale in comparison with their alternatives.

## Overview

We hope that an efficient and reliable data collection method will be a prominent feature of your behavior change project. The method should provide data on the target behavior(s) throughout the various stages or conditions of your project: first during the baseline condition that occurs prior to any formal treatment intervention and thereafter during treatment and control conditions as well as during follow-up.

A comparison of baseline rates of the target behavior with rates obtained during and following treatment will allow you to determine whether your child-client has improved; other comparisons will assist you in assessing the durability and generality of the change as well as whether the change can be attributed to the specific techniques you employed. (A more extensive discussion of methods for identifying the effective therapeutic ingredient is presented in the following chapter on experimental control.)

The generally accepted steps to be followed in developing an effective method of data collection (see, for example, Hartmann & Wood, 1982; Wright, 1967) include the following:

1. Define the target behavior(s) in a way suitable for measurement.

2. Develop a measurement procedure.

3. Select settings for observation.

4. Schedule observations.

5. Assess reliability and observer bias.

It is the purpose of this chapter to provide a detailed description of how each of steps one through four can be successfully accomplished; issues concerned with reliability will be discussed in Chapter 8. You may find some of the tasks we suggest time-consuming and even tedious. We believe, however, that the added information provided by good data makes the effort well worthwhile.

## Define the Target Behavior

Once you have selected a target behavior, define it in a way suitable for your project. As Chapter 2 pointed out, one cannot safely assume that the caretaker's initial description of the target behavior will be satisfactory. Your aim is to achieve a response definition that is meaningful and that produces reliable data.

Meaningful, as used here, resembles the term *valid*, as used in the test and measurement literature. Although there are many different conceptions and methods of validation, Campbell and Fiske (1959, p. 81) point out that "validation is typically convergent." Thus, your response definition should converge or generally agree with the target response as defined by the child's caretakers; if possible, it should be consistent with the definition used in related behavior change projects. While concerns with validity have not been prominent in the writings of behavior modifiers, the relevance of validity issues is highlighted in papers by Johnson and Bolstad (1973, pp. 50–58), and by Cone (1982).

The second characteristic of a good definition is that it produces reliable data. Reliability in this context refers to the degree to which *independent observers agree* on the occurrence and nonoccurrence of the target response. Hawkins and Dobes (1977) propose to remedy interobserver disagreements and other definitional problems by making definitions *objective*, *clear*, and *complete*. Objective definitions refer only to observable characteristics of the target behavior. You already have experience in making narrative accounts of your child-client's observable behavior in naturalistic situations, and you should be aware of the pitfalls of making inferences about intent, internal states, and other private events. Apply the same precautions when you define the target behavior(s). Clear definitions are unambiguous and easily understood. If you and your partner can accurately paraphrase your definition, it meets the clearness requirement. A complete definition includes the boundaries of the behavior so that an observer can discriminate it from other, related behaviors. Complete definitions include the following components (Hawkins, 1982): a descriptive name; a general definition, as in a dictionary; an elaboration that describes the critical parts of the behavior; typical examples of the behavior; and questionable instances — borderline or difficult examples of both occurrences and nonoccurrences of the behavior. Your definition might be prepared in a manner similar to the material presented in Table 3-1. If decisions about novel questionable responses must be made after data collection has begun, note your decisions in some convenient and accessible place, such as an observer's logbook or on the data sheet itself.

**Table 3-1.** A Sample Definition

| | |
|---|---|
| Target Behavior: | Peer interaction. |
| Definition: | Peer interaction refers to a social relationship between agemates such that they mutually influence each other (Chaplin, 1975). |
| Elaboration: | Peer interaction is scored when the child is (a) within 3 feet of a peer and either (b) engaged in conversation or physical activity with the peer or (c) jointly using a toy or other play object. |
| Example: | "Gimme a cookie" directed at a tablemate; Hitting another child; Shouting to a friend across the playground; Sharing a jar of paint. |
| Questionable Instances: | Waiting for a turn in a group play activity (scored); Not interacting while standing in line (not scored); Two children independently but concurrently talking to a teacher (not scored). |

## *Additional Considerations*

Remember, most target responses can be defined in a variety of ways. A target behavior such as aggression-toward-teacher could be defined in terms of (a) the number of bites, scratches, and hits, (b) the amount of time spent biting, scratching, and hitting, or (c) the intensity of the bites, scratches, and hits. These are all *direct* measures of aggression. Another tactic that may work is to measure the number of bandaids applied to the victimized teacher. This is an indirect measure, and its acceptability as a measure of aggression must be demonstrated by showing its relationship to a direct measure (e.g., Cone & Foster, 1982). For example, the teacher may apply a bandaid each time little Timmy has drawn blood — a direct measure; so there is a reliable relationship between depth of abrasion and number of bandaid applications. While direct measure may be preferred because they require fewer inferences, they may be so complex or expensive that indirect measures are chosen. For example, studying may be assessed indirectly by counting the number of problems correctly solved, rather than directly by measuring the duration of the joint occurrence of buttocks-on-chair, eyes-on-book, and pencil-on-paper.

Target response definitions can also differ in other ways. Response categories may be either molar or molecular. Molar response categories are used to observe global units of behavior, such as "plays" or "aggresses." Molecular response categories are used to observe narrowly defined behaviors, such as "kicks" or "bites." Molar categories may be troublesome since they require observers to make complex inferences in order to sort events into appropriate response classes. Molecular categories are easier for observers to use, but may be more difficult to interpret subsequent to data collection (Hollenbeck, 1978). For example, the meaning of 10 kicks is quite different if they were delivered to a soccer ball on a playing field than if they were delivered to the family's pet dog or to a favorite aunt.

Responses also differ in whether they are defined in terms of *topography*, the movements comprising the response, or in terms of *function*, the effects of the response on the environment (Hutt & Hutt, 1970). Consider the examples of thumb-sucking and window-breaking. Thumb-sucking would be defined topographically, for example, as the child's having his thumb or any other finger touching or between his lips or fully inserted into his mouth between his teeth. This definition informs observers that the child's having his thumb to his chin or near his mouth does not constitute thumb-sucking. Any disagreement among observers might then be due to failure to observe accurately rather than to disagreement on definitions. Window-breaking, on the other hand, would be defined functionally, and the definition would focus on what constitutes a broken window. The definition need not specify the precise movements or responses required to break a window — a task that might prove difficult when working with an inventive and persistent child-client. Which of these two definitional approaches you take will depend largely on the nature of your target behavior. As Hutt and Hutt (p. 33) indicate, "some behavioral abnormalities are manifested primarily in the morphological (topographical) characteristics of behavior, and others by the specificity of the changes wrought upon the environment."

Additional information on response definitions can be found in a number of sources, including Arrington (1939), Hartmann and Wood (1982), Hawkins (1982), Hutt and Hutt (1970), and Wright (1967).

## Probe Questions for Chapter 3, Section 1

1. *What are the functions of assessment data?*

2. *It is sometimes argued that data collection requires more time and effort than it is worth. What are the primary advantages and disadvantages of data collection?*

3. *If target behaviors for modification programs are typically identified by parents or teachers, why shouldn't we accept their descriptions (or definitions) of the troublesome behaviors without change?*

4. *Describe and explain the requirements of a good target response definition.*

5. Why might one not wish to define "appropriate care of pets" in terms of the longevity of the family goldfish?

6. Why is it usually a good practice to accompany a definition with instances and noninstances?

7. What is a molar response class? What is a molecular response class?

8. What is a topographic definition? What is a functional definition?

## Behavioral Objectives for Chapter 3, Section 2

*After study of Section 2 of this chapter, you should be able to:*

1. *Select an appropriate response characteristic for measurement, such as frequency or duration.*

2. *Decide upon a level of quantification suitable for your target behavior.*

3. *Select an appropriate response recording technique.*

4. *Develop behavioral codes and design useful data sheets.*

# SECTION 2. DEVELOPING A MEASURING PROCEDURE

We have available to us an extremely wide variety of methods of obtaining response data — an observation familiar to those who have completed courses in experimental psychology. Finding one's way through the thicket of alternatives requires attention to three questions: First, what characteristic of the response should be measured? Second, what level of measurement should be employed? And third, what kind of recording procedure should be used?

## Select the Appropriate Response Characteristic

Some responses, such as problem-solving, are measured in terms of frequency or number; others, such as crying, are better measured in terms of duration; still others are best measured in terms of latency (delay in responding to requests), volume (amount of milk drunk), amplitude (loudness of screams), or extension (distance crawled). The definition you developed in the previous section will probably limit the response characteristics appropriate for inclusion in your study. Practical considerations, such as time and the availability of suitable measuring instruments, will further narrow the alternatives.

Consider a response such as napping. Napping would not ordinarily be measured in terms of volume, extension, or amplitude. But the frequency of naps, their latency (time taken to fall asleep), or duration (time slept) might be suitable characteristics to measure. The frequency or number of naps may be the easiest of the three characteristics to measure, but before you choose this response characteristic be sure that it will be sensitive to the changes your treatment is intended to produce. When frequency is the characteristic of naps measured, a 1-minute nap may be equivalent to a 3-hour nap. If this equivalence is undesirable, you may wish to choose an alternative characteristic to measure nap-taking.

## Select a Level of Measurement

Once you have decided which response characteristics to measure, you must decide what level of measurement to use. Assume that your target behavior was spilling food and you were trying to decrease it. The response characteristic of interest was amount of spilling. The most precise measure of amount of spilling might be obtained by weighing the child and the food on his plate before the meal and again after the meal. The preweight minus the postweight would then give a *quantitative, continuous* measure of the amount (weight) of food spilled. If spilling had been restricted to the tablecloth, you might count the number of soiled spots. This would provide a *quantitative, discrete* (only integer values allowed) measure of the amount of food spilled. And there are still additional alternatives. You could determine for each meal whether spilling occurred or not. This would provide a *dichotomous* (two category), *discrete* measure of spilling. While this does not exhaust the possibilities, the important point to note is that each successive example was cruder in terms of measurement than the prior examples. That is, the earlier examples included more information and allowed for finer discriminations. This increased precision has a drawback, however; generally, the more precise the measurement, the more expensive and time consuming it is to obtain.

It is important, then, in deciding upon a useful level of measurement to consider both precision and expense. The measure must be precise enough to show changes in the target behavior, but inexpensive enough not to be a burden on you, the child, or his caretakers. In the example of spilling described above, the first measure that involved weighing of the child might be quite inconvenient, whereas the measure of spilling that required a yes-no response to each meal might not be sensitive to changes in the child's eating behavior. For example, you may reduce spilling from 15 times per meal to once per meal, but the dichotomous measure of spilling would not reflect this change. An acceptable compromise might be to use some intermediate level of measurement, such as counting the number of times the child spilled food during each meal.

## Select a Recording Technique

After you have decided what to observe and how to observe it, you must then decide what kind of recording technique to use. If your target response leaves a record, you are in luck; all you need to do is examine the record and tabulate the response.[1] The number of responses leaving natural records

---

[1] At times, the processes intervening between examining the record and tabulating the response are somewhat more complicated. For example, if the target behavior was writing one's name legibly, a perhaps complex judgment would have to be made of the product to determine its legibility score. Methods of arriving at qualitative assessments of behavioral products are described in Anastasi (1976); also see Cone and Foster (1982). Examples of how such complex judgments can be made reliably are found in Goetz and Baer (1973) and in Hopkins, Schutte, and Garton (1971).

is surprisingly large: Soiled diapers, unmade beds, solved math problems, dampened tooth brushes and face cloths, heated TV sets, dirty dishes, and empty pop cans all indicate the occurrence of potentially interesting behaviors. Still other responses can be induced to leave incriminating tracks: Cries and other distinctive noises can be audio-recorded at slow speed, and rapidly detected by a fast-forward search; the use of radios, TVs, and similar appliances can be detected by changes in an electrical meter; and door openings (including refrigerator door openings) can be identified by examining whether or not inconspicuous seals remain intact. In addition, if these relatively permanent behavioral products can be collected unobtrusively, problems of reactivity are avoided. A number of intriguing examples of trace or record-leaving responses can be found in Webb et al. (1966, 1981).

If, instead, your target behavior is ephemeral and leaves no record, the recording techniques most frequently used by clinical researchers require a human observer armed with a clipboard, stopwatch, and data sheets of one type or another (Kelly, 1977). The following sections describe the four methods most commonly used with human observers: event and duration recording, momentary time sampling, and interval recording (Kelly, 1977).

*Event recording.*    For many behaviors, the easiest method of gathering data is simply to count or tally the number of occurrences of the behavior, as you have defined it, during some observation period. For example, the event recording method might be used in observing a young child who has an inappropriately high rate of squealing. You would count each time the child squeals between 9:00 and 11:30 a.m., or within each of 30 five-minute time intervals spread throughout the school day. The latter method might be preferable because of the more representative data it provides. A variant of event recording, called *trial-scoring*, requires the observer to note whether a response is performed, or performed correctly, on each of a number of occasions or trials. This counting method is used to record compliance with requests, such as "wash your hands" or "set the table." It is also used to record correct responses to language (e.g., "say 'mama'"), academic (e.g., number of questions answered), as well as other discrete tasks (e.g., proportion of free-throws made).

In applied behavioral work with children, event recording has been used to assess a variety of discrete behaviors, such as vomiting, jaywalking, sharing, the occurrence of seizures, and various social behaviors. Event recording has also been used to track multiple behaviors in a single child (e.g., Lovaas & Simmons, 1969). This complex recording task is most easily performed with behaviors that have been videotape-recorded, and when observers have been provided with sophisticated keyboards and event recorders (see Holm, 1978; Simpson, 1979). Additional information on event recording can be found in Bijou, Peterson, and Ault (1968), in Nay (1979), and in recent issues of major behavioral journals including *Behavioral Assessment*, *Behavior Therapy*, the *Journal of Behavioral Assessment*, and the *Journal of Applied Behavior Analysis*.

*Duration recording.* This method is used in cases in which a temporal aspect of the behavior (duration, latency, or interresponse times) rather than its daily frequency is the essential feature. To record response duration, run a stopwatch continuously while the behavior is occurring during an observation period of a specified length. An example of the use of this method would be recording the amount of time a child sucks his thumb. While the child sucks his thumb, the watch is running; when he stops sucking, the watch is stopped. To get adequate duration data, use a watch to time the total duration of the observation session and a stopwatch to record duration of the target behavior.

Duration recording has been used to chart temporal changes in thumbsucking, student off-task responding, proximity to other children, and delays in returning home from school and in compliance with instructions (see Kazdin, 1982b). While these target behaviors represent only a fraction of those assessed using duration recording, it nonetheless is the least used of the common response measures (Kelly, 1977). We suspect that this is due in part to the belief that frequency is a more basic response characteristic (Bijou et al., 1969; Skinner, 1966) and in part to the apparent ease of estimating duration by either of the two methods discussed below.

*Note*: If you decide that either event or duration recording is appropriate for your study, the daily observation period (say 20 minutes) might be divided into 8 to 12 intervals of *equal* length for purposes of reliability assessment. The necessity for doing so will become apparent in the chapter on reliability (Chapter 8).

*Momentary time sampling.* This technique assesses duration by noting whether or not the target behavior is occurring at specified brief observation periods, for example at each quarter hour. The brief observation periods that give this technique its name can be signaled by a fixed or variable time signal on a digital watch, an oven-timer, or an audio-tape played through an ear plug.

Momentary time sampling has been used to code an individual's location, facial expressions, activities, and a variety of appropriate and inappropriate behaviors in groups as diverse as students and chronic mental patients (e.g., Power, 1979). The duration of responses such as those are estimated on the basis of the proportion of time samples during which occurrences are observed. This technique resembles taking a series of still photographs and inspecting each one to see whether a particular behavior has occurred. By contrast, event and duration recording resemble taking a continuous film of the subjects and inspecting it for response onsets and offsets (e.g., Hawkins, 1982).

*Interval recording.* To use the interval method of recording, break the observation period into small *equal* intervals and record whether or not the behavior is observed to occur in each interval. The interval size will usually be from five seconds to one minute in duration, depending upon (a) the rate of the response, (b) the average duration of a single response, and (c) practical considerations such as the nimbleness and experience of the observer. For high-rate behaviors, the interval should be sufficiently small so that two complete responses could not occur in a single interval. On the other hand, the interval should be at least as long as the average duration of a single response. The use of excessively long intervals would obviously result in an underestimate of the occurrence frequency of the target behavior, and might result in your underestimation of the size of the reduction of an undesirable behavior as a result of a deceleration program. The use of very small intervals would have the opposite effect.

Interval-recording techniques are popular because of their presumed ability to measure both response frequency and duration.[2] They are applicable to a variety of target behaviors, so you may find them useful in your project. The interval method has been used to record changes in mealtime behavior, studying, attending, talking, playing, as well as disruptive behaviors (Gelfand & Hartmann, 1975). For further details on the specific interval-recording technique employed, refer to the papers cited there.

With the interval-recording method, as with any of the other methods, you must adopt consistent rules on when to record behavior. The rule may be either that behavior is recorded only when it occurs during (a) the entire interval, or (b) at any time during the interval. Otherwise you may get fluctuating standards for rating occurrences and consequent lowered interrater agreement. Of these two rules governing rating the occurrence of a behavior, the latter requires less judgment and is perhaps the easier procedure to employ, although it may give an overestimate of absolute frequency or duration of the target behavior.

If your intervals are short and you are observing more than one behavior, you might find that your agreement is lowered because you and your fellow observer are not coordinating your observing and tabulating time. If this is a problem, you might try a slight variation of these procedures: Use one interval for observing and the next for recording. Or, if the intervals are longer (say 20 seconds), the first 15 seconds might be used for observing and the final five seconds for recording. The use of a strategy such as this might substantially improve the quality of your data.

---

[2]A note of caution should be sounded regarding interval recording. The chief virtue of this technique — its sensitivity to both frequency and duration — also may be its major vice. The technique does not provide fundamental or pure measures of either frequency or duration; instead, it measures some combination of the two response characteristics. Furthermore, recent research indicates that under certain circumstances interval recording may seriously distort estimates of both frequency and duration (Hartmann & Wood, 1982).

If you intend to use time intervals shorter than 30 seconds, you will find it necessary to develop some signaling device that alerts you to the end of one interval and the beginning of the next. We have found the use of a portable cassette audio-tape recorder to be an efficient and unobtrusive means of signaling observation and recording intervals. To use the recorder, first prepare a tape on which you speak the number of each observation and recording interval. A tape so constructed might begin with "Interval 1, observe" (ten seconds of silence or whatever the length of your observation interval), "Interval 1, record" (5 seconds of silence or whatever the time required to record your observations), "Interval 2, observe," etc. Then, while you make the behavior observations, carry the tape recorder and use an earpiece speaker to listen to the prerecorded interval signals. If the intervals on your recording sheets are similarly numbered, you need not worry about tabulating your entries in the wrong recording interval, as sometimes happens when beeps or tones, rather than recorded numbers, are used to signal intervals (Whelan, 1974).

After this brief discussion of recording techniques, you may find it difficult to decide on the recording method that is best for your study. Clearly the factor most important in choosing a method is whether it will provide the kind of data that are consistent with the aim of your project. Once that factor is accommodated, then guidelines such as those provided by Gelfand and Hartmann (1975), Nay (1979), and Sulzer-Azaroff and Mayer (1977) should be consulted. Table 3-2 summarizes the most important of these guidelines. Additional suggestions for dealing with special recording problems, such as those involved in observing more than one child are available in Bijou et al. (1968), in Boer (1968), and in Paul (1979).

**Table 3-2.** Factors to Consider in Selecting an Appropriate Recording Technique

| Method | Advantages (✔) and Disadvantages (O) |
|---|---|
| Permanent Product | ✔ Time-saving and convenient. |
| | ✔ Information available for reliability anlaysis and for reanalysis if definitions are revised. |
| | O Permanent product not available without the aid of costly equipment. |
| Event or Duration Recording | ✔ Measures are of a fundamental response characteristic (i.e., frequency or duration). |
| | ✔ Can be used by participant-observers (e.g., parent or teacher) with low rate responses. |
| | O Requires responses to have clearly distinguishable beginnings and ends. |
| | O Unless responses are located in real time (e.g., by dividing a session into brief recording intervals), some forms of reliability assessment may be impossible. |
| | O May be difficult with multiple behaviors unless mechanical aids are available. |

| Momentary Time Sampling | ✓ | Response duration of primary interest. |
| | ✓ | Time-saving and convenient. |
| | ✓ | Useful with multiple behaviors and/or children. |
| | ✓ | Applicable to responses not having a clear beginning or end. |
| | O | Unless samples are taken frequently, continuity of behavior may be lost. |
| | O | May miss most occurrences with brief, rare responses. |
| Interval Recording | ✓ | Sensitive to both response frequency and duration. |
| | ✓ | Applicable to wide range of responses. |
| | ✓ | Facilitates observer training and reliability assessments. |
| | ✓ | Applicable to responses without clearly distinguishable beginnings and ends. |
| | O | Confounds frequency and duration. |
| | O | May under- or overestimate response frequency and duration. |

Whatever recording device you select, be sure that it is in good working order. With human observers, this implies — among other things — that you should attend to elementary rules of human engineering. For example, the use of trained, and relatively alert observers, of behavioral codes, and of well-constructed data sheets may make the difference between confusing, poor quality data and useful data. Similarly, attention to such seemingly trivial details as availability of clipboards with attached pencils and coordination of stopwatches can spare you from data loss and unexplained poor reliability.

## Develop Behavioral Codes

Develop a coding system to save observer writing and recording time. If a single target behavior is being recorded, a simple tally mark or activation of a wrist golf-score counter can be used to indicate each occurrence. If several behaviors are being studied, a single-letter abbreviation for each behavior is useful — e.g., P to indicate play behavior. Keep the code simple by minimizing the number of pencil strokes required for each tally, by using a unique and easily discriminated symbol for each behavior, and by using symbols that remind you of the behaviors they signify — e.g., use $\Delta$ for smiles and $\nabla$ for frowns. That way the symbols won't be confused. Helpful information on behavioral codes can be found in Hart (1983), in Hawkins (1982), in Haynes (1978, Chapter 4), in Haynes and Wilson (1979, Table 1), and in Johnston and Harris (1968).

## Design and Duplicate Data Sheets

A well-designed data sheet is an indispensible part of a high quality data collection method. A sample data sheet is shown in Table 3-3. Be certain to date each data sheet and indicate the time and situation, including the

**Table 3-3.** Sample Data Sheet

Date _____ Session number _____ Child _____ Therapist _____

Time started _____ Time concluded _____ Observer _____

Setting: (e.g., tutoring booth, classroom, family dining room) _____

Activity _____

BEHAVIOR CODES: (e.g.,  I = interactive play
                          S = solitary play)

| 1 | 2 | 3 | 4 | 5 | 6 | 7 | 8 | 9 | 10 | 11 | 12 | 13 | 14 | 15 |
|---|---|---|---|---|---|---|---|---|----|----|----|----|----|----|
|   |   |   |   |   |   |   |   |   |    |    |    |    |    |    |

| 16 | 17 | 18 | 19 | 20 | 21 | 22 | 23 | 24 | 25 | 26 | 27 | 28 | 29 | 30 |
|----|----|----|----|----|----|----|----|----|----|----|----|----|----|----|
|    |    |    |    |    |    |    |    |    |    |    |    |    |    |    |

| 31 | 32 | 33 | 34 | 35 | 36 | 37 | 38 | 39 | 40 | 41 | 42 | 43 | 44 | 45 |
|----|----|----|----|----|----|----|----|----|----|----|----|----|----|----|
|    |    |    |    |    |    |    |    |    |    |    |    |    |    |    |

| 46 | 47 | 48 | 49 | 50 | 51 | 52 | 53 | 54 | 55 | 56 | 57 | 58 | 59 | 60 |
|----|----|----|----|----|----|----|----|----|----|----|----|----|----|----|
|    |    |    |    |    |    |    |    |    |    |    |    |    |    |    |

| 61 | 62 | 63 | 64 | 65 | 66 | 67 | 68 | 69 | 70 | 71 | 72 | 73 | 74 | 75 |
|----|----|----|----|----|----|----|----|----|----|----|----|----|----|----|
|    |    |    |    |    |    |    |    |    |    |    |    |    |    |    |

| 76 | 77 | 78 | 79 | 80 | 81 | 82 | 83 | 84 | 85 | 86 | 87 | 88 | 89 | 90 |
|----|----|----|----|----|----|----|----|----|----|----|----|----|----|----|
|    |    |    |    |    |    |    |    |    |    |    |    |    |    |    |

| 91 | 92 | 93 | 94 | 95 | 96 | 97 | 98 | 99 | 100 | 101 | 102 | 103 | 104 | 105 |
|----|----|----|----|----|----|----|----|----|-----|-----|-----|-----|-----|-----|
|    |    |    |    |    |    |    |    |    |     |     |     |     |     |     |

| 106 | 107 | 108 | 109 | 110 | 111 | 112 | 113 | 114 | 115 | 116 | 117 | 118 | 119 | 120 |
|-----|-----|-----|-----|-----|-----|-----|-----|-----|-----|-----|-----|-----|-----|-----|
|     |     |     |     |     |     |     |     |     |     |     |     |     |     |     |

Comments: (Include descriptions of unusual events, indications of child's ill health, competing activities, etc., that might have an impact on the child's behavior.)

names of other people who may be present. If more than one child or more than one behavior is being observed, also indicate the appropriate additional names and behavioral codes. Nothing is quite so discouraging as concluding a study and finding a set of unlabeled (hence uninterpretable) data sheets. You should also *number the recording intervals*, as this will ensure correspondence between the intervals indicated by the signaling device and the interval to be used on the data sheet. It will also facilitate data retrieval and comparison of data following reliability checks. Don't forget to include a "comments" section on the data sheet. Use this space for noting hunches about possible controlling variables, noteworthy therapist behaviors, and any irregularities that might affect the results; see the example by Weinrott, Reid, Bauske, and Brummett (1981) on the advantages of observer hunches.

## Probe Questions for Chapter 3, Section 2

1. The target behavior to be increased is compliance with requests. Which response characteristic (e.g., frequency, duration, latency, strength) might be most appropriate for measurement purposes?

2. Tom's mother has defined "picking-up clothes" as the target behavior for an acceleration program. She has a number of options available for measuring the amount of clothing not picked up, including weighing them, counting them, and simply indicating whether or not all the clothing has been picked up. What kind of measurement does each procedure provide? What are their advantages and disadvantages?

3. Give examples of trace or record-leaving behaviors and of ephemeral behaviors.

4. What is event recording? How is it similar to a motion picture film and when might you want to use it?

5. Which of the methods of taking observational data (e.g., event and duration recording, momentary time sampling, and the interval method) has the widest applicability? Why?

6. What are the characteristics of a good behavioral code?

7. Assume that you want to record whether a child is playing alone, interacting with peers, or interacting with teachers, and whether peers or teachers attend to his approach attempts. Select a simple, easily discriminated code symbol for each of these five events.

## Behavioral Objectives for Chapter 3, Section 3
*When you have read Section 3 of this chapter, you should be able to:*

1. *Determine when to collect data on the target behavior during your study.*

2. *Distinguish between free and discriminated operants.*

3. *Distinguish between continuous and sampling data collection techniques.*

4. *Describe the advantages of data probes.*

5. *Distinguish among the various kinds of generalization that have relevance to a treatment study.*

## SECTION 3.
## DETERMINING THE TIME AND
## CONTEXT OF DATA COLLECTION

In a broad sense, the answer to the question "when to collect data" has already been given: during the baseline, treatment, and control conditions, and, if possible, some time (perhaps two weeks to a month) following the termination of the last treatment phase. A week of data collection during this follow-up period is a small cost to pay for information on the durability of the behavior change you produced, and it is usually worthwhile (Mash & Terdal, 1977, 1980).

Given that data should be collected during each of these various phases, a problem still remains concerning when during these phases of your study the data should be collected. Unfortunately, there are few useful generalizations that can be given to this question. You might think that an ideal answer is "all the time," but this may not be the case. Consider, for example, the target behavior of wearing a seat belt. It would be foolhardy to collect data on that behavior at times other than when the child is located in a moving automobile. It would be equally inefficient to collect data on the target behavior of setting the table at a place other than the dining area and at a time other than mealtime.

You must decide when to schedule observation periods and when during the observation periods to collect data. At one extreme the entire day could constitute the observation period, while at the other extreme a small segment of the day (such as lunch time) could constitute the period of data collection. Within the selected observation period, data could be collected *continuously* or *sampled* on some basis during that period of time. Your decision on when to collect data hinges on (a) the nature of the target behavior, (b) the nature of your treatment interventions, (c) the purpose of your study, and finally (d) various practical considerations such as the amount of observer time available and the extent and regularity of your access to the child-client.

*Nature of the target response.* A method of classifying target responses that is useful in determining when data should be collected is the extent to which the behavior is under specific and known stimulus control. At one extreme are behaviors (such as walking, thumb-sucking, and crying) that are not under tight stimulus control; they occur almost any time and any number of times. These responses, if they are under the control of consequences, are sometimes called free operants. Free operants can be measured either *continuously* or by means of a *sampling* procedure. Consider the target behavior of crying. A caretaker, almost certainly a parent or staff member of an institution, could stay within the range in which crying can be detected, armed with a stopwatch, clicking the watch on and off with the beginning and end of each crying episode for 24 hours of a child's day. Or, instead, crying might be measured by noting whether it occurred during each hourly strike of a clock chime or an oven timer. You may recognize this as an example of momentary time-sampling as discussed in the previous section. For an old, but good review of time-sampling procedures, see Arrington (1943); also see Weick (1968).

On the other extreme of the continuum are behaviors that ordinarily occur only under highly limited stimulus conditions. These responses, sometimes referred to as discriminated operants, include responses such as appropriate eating behavior, fighting with siblings, and leaving the tub during bath time. Such responses may vary in rate, but they occur only in specific stimulus situations. Consequently, it makes little sense to observe these behaviors continuously throughout the day. They may, however, be observed continuously throughout the situation in which they occur. Data could be taken throughout mealtime, or bath time, or, in the case of sibling aggression, whenever a sibling is present. Alternatively, data could be sampled within these occasions. For example, the child could be observed every 5 minutes during his three meals and data taken on the proportion of time during which he was engaged in "pigging" (Barton, Guess, Garcia, & Baer, 1970).

A subclass of discriminated operants alluded to in the previous material on trial-scoring is sometimes referred to as *discrete trial responses*. In discrete trial responding, only a single response is given to each presentation of a specific stimulus, for example, catching or not catching a ball when it is thrown, compliance or noncompliance to a request such as, "Close the door," greeting a playmate when she enters the house, and flushing the toilet after using it. It should be obvious that data on discrete trial responses should be taken only when a trial occurs. Again, data could be gathered during each trial or only sampled on some trials.

A sample of a child's discrete trial performance, obtained at the beginning or end of a training session or periodically throughout the session, sometimes is called a *data probe*. Probing has much to recommend it in contrast to taking data continuously during a training session — a task that is best performed by either an observer or by a practiced trainer with unusual dexterity. Consider a training session in which you are training a child to say "baby" (or to swim, throw a ball, or climb a tree). The specific techniques you use during a training session might include prompting, modeling, guided participation, in addition to various consequating procedures (see Chapter 5). To attempt to tabulate only the child's responses into categories of no-response, partially correct response, prompted response, and correct response while managing both the stimuli and the consequences would be an almost unmanageable feat. Contrast this with the relative ease of probing the child's responses — perhaps at the end of the session — by noting how he responds to three unreinforced presentations of the instruction, "Say, 'baby.'" Unless you can conveniently use continuous data collection techniques during training, use probes. As we will discuss later, data probes also may be useful when assessing treatment generalization or when the child-client would otherwise be exposed to long series of unreinforced trials (see the section on multiple baseline designs in Chapter 4).

*Nature of the intervention procedures.* At one extreme, your intervention procedures might be in effect throughout the child's entire day, such as might be the case if you were trying to train toileting behaviors in a young child. At the other extreme, treatment might only be applied for a very limited part of a child's day, as would be the case if the target behavior were swimming or table manners.

In the case of behaviors trained throughout the day, data might be either sampled or gathered continuously throughout the day. In the case of more discrete training programs, data again could be obtained continuously or sampled (probed), but during the occasions when training is taking place.

*Purposes of the study.* If the purpose of your study is only to demonstrate that a response has been changed in a highly specific situation (such as a one-half hour training session), then all you need do is collect data during that training session. If, instead, your horizons are broader and you want to assert that improvements in the child's behavior have generalized beyond the specifics of your training procedure, you must collect additional data. (See Chapters 7 and 10 for a discussion of the advisability of including generalization training in your treatment program.)

Before examining the types of additional data to be collected and where, a number of types of generalization should be distinguished (see Stokes & Baer, 1977). One might be interested in knowing whether the target response improves in settings other than the training setting (setting or situational generality), or in response to other training stimuli (stimulus generalization or concept formation). The latter type of generalization would be demonstrated if, after a child correctly labeled as blue a blue ball (the training stimulus), he also correctly labeled as blue the sky, a blue shirt, and a blue truck.

Obviously, the data collection requirements of these forms of generalization differ. Situational generalization requires you to assess the child's performance in a situation different from the training room or training booth (e.g., another room), while stimulus generalization requires probing the child on additional test stimuli — perhaps during the regular training session. These generalization assessments, particularly if conducted intermittently, are referred to as *generalization probes* (e.g., Stolz, 1976).

Let us examine an example of situational generality more closely. Assume, for example, that training was directed at increasing a child's "attention span" for two daily 20-minute sessions and that changes were observed during those sessions. It may not be true, however, that the child's "attention span" had changed during other periods of time. (It is entirely acceptable and well within the tradition of much behavior modification work with children to observe the target behavior only during training sessions. However, the change has much greater social relevance or validity if it also occurs outside of the training session, and observations taken outside of the session may be worth the brief time required.) In order to conclude that the target behavior has generalized broadly, data must be obtained either continuously throughout the day (which is difficult at best) or from representatively sampled occasions. Less broad but nonetheless useful conclusions about generalization can be made by observing the target behavior in but one extratreatment situation in which it is likely to occur. For example, instruction-following, trained in a limited treatment setting, could also be observed at home during a time when instructions are regularly given.

*Convenience.* The last consideration, convenience, requires little amplification. If data are to be gathered by human observers (rather than from behaviors yielding permanent products, or by electronic or mechanical devices), convenience for the observers is a crucial determinant of the amount of data that can be obtained. Continuous data obviously cannot be gathered throughout the day unless the child is young and a member of one's own family. Complex data can only be obtained from an independent observer. You should carefully consider the practical demands placed on the data collector; unreasonable demands will probably result in disgruntled, demoralized observers and poor quality data. Table 3-4 presents some general rules that you may find useful in deciding when and how often to collect data.

If during data collection you are a classroom or home visitor, or if your presence as an observer represents a novel situation for the child, some added precautions are warranted. The child will probably react to your presence.

**Table 3-4.** General Rules for When and How Often to Collect Data

| | | |
|---|---|---|
| A. | If your treatment intervention occurs during a brief training session, but it is desirable that the behavior occur in other situations: | |
| | DO | take data during the training session. |
| | DO NOT | attempt to take *continuous* data during a complex training session if you are both trainer and observer; instead use data *probes.* |
| | DO | include *generalization probes* if at all possible. |
| B. | If the target behavior is a discrete trial or other discriminated response: | |
| | DO | take data in the stimulus condition in which the behavior occurs. |
| | DO NOT | take data at random periods throughout the day. |
| C. | If the target behavior is a free operant: | |
| | DO | take data at random periods throughout the day. |
| | DO NOT | use a few long observation periods if you are able to use many short observation periods. |
| D. | And, finally, whatever the nature of the target response: | |
| | DO NOT | make unreasonable demands on the observers (or on the child and his caretakers). |

Consequently, the first few days of observational data may be unrepresentative of the child's natural behavior and probably should be discarded. (That's just as well because the procedures you use during your first few days of data collection may require modification and, even if unchanged, your skills in using them will probably improve substantially with initial practice.) In order to reduce the effects of the observer on the data, review and follow the guidelines for observer conduct offered in Section 3 of Chapter 2.

You should make some tentative decision about what should be done in the event of unforeseen interruptions or other distracting events. Will you continue to record data, move the child to another room, discontinue data collection for a short period, or terminate the day's observation session? Not all untoward events can be foreseen, but those that can should be planned for.

This concludes our discussion of the basic development of a data collection method. Many of the issues are perhaps even more complicated than we have indicated. If you are interested in gaining more information on these topics, you may want to examine Cone and Foster (1982), Hartmann (1982b), Hartmann and Wood (1982), Hutt and Hutt (1970), Johnston and Pennypacker (1980), Kazdin (1981a), Mash and Terdal (1981), Weick (1968), or Wright (1960).

# Probe Questions for Chapter 3, Section 3

1. *Alternative methods of data collection are being discussed as part of a program to teach shoe-tying. Would this behavior be considered a free operant? If a sampling method were to be used, would it be a time-sampling or event-sampling method?*

2. *What do the responses of catching a ball, responding to a request, and closing a door all have in common?*

3. *What factors should be considered in determining when to collect data?*

4. *What rules of conduct are relevant when observing children in either a home or school setting?*

5. *What are the primary advantages of using data probes?*

6. *Name two forms of generalization. What implications for data collection do these forms of generalization have?*

7. *You are requiring a reluctant observer to travel to a child's home on Sunday evening to record the child's completion of homework assignments. What are the probable effects on the observer's behavior and the data collected? What other methods might be used to collect the same data?*

# Chapter 4
# DEMONSTRATION OF
# EXPERIMENTAL CONTROL

## Behavioral Objectives for Chapter 4, Section 1

*After studying Section 1 of this chapter, you should be able to:*

1. *State the major purpose of demonstrating experimental control.*

2. *State the major threats to internal validity and know how they might occur in a pre-post study.*

## SECTION 1.
## INTRODUCTION AND
## THREATS TO INTERNAL VALIDITY

### *Introduction*

Up to this point in your treatment program, you have set up appropriate contacts with the child's caretakers, completed a detailed behavior assessment (including narrative observations of the child in his natural environment and discussions with the child and his caretakers), and perhaps selected a tentative treatment strategy. Before beginning your program, you should study this and the preceding chapter on developing a data collection system, because they provide the backbone for the scientific portion of your study.

Any mention of experimental design recalls for some students their disinterest in learning about rodents either scampering down runways or awaiting the approach of desensitized sophomores. For some, the mention of data and the numbers used to represent them can precipitate an anxiety attack. But take heart. We have tried to minimize these effects — first by directing our discussion of experimental designs to those directly relevant to your work with children, and second, wherever possible, by avoiding esoteric, technical jargon. The closest we come to things statistical in this section is the interocular test (your eyes), and you already have the equipment for that.

We hope that you integrate the material in this and the following chapter into your project; your failure to do so would simply result in one more uncontrolled case study in behavior modification (Pawlicki, 1970). If, on the other hand, you do include this material, you will have acted in a manner consistent with current emphases on accountability which we discussed in Chapter 3, and your study will qualify as an experiment in the best sense of that term.

There are several interdependent questions that you will want to consider in evaluating your project.

1. Did you target behavior's rate change reliably during the study? In order to answer this question, the target behavior must be carefully defined and reliably measured during the course of the study. A functional presentation of the material on definitions, reliability, and methods of developing continuous data collection procedures is given in Chapters 3, 8, and 9.

2. If reliable changes in the target behavior have occurred, can these changes be attributed to your treatment procedures (those child management changes that occurred between baseline and treatment)?

3. Finally, if the changes can be attributed to your treatment procedures, can you specify unequivocally which of the child management techniques was the effective change ingredient? Very few published papers meet this criterion, so don't feel obligated to try for it.

If you are able to answer either of the latter two questions affirmatively, and we think you will, you will have achieved a fundamental goal of science — that is, you will have established a cause-effect relationship between variables. In your case the cause-effect relationship will be between a child behavior — the target behavior — and an intervention technique or set of techniques.

The methods of demonstrating cause-effect relationships are discussed in texts on general experimental design (e.g., Campbell & Stanley, 1963; Cook & Campbell, 1979) as well as in more specialized monographs on individual subject methodology (e.g., Bloom & Fischer, 1982; Hersen & Barlow, 1976; Jayaratne & Levy, 1979; Kazdin, 1982b; Kratochwill, 1978b). Before providing information to aid you in selecting an experimental design appropriate for your study, we will examine the factors that must be controlled if you are to be confident that your treatment effects are genuine and your cause-effect statements accurate.

## Threats to Internal Validity

A good experimental design should protect against the major threats to internal validity. These threats are *systematic* biasing factors or confounding variables. If not controlled, they might be mistaken for a treatment effect (a false positive) or obscure a real treatment effect (a false negative). Those factors that threaten the internal validity of individual subject studies include the following (Cook & Campbell, 1979, pp. 51–55; Kratochwill, 1978a, pp. 12–20):

1. History — the specific events occurring to the child such as illnesses and changes of teacher, or even treatments initiated by other therapists and producing changes mistakenly attributed to the treatment of interest.

2. Maturation — processes within the child operating as a function of time and effecting changes in the target behavior, e.g., becoming less afraid of a neighborhood bully because of increased size or strength.

3. Testing — the effects of an initial measurement upon subsequent measurements, e.g., remembering answers from the last quiz or becoming bored with repeated exposure to the same material. In the former case "testing" would improve performance while in the latter case "testing" would worsen performance.

4. Instrumentation — changes in the criteria used by observers that produce changes in the obtained measurements (e.g., instrument decay). For example, in a speech training program the criteria for a scorable initial "r" sound may change during the course of the program. Consequently, lower rates of mispronounced "r"s observed at the end of the study are due not to changes in the child but to changes in the response definition.

5. Statistical regression — a variety of related phenomena which have in common illegitimate exploitation of chance. One form of statistical regression occurs when a child is selected for treatment because of his extreme performance (due in part to a measurement fluke). The child later scores less deviantly when evaluated because the same random or chance measurement error is not present. Two other effects of statistical regression can be observed in extended time series designs. A threat due to *instability* occurs when a random improvement in the target response during a treatment phase is interpreted as treatment produced. A threat due to *reactive interventions* occurs when treatment is initiated following an atypically extreme pre-intervention measurement. Perhaps the target child engaged in severe tantruming as a result of having to return a lost pet. The return to more typical responding is then mistakenly interpreted as a treatment effect.[1]

---

[1]Other threats to validity are one of three types. (1) They are a subclass of those threats to validity already mentioned, such as compensatory equalization of treatment. This threat is illustrated by a socializing agent who changes her behavior during a withdrawal-of-treatment phase to compensate for the target child's loss of treatment. (2) They are relevant largely to group, rather than $N= 1$ investigations, such as biased selection of subjects and non-random loss of subjects from various treatment and control groups. (3) They are threats to other forms of validity such as external, statistical-conclusion, or construct validity (e.g., multiple treatment interference). These other forms of validity are discussed in some detail by Cook and Campbell (1976, 1979) in the context of quasi-experimental designs.

Consider how the five threats of history, maturation, testing, instrumentation, and statistical regression might operate in a traditional, but weak, experimental design for evaluating change in a single subject. The design could be diagrammed as O × O, where the Os represent pre- and post-measures and X is the treatment. Assume that the problem behavior was sibling aggression and that the rate of aggression decreased between the pretest and posttest. Can we safely attribute this change to treatment? Definitely not! Lower rates of aggression observed at the second O could be due to some environmental event (i.e., history) that occurred at approximately the same time but independently of treatment — for example, the visit of a doting grandparent, or the departure of a troublesome sibling for summer camp.

Perhaps the child has undergone a growth spurt (maturation) coincidentally with treatment, so that an older brother is no longer physically superior and consequently no longer bullies the child-client. Perhaps the initial measurement of peer aggression sensitized the child to his own aggressive behavior, and this alone resulted in lower rates of aggression on the posttest (testing). Perhaps the observer, who might also have been the therapist, developed a more stringent definition of aggression at the time of the second testing (instrumentation); that such calibration changes in observers are possible is suggested by the work of Rosenthal (1966) on experimental bias. Finally, perhaps the child's initial rate of aggressive behavior during the pretest was the highest rate he had ever displayed. If his selection for treatment was based on that high rate, the posttest rate would almost certainly decrease (regression).

In order to avoid mistaking these five factors for a treatment effect, it would be necessary to include additional experimental design features over and above the O × O features of the design described above, a topic to which we turn in Sections 2, 3, and 4 of this chapter. Readers interested in general design issues in child treatment might consult the chapters by Furman and Drabman (1981), by Hartmann, Roper, and Gelfand (1977), and by Kazdin and Marholin (1978).

## Probe Questions for Chapter 4, Section 1

1. *What are the questions that should be answered by a good experimental design?*

2. *What are the five primary threats to internal validity?*

3. *Why would an interpretation problem be created by replacement of a classroom teacher that occurred coincidentally with treatment?*

4. *Give at least two illustrations of regression effects.*

5. *Name at least one useful resource for finding out more about threats to validity.*

# Behavioral Objectives for Chapter 4, Section 2

*After reading Section 2 of this chapter, you should be able to:*

1. *Describe how individual subject designs guard against threats to internal validity.*

2. *State the defining characteristics of the reversal or ABAB procedure and the advantages and limitations of this design.*

3. *State the type of problem behaviors for which the ABAB design is most appropriate.*

## SECTION 2. WITHIN-SUBJECT DESIGNS: ABAB DESIGNS

### *Within-Subject (N = 1)* Designs

At least four general families of experimental designs might be employed in demonstrating control with a single subject. These design families include the ABAB designs, multiple baseline designs, multiple treatment designs, and changing criterion designs. Detailed presentations of these designs are given in Hersen and Barlow (1976), in Kazdin (1982b), and in Jayaratne and Levy (1979); Kratochwill (1978a) provides summary descriptions, examples from the literature, and extensive citations. While the design families differ in detail, they accomplish the common purpose of protecting against internal validity threats by *continuously measuring* the target behavior throughout the study and by *repeatedly varying* conditions within the individual subject. The ability to produce changes at will — either by systematically (a) introducing, (b) introducing and then removing, or (c) introducing and then changing treatments — is the crucial and common characteristic of experimentally sound individual subject designs.

### *ABAB Design*

The basic characteristics of the ABAB, reversal or withdrawal design[2] are as follows: During the first A phase, a series of baseline observations are obtained on the target behavior; during the first B phase, the treatment or

---

[2]Leitenberg (1973) distinguished between withdrawal designs in which change from B to A involves a withdrawal of treatment, and reversal designs in which the change from B to A involves switching or reversing contingencies from one behavior to another. This distinction generally is not maintained in the behavior modification literature; instead, the two terms are used generically and interchangeably to refer to ABAB designs (see Hersen & Barlow, 1976, pp. 92-94).

independent variable is manipulated while continual observations are taken on the target behavior; during the second A phase, or return to baseline, the treatment variable is removed, the procedures that were in effect during baseline are reinstituted, and observations continue. The last B phase is a return to the treatment procedure. (These phases or stages are depicted in Figure 4-1.)

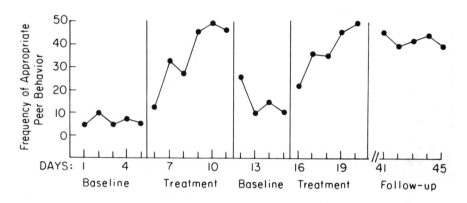

**Figure 4-1.** Frequency of appropriate peer play (fictitious) during baseline and treatment (contingent parental attention) phases using an ABAB design and a follow-up observation period. Figure adapted from Hartmann (1975).

If the target behavior is controlled by the experimental manipulations, it should rise and fall with each introduction and removal of the independent variable. (This is the pattern hoped for with acceleration programs. With deceleration programs, the opposite change direction would occur with each introduction and removal of the treatment variable.) Thus, in contrast to group designs where control is demonstrated by replicating *across subjects*, control in a reversal design is demonstrated by replicating *across conditions* for a single subject.

*Illustration of ABAB design.* We will illustrate the use of an ABAB design with an example in which the target behavior is the child's bed-making.

During the baseline period, daily observations are made as to whether or not the child makes his bed. These data serve to describe current performance and to predict the likely course of responding in the absence of treatment. (If the child never makes his bed, we might decide to use a *retrospective baseline* rather than spending a week obtaining actual baseline, when that week could be better spent increasing bed-making. A retrospective baseline is one based on the verbal report of some responsible person such as the child's parent or teacher, rather than on formal observational procedures. Retrospective baselines should *only* be used when you can be certain that the behavior has either a zero rate or a 100% rate of occurrence.) The number of days of baseline observations required is discussed in some detail in the chapter on data collection (Chapter 9).

During the B stage, the treatment manipulations (such as the use of instructions in conjunction with a point system for bed-making) are instituted. The duration of the treatment may vary from 2 or 3 days to 2 or 3 weeks or longer depending upon the success of the treatment, the stability of the target behavior, and the method used for graphing the data. (If your target behavior can occur only once each day or if your baseline data are quite irregular, you may decide to graph or plot weekly data points rather than daily data points. If you decide to graph by weeks, you would want to carry out your treatment manipulation for two or more weeks to get some idea of the weekly stability of the target behavior during treatment. Further information on graphing is included throughout the text and more specifically in Chapter 10 on data analysis.)

During the second A condition, the instructions and point system are withdrawn and the conditions present during the baseline (such as requests and nagging) are reestablished. Again, observations are continued throughout this phase until the behavior either reaches baseline level or has stabilized at some other level. Finally, during the last condition, instructions and the point system are reinstated, and the desired rate of the target behavior recaptured.

The ABAB design is the most commonly used individual subject design in child behavior modification (Kazdin, 1975). The design has been used to demonstrate experimental control over behaviors as diverse as littering in a forest campground, proper eating, disruptive classroom behavior, question-asking, isolate behavior, and racially integrated play. Additional examples of target behaviors and treatment techniques analyzed by means of the ABAB design and its variants can be found in recent issues of the *Journal of Applied Behavior Analysis*, *Behavior Therapy*, and other applied behavioral journals. Cumulative indexes for these journals, such as the supplement to Volume 10, Number 4 of the *Journal of Applied Behavior Analysis*, can be particularly useful for identifying relevant studies.

*Advantages of the ABAB design.* The basic advantage of a successful ABAB design is that it insures that changes in the child's behavior are due to the treatment manipulation rather than to some confounding variable (see section on threats to internal validity). For example, a rival interpretation to a treatment effect in a simple baseline-treatment or AB design is that the child changed because of some coincidental happening in his environment.

However, each time we make a dramatic change in the rate of the target behavior, by introducing or removing the independent variable, the reasonableness of such an interpretation decreases. On occasion, we may want to expand the ABAB design by adding additional AB segments. Such expansion would be desirable when extraneous factors, which might conceivably be responsible for change in the child's behavior, occur simultaneously with our initial change from A to B and back to A. With the inclusion of enough AB segments, even the most skeptical become believers!

Another "rival" hypothesis or alternative interpretation in the simple AB design is that the repeated testing itself results in changes in the dependent variable. However, if treatment is introduced and removed a number of times with a subsequent rise and fall in the target behavior, the interpretation of repeated testing also loses credibility. If conducted properly, the ABAB design also controls for the other previously described threats to internal validity, including maturation, instrument decay, and regression.

In addition to the technical advantages the ABAB design has for demonstrating control, it also may have assessment and therapeutic advantages (cf. Hayes, 1981, pp. 200–201). Each treatment withdrawal functions as an assessment or test of whether the child is able to respond appropriately in the absence of treatment or whether additional treatment is required (Jayaratne & Levy, 1979).

Baer et al. (1968, p. 94) suggest that repeated withdrawals or reversals may have a positive effect on the child subject by "contributing to the discrimination of relevant stimuli involved in the problem." Baer (1968) also suggests that the repeated withdrawals provide behavior modifiers with increased confidence in their ability to control behavior.

*Limitations of the ABAB design.* The most important limitations of the ABAB design are due to the *undesirability* of reversing some behaviors and the *"irreversibility"* of others. Without the ability to reverse the target behavior the ABAB design is unable to demonstrate experimental control — to establish a functional relationship between independent and dependent variables.

Some behaviors such as fire-setting or self-destructiveness may be so serious that even a temporary resumption of these behaviors is totally unwarranted. Although you won't choose behaviors as serious as these to work with until you have moved from novice to journeyman status, the child's caretakers may be unwilling to approve of a temporary resumption of even a much milder problem behavior; be sure to discuss this matter with them early in your project. Even with minor problem behaviors and caretaker approval, one should be cautious in using this design repeatedly with a single child because inconsistency in child management techniques can be upsetting to the child. Although this typically may not be the case, you should be alert for emotional upset as a possible undesirable side effect.

Behaviors may be "irreversible" due to a number of causes:

1. Initial changes in the target behavior may have been produced by an extraneous variable. Consequently, treatment withdrawal would not be expected to produce a change in performance.

2. Treatments may produce direct and irreversible behavior changes. For example, a surgical intervention may change the child's bodily structure so as either to prevent or to dramatically alter his capacity to emit certain target responses. Other more "psychological treatments" may result in the acquisition of skill, such as reading or bicycle riding, which are not easily lost once acquired.

3. Treatments may continue to exert temporary effects even after they are withdrawn — referred to as *treatment carryover*. Some drugs, for example, as well as certain intermittent schedules of reinforcement may continue to exert control over a behavior long after they have been withdrawn. Punishment procedures also might continue to control a behavior even though they are no longer available. If a target response does not occur, the child may never discover that the contingencies have changed (e.g., Kazdin, 1978).

4. Finally, it may not be possible to reinstitute all relevant baseline procedures. For example, low levels of peer interaction may be modified by generous teacher attention for appropriate play behavior. When this attention is withdrawn, peer interactions may persist as this behavior is "trapped" (Baer & Wolf, 1967) by natural contingencies, such as peer approval, that are not susceptible to our control.

Some investigators have suggested that the likelihood of irreversibility can be lessened by withdrawing interventions as soon as a change in behavior is apparent (e.g., Bijou et al., 1969). Other behavior modifiers have adopted alternative control procedures when a reversal is undesirable or difficult to achieve. Some of these procedures such as the DRO (Differential Reinforcement of Other behavior) and other rate-changing techniques described in Chapters 5 and 6 are employed when the behavior is reversible but not simply through reinstatement of baseline conditions (Baer & Wolf, 1970; Gelfand & Hartmann, 1968, p. 211; Sidman, 1960). Still others, such as the multiple baseline procedures, are employed when the behavior either cannot or should not be reversed. The following section describes multiple baseline procedures, which fortunately, achieve control without temporarily decreasing the rate of desired behaviors.

## Probe Questions for Chapter 4, Section 2

*1. What functions are served by each phase of an ABAB design?*

*2. What is a retrospective baseline? When can a retrospective baseline be used safely?*

3. Describe a situation in which more than two AB segments should be used in an experimental design.

4. What aspect of a reversal design might prove difficult for socializing agents to accept?

5. How might an ABAB design be therapeutic?

6. Why might a target behavior be irreversible?

## Behavioral Objectives for Chapter 4, Section 3

*After reading Section 3 of this chapter, you should be able to:*

1. *State the defining characteristics of multiple baseline designs and the advantages and limitations of these designs.*

2. *State the kinds of problems for which the various types of multiple baseline designs are best suited.*

## SECTION 3. WITHIN-SUBJECT DESIGNS: MULTIPLE BASELINE DESIGNS

### *Multiple Baseline Designs*

Multiple baseline designs typically involve keeping data on two or more behaviors that will be modified *sequentially* with the *same* treatment procedure. During the first step, then, baselines need to be obtained on each of the behaviors. During the next steps, one behavior at a time is manipulated, while observations continue on treated and untreated behaviors alike. Thus, if you were employing a positive reinforcement program to increase rates of three prosocial behaviors, you would consequate one of the target behaviors while continuing to take data on all three. After a stable rate is achieved on the first treated behavior, consequate behavior two while continuing to take data on all three. Finally, consequate behavior three.

Multiple baseline data, plotted for three-day averages on correct pronunciation of "r," "l," and "w" are shown in Figure 4-2. (*Note*: It is usually best to "piggyback" graphs when plotting the data from multiple baseline design studies — that is, each behavior is represented in one of separate, but interconnected panels. The panels are aligned for easy comparison of rates of the different responses at the same moment in time. Putting several behaviors on a single graph often results in serious eyestrain for your readers. Compare, for example, Figure 4-2 with the much "busier" Figure 4-3.)

Figure 4-2 indicates how the base rate of each behavior is maintained until that behavior is itself manipulated. Control is then demonstrated by replicating a procedure *sequentially across a set of behaviors*. If each baseline (behavior) remains at a fairly stable rate prior to treatment, and only improves following treatment, you can safely assume that the treatment was responsible for the change in rate of that behavior.

Two other variants of the multiple baseline design commonly are used in behavior modification studies. One version of this design requires the application of a treatment to one target response of a child under two or more settings or stimulus conditions. Control is demonstrated by replicating a pro-

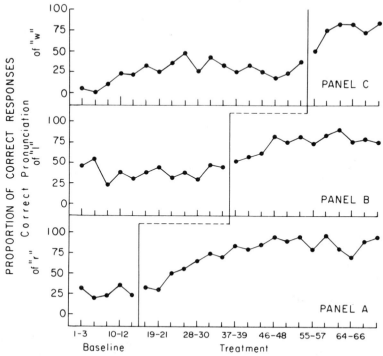

**Figure 4-2.** Data on correct pronunciation modified in a multiple baseline design. Panel A shows data on "r" sound; Panel B shows data on "l" sound; Panel C shows data on "w" sound. (Data plotted are three-day averages.)

cedure *sequentially across several settings* for a single behavior. The final version requires the application of a treatment to two or more subjects with the same target response and under the same environmental or stimulus conditions. Control is demonstrated by replicating a procedure *sequentially across a number of subjects* for a single behavior. These three types of multiple baseline designs are summarized in Table 4-1.

**Table 4-1.** Summary of Types of Multiple Baseline Designs

| Control demonstrated by replicating across: | Responses | Number of Settings | Subjects |
|---|---|---|---|
| Responses | ≥2 | 1 | 1 |
| Settings | 1 | ≥2 | 1 |
| Subjects | 1 | 1 | ≥2 |

Note: With each design, the same treatment procedure must be used consistently, whether across behaviors, across settings, or across subjects.

The three types of multiple baseline designs have gained increasing popularity in applied behavioral work with children, and their use is almost certain to increase. Surprisingly, most multiple baseline designs have employed multiple behaviors in a single setting, rather than a single behavior in multiple settings (see Jackson, 1973). Because the most commonly used form of this design requires the use of two or more behaviors that are likely to be similarly affected by a *single* treatment strategy, the range of behaviors for which this design is suitable is somewhat more restricted than is the case with the ABAB design. The behaviors over which control has been demonstrated in multiple baseline demonstrations are quite varied, and include arithmetic problem solving, letter printing, articulation errors, imitative responding, and fetishes. The rationale for multiple baseline design and additional examples with children are described by Cuvo (1979), Hall, Cristler, Cranston, and Tucker (1970), and Risley and Baer (1973).

*Illustration of a multiple baseline design.* We will use the target behavior of aggressive play with peers to illustrate the details of multiple baseline designs. This example demonstrates the second type of multiple baseline design in which a single response is modified in multiple settings or stimulus conditions: In this case, when mother is the principal caretaker, when father is the principal caretaker, and when babysitter is the principal caretaker. The therapist would first obtain base rates on aggressive play with peers in each of the three settings. It is important that interobserver reliability figures are obtained in each of the three settings — this is crucially important if the primary data gatherer is a different person in each of the three settings, as would be the case if mother, father, and babysitter functioned both as trainers and as data collectors. (This reliability point will be amplified in Chapter 8, "Reliability.") When the baselines become orderly (see Panel A in Figure 4-3), the therapist introduces the treatment into one of the three caretaker conditions. Which condition is treated first should be determined either randomly or, in this case, on the basis of whichever caretaker is least likely to produce generalized improvement across all settings. Our best guess as to which caretaker this is, is the one least often responsible for the children. (See the section entitled "Limitations of the multiple baseline design" for an elaboration of this point.) In this example, we will assume a "traditional" household, and thus the child would probably be treated first when either father or babysitter was responsible for child care. Data would continue to be collected in all three caretaking conditions. When the data have restabilized in the first treated setting or condition (see Panel B of Figure 4-3), the therapist would introduce the treatment manipulation in the second condition, using a consistent criterion for selecting the second condition. If the choice of the first treatment setting was based on frequency of caretaker contact, this criterion would be used for selecting the second condition; if, instead, the random selection criterion had been used, it would continue to be used. When the rate had stabilized in this second condition (see Panel C of Figure 4-3), the therapist would introduce the treatment in the remaining condition. Data would be collected until the rate in this condition had also stabilized (see Panel D of Figure 4-3).

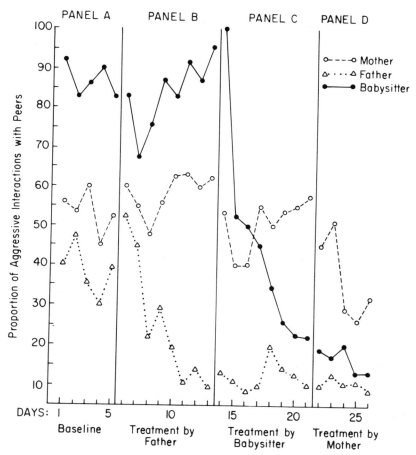

**Figure 4-3.** Example of multiple baseline design showing proportions of aggressive peer interactions relative to total sibling interactions in three stimulus conditions: with father, with babysitter, and with mother as caretaker.

*Advantages of the multiple baseline design.* Whenever feasible in treatment demonstrations, it is safer to employ a multiple baseline procedure than an ABAB design since it may be difficult or impossible to recapture baseline levels of performance with the latter designs (Risley, 1969; Sidman, 1960;

and sad personal experience). If you have kept records on two or more target behaviors, you can always resort to the multiple baseline model if your reversal procedure fails to produce the desired rate changes.

A second, and equally important, advantage of the multiple baseline approach is that everyone is spared the painful process of reinstating some undesirable behavior (for example, lying), solely in order to demonstrate the efficacy of the treatment procedure. Caretakers are usually only too glad to testify to the value of any intervention that has dealt successfully with a troublesome behavior, and they frequently don't appreciate the scientific and professional importance of an experimental demonstration. Caretakers are happier with a multiple baseline design. Not only is there no need to return to the old, unsatisfactory performance, but two or more desirable behaviors are instated for the price of one — a public relations dream come true.

The final advantages of the multiple baseline designs are a consequence of the long baselines required for the later-treated behaviors (Strain & Shores, 1979). Long baseline series allow us to detect performance trends, and hence provide superior estimates of future responding. They also may allow us to make more subtle performance assessments. For example, a long series of baseline trials may aid us in distinguishing various types of errors made by a child in completing subtraction problems; this additional information may suggest refinements in our treatment procedures for each of the types of error. With a shorter baseline — and fewer attempted problem solutions — the types of errors made by the child may not be discernible.

*Limitations of the multiple baseline design.* The extended baselines in multiple baseline designs also can be problematic. The long periods of unreinforced (baseline) responding may cause upset, boredom, or fatigue, and as a result, seriously disrupt performance. According to Cuvo (1979) these *reactive effects* produced by long baselines might be counteracted in the following ways.

1. Make performance assessments intrinsically interesting. For example, assess a child's color-naming skills by creating a game atmosphere involving surprise and excitement.

2. Use non-contingent rewards such as telling the child that she "sure tried hard" once during each minute of the assessment.

3. Divide up the assessment period into shorter sections, each of which is followed by brief access to some enjoyable activity.

Other disadvantages of this design strategy involve time and effort. Additional time and effort are required to collect data on more than one baseline, and to ensure that the baseline rate of each behavior is relatively stable before treatment is initiated for that behavior.

If you intend to use two or more behaviors, it may be difficult to find enough behaviors that can be treated with the same technique — a necessary prerequisite to using the multiple baseline approach. In general, behaviors of a single child that will be responsive to similar treatment strategies will be either topographically similar (e.g., saying "a," "o," and "u") or functionally similar (e.g., gaining attention by pulling on mother's apron, screaming at her, and kicking her in the shins).

It may also be difficult to find several behaviors that are independent, another requirement for a successful multiple baseline demonstration of control. By independence we mean that each behavior can be separately modified without changing the rate of the remaining unmodified behavior(s). An empirical approach to estimating the likely independence of behaviors involves examining the degree to which the behaviors covary during baseline assessments. If the target behaviors covary — increase and decrease in rate together from one occasion to another — they may not display the kind of independence required for demonstrating experimental control (cf. Kazdin & Kopel, 1975). Incidentally, our concern with independence explains why we chose to manipulate aggressive peer play (see Figure 4-3) initially in the least frequently occurring childcare setting — with father as caretaker. If, instead, we had first applied our treatment in the most frequently occurring caretaking setting (with mother as caretaker), the treatment effect may have been more likely to generalize to the remaining untreated settings. If generalization had occurred, the opportunity to demonstrate experimental control may have been lost. For similar reasons, it would be unreasonable to use a multiple baseline design with a small child when the three target behaviors were tearing magazines, books, and papers. The child probably does not discriminate among the three objects, and so modifying book-tearing would probably also affect magazine-tearing.

Independence as a requirement also implies that the behaviors should not be developmental prerequisites for one another (Risley & Baer, 1973). For example, it might not be appropriate to choose standing, walking, and running as the three behaviors in a multiple baseline design for a one-year-old child. Because these behaviors occur in a developmental sequence, they would have to be "treated" in the order of standing, walking, and running. Furthermore, the earlier baseline trials for running (those conducted prior to completing the training of standing and walking) provide little useful information. That is so because the rate of running during these trials has to be zero because running has no *opportunity* to occur before the acquisition of both standing and walking.

Horner and Baer (1978) have developed a version of the multiple baseline design that overcomes both the problem posed by developmental sequences and by extended (and possibly reactive) baseline phases. This design variant replaces the long series of baseline trials with strategically placed baseline probes (see Chapter 3, Section 3); hence its name, the multiple probe technique. The multiple probe technique is especially useful in demonstrating control for programs involving the acquisition of successive approximations and of behavior chains such as shoe-tying or ball-throwing.

## Probe Questions for Chapter 4, Section 3

1. What are the requirements for a multiple baseline design?

2. How do the types of multiple baseline design differ?

3. Why might a multiple baseline design foster good relations with parents and teachers?

4. Why might a multiple baseline design be preferred to a reversal design when peer aggression is the target behavior?

## Behavioral Objectives for Chapter 4, Section 4

*After reading Section 4 of this chapter, you should be able to:*

1. *Give the defining characteristics of the multiple treatment designs and the advantages and limitations of these designs.*

2. *State the types of problem behaviors for which multiple treatment designs are most suitable.*

3. *Define multiple treatment interference and describe how it limits the interpretations of individual subject designs.*

## SECTION 4. WITHIN-SUBJECT DESIGNS: MULTIPLE TREATMENT DESIGNS

### *Multiple Treatment Designs*

Multiple treatment designs enable you to compare the effects of two or more interventions or treatments that are implemented during a single treatment phase. Thus, unlike most applications of other individual subject designs, multiple treatment designs allow direct experimental comparisons among treatments. In other ways, however, multiple treatment designs have much in common with the individual subject designs previously discussed. They share with between-settings multiple baseline designs the use of two or more baselines on the same target behavior; and they share with ABAB designs alternations in conditions — though the alternations are much more rapid with multiple treatment designs.

Because the members of this design family vary somewhat more than do members of the other design families, we must limit our comments to a commonly used multiple treatment design, the alternating (sometimes called the simultaneous) treatments design (Barlow & Hayes, 1979; Kazdin & Hartmann, 1978).[3] Both names are descriptive of this design: "simultaneous" because two or more interventions are applied during the same treatment phase; "alternating" because the interventions are presented in an alternating fashion during that treatment phase: In the first phase of the alternating treatments designs, baseline observations are taken on the target behavior. After stability is achieved, the first or comparative treatment phase is begun. During this phase two or more interventions are presented repeatedly in a rapidly altern-

---

[3]Other members of this design family, according to Kazdin (1982b) include multiple schedule designs, concurrent schedule designs, and randomization designs (also see Browning, 1967; Edgington, 1980; Hersen & Barlow, 1976; Ulman & Sulzer-Azaroff, 1975).

ating pattern (e.g., BCCBCBBC). When two or more interventions are applied to an individual's behavior during a treatment phase, there may be some danger that the factors associated with treatment administration, such as class period or teacher, might produce changes in the target behavior that erroneously are attributed to the treatments. If this occurs, treatments are said to be confounded with the conditions of their administration. In order to insure that such confounding does not occur in your project, each intervention should be implemented equally often during each condition of administration, such as time-of-day, class period, or teacher.

Assume that two reward conditions — call them B and C — were implemented during math and during spelling each day by either the classroom teacher or by the teacher aide. In order to avoid confounding, each of the two reward conditions would be administered equally often, and in a counterbalanced order, in each of the following four conditions of treatment administration: math class with classroom teacher, spelling class with classroom teacher, math class with teacher aide, and spelling class with teacher aide. The sequence of treatments and conditions over a 2-day period might be:

• Day 1: B (Math/teacher) and C (Spelling/teacher aide);

• Day 2: C (Math/teacher aide) and B (Spelling/teacher).

For the following 2-day period, the sequence might be:

• Day 3: C (Math/teacher) and B (Spelling/teacher aide);

• Day 4: B (Math/teacher aide) and C (Spelling/teacher).

After the more effective of the two treatments has become clear, the final treatment phase is implemented. In this final phase, the more effective treatment is applied in all conditions to maximize treatment gains. In our example, the more effective treatment would be implemented during both class periods whether taught by the teacher aide or by the regular classroom teacher.

Control is demonstrated in the alternating treatments design in two ways. First, control is demonstrated by changes in the target behavior that occur with changes in phase — primarily as a result of changes in the rate of the target behavior from the baseline phase to the first treatment phase, but also as a result of performance changes from the first (comparative) treatment phase to the final treatment phase. Second, control (or differential control) is demonstrated by differences in rate of the target behavior associated with each of the two or more interventions that are implemented in the comparative treatment phase.

Applications of multiple treatment designs are not yet common in the child treatment literature. Those studies available have used one or another form of the design for modifying various classroom behaviors such as attending, phonics, telling time, numbers, and reading; cooperation; generalized imitation; stereotyped repetitive movements; and appropriate verbalizations (see, for example, Barlow & Hayes, 1979; Kazdin, 1982b; Ulman & Sulzer-Azaroff, 1975).

*Illustration of a multiple treatment design.* Data illustrating the alternating treatments design version of the multiple treatment design are shown in Figure 4-4. In the baseline phase, data are gathered on the percent attending displayed by the target child during reading and during science when these classes were conducted by either of two teachers. This phase was continued until attending was observed to occur at a relatively stable rate of approximately 20%. As in previous designs, these baseline data provide descriptive information on the extent of the problem; they also provide the basis for predicting what the rate of responding would be if treatment had not been implemented. In the next (comparative treatment) phase, tokens earned for attending could be exchanged either for rewards for the target child (self-rewards) or for the entire class (class-rewards). The two treatments would have been counter-balanced across class periods and teachers as previously illustrated, so that the conditions associated with the administration of treatment would not be confounded with the treatments themselves. Attending improved under both reward treatments, although more in the class-reward treatment (approximately 60%) than in the self-reward treatment (approximately 40%). During the final treatment phase the more effective treatment, tokens exchanged by the target child for class-rewards, is implemented during both science and reading when these classes are conducted by either teacher. The improvement in attending seen in this phase provides additional evidence for the control exerted by the class-reward intervention.

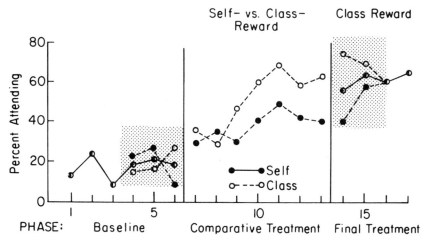

**Figure 4-4.** Illustration of the alternating treatments design showing the proportion of attending across baseline, comparative treatment phase (tokens exchanged for self vs. class rewards), and a final treatment phase (tokens exchanged for class rewards during all periods). Shaded areas represent data graphed as though all measurement occasions were associated with either self-or class-rewards (see text). Data modeled on Figure 1 from Kazdin and Hartmann (1978).

In some displays of data obtained from alternating treatments designs, data from the baseline phase and from the final treatment phase are presented as in the shaded portions of Figure 4-4. That is, all measurement occasions are identified as being associated with one or another of the interventions even though neither intervention is implemented during the baseline phase and only the most effective intervention is implemented during the final treatment phase.

*Advantages of multiple treatment designs.* The multiple treatment designs can be used to compare different treatments, or to compare a treatment with a control (baseline) condition. The first purpose, that of comparing different treatments, can perhaps *only* be served by multiple treatment designs. Thus, if treatment comparisons are part of your project plan, the alternating treatments design, or another variant of multiple treatment design almost certainly will be required.

The second purpose, that of comparing a treatment and a control or baseline condition, also can be served by ABAB and multiple baseline designs.[4] However, the alternating treatment design does so most efficiently of the three designs because critical comparisons are made primarily within a single phase rather than across successive phases. Efficiency sometimes can be improved even more by omitting completely the initial baseline phase of the alternating treatments design (Ulman & Sulzer-Azaroff, 1975). Think carefully before omitting this phase, however, since the increased efficiency may come at the cost of a less compelling demonstration of control.

Another important advantage of multiple treatment designs is that they do not require a return-to-baseline or reversal phase. Thus, they avoid the ethical and public relations problems associated with a phase in which treatment gains may be temporarily lost. Other minor advantages of multiple treatment designs are described by Kazdin and Hartmann (1978).

*Limitations of multiple treatment designs.* Because members of this design family compare rapidly alternating conditions within a treatment phase, there are definite limitations on the kinds of treatments and behaviors to which they apply. Consider an alternating treatments design in which each of two eating reduction treatments are implemented during either lunch or dinner each day. For the study to be effective, the treatments must have relatively immediate effects, and the effects must be limited to a relatively brief time that does not include the next meal. If the treatments were slow acting, their

---

[4]When the primary interest is in comparing control (baseline) and treatment conditions, the alternating treatments design is very similar to a between-settings multiple baseline design (see Kazdin, 1982b).

effects on behavior might not be observable before the next treatment was applied and thus the individual effects of the two treatments could not be distinguished. As a result, the effects of each treatment would be *confounded* by the carryover effects of the other treatment. An example of treatments having carryover effects are medications that continue to be present in the bloodstream during an entire day, so that when a second medication is taken later in the day, the first medication still is effective. Carryover effects of this kind are but one of the forms of *multiple treatment interference* that may be troublesome in individual subject designs.[5]

Multiple-treatment interference is a threat to *external validity* (Cook & Campbell, 1979), or the extent to which the results of a study can be generalized to other conditions. For example, would the effects of treatment generalize to applications in which treatments were separated by a longer period of time that reduced the likelihood of carryover effects? These external validity threats caused by multiple treatment interference can be reduced by balancing conditions of administration across treatments, as we have previously discussed; by avoiding very long treatment sessions; and by using only one treatment in each session (Barlow & Hayes, 1979).

The nature of target behaviors also may limit the use of multiple treatment designs. Consider weight loss as the target behavior in the mealtime program just discussed. Weight loss is far too slow in reacting to typical weight modification treatments to be used with multiple treatment designs. Caloric intake, however, would not have the same problem as weight loss, and might permit use of a multiple treatment design. (See Kazdin, 1982b, p. 189 for a discussion of the kinds of target behaviors that are good candidates for use in treatment studies using multiple treatment designs.)

Multiple treatment designs also may require certain discriminations on the part of the target child. For example, if the effects of two different contingencies are to be compared, such as two lengths of time-out or two magnitudes of reinforcer, the child must be able to distinguish which contingency is in effect during which period of time. These discriminations often can be facilitated by the use of instructions. Instructions, such as "Timmy, two minutes in the time-out booth for kicking while we do numbers this morning," tell the target child exactly which treatment is in effect and for which period of time.

---

[5]Two other forms of multiple treatment interference also may be of concern (Barlow & Hayes, 1979): *alternation effects*, in which the effects of a treatment are dependent upon the treatment being applied in alternation with some other condition; and *sequence effects*, in which the effects of a treatment are dependent upon the specific sequence in which treatments are alternated. While there is little evidence that these forms of multiple-treatment interference seriously threaten typical applications of multiple-treatment designs (Shapiro, Kazdin, & McGonigle, 1982), it is important to understand the nature of the threat they pose, and how the threat might be reduced.

The final limitation in the use of multiple-treatment designs occurs if the conditions of treatment administration such as the time of day, class period, teacher, or the like are strongly associated with different rates of performance of the target behavior. Imagine that the base rate of thumb-sucking averaged 50% in the morning and averaged 30% in the afternoon. The large differences in rate of thumb-sucking in morning and afternoon time periods might make it difficult to distinguish between differences in rate associated with treatments and differences in rate associated with the morning and afternoon conditions of treatment administration. Sometimes the effects of these large performance differences between conditions of treatment administration can be reduced with a little mathematical magic. That is, express the rate of performance during treatment relative to the rate of baseline performance in the same condition. In our thumb-sucking example, treatment phase scores obtained in the morning would be expressed as a percent deviation from the morning baseline rate of 50% [e.g., $(50\% - X\%)/50\%$], and treatment phase scores obtained in the afternoon would be expressed as a percent deviation from the afternoon baseline rate of 30%.

## Probe Questions for Chapter 4, Section 4

1. *How many separate conditions of treatment administration would be necessary if an alternating treatments design was used to assess the effectiveness on food-spilling of two response-cost interventions and a control procedure implemented daily?*

2. *What are the primary means by which control is demonstrated in an alternating treatments design?*

3. *Name a possible source of multiple treatment interference in an alternating treatments design investigating the effects of three medications on caloric intake.*

4. *What is external validity? Why should threats to external validity concern us?*

## Behavioral Objectives for Chapter 4, Section 5

*After reading Section 5 of this chapter, you should be able to:*

1. *State the defining characteristics of the changing criterion design and its advantages and limitations.*

2. *State the kinds of target behaviors and treatment interventions for which each of the individual subject designs are best suited.*

3. *Select an appropriate design for your study.*

## SECTION 5. WITHIN-SUBJECT DESIGNS: THE CHANGING CRITERION DESIGN AND SELECTING A DESIGN

### *The Changing Criterion Design*

With the changing criterion design, a target response is gradually modified in increments in a series of treatment subphases. With the introduction of each subphase, the requirements or criteria for acceptable performance are increased. For example, a child might be required to go progressively longer each week without tantrumming in the grocery store, or lose a special treat such as a 5-minute pony ride. During the first week the criterion may be set at 5 minutes, during the second week at 10 minutes, and so on for a 2-month treatment period. Control is demonstrated using the changing criterion design when performance repeatedly changes to match changes in the criterion, hence the name, changing criterion design.

According to Hartmann and Hall (1976), the changing criterion design shares a number of important characteristics with multiple baseline designs. Each treatment subphase provides a baseline against which to assess change when the criterion of acceptable performance has once again changed in the subsequent subphase. And the improvements in behavior that (we hope) occur with each change in criterion are similar to the replicated changes found in successive treatment phases of a successful multiple baseline design. However, unlike multiple baseline designs, the changing criterion design does not require extended baseline phases during which treatment is withheld (and then abruptly introduced); instead, treatment changes are made continuously in a series of gradual steps or stages.

The changing criterion design has seen only limited use in published child behavior change studies, perhaps due to the recency of the design's description in the behavioral literature (Hartmann & Hall, 1976). The studies currently available using changing criterion designs tend to focus on academic target behaviors such as number of math problems solved or work sheets completed (Hall & Fox, 1977). However, the changing criterion design has been advocated for demonstrating the effectiveness of shaping programs, and for behaviors which are desirable to change (either upward or downward) in an incremental manner. The many behaviors that fit this description include exercise and eating, academic problem-solving, reading, compliance, and motor skills such as ball-throwing. Because of the wide applicability of the changing criterion design, we can expect to see many more studies in which this design is used. Detailed presentations of how the design might be implemented successfully with a broad range of target behaviors are given in Hartmann and Hall (1976) and in Kazdin (1982b).

*Illustration of the changing criterion design.* The changing criterion design is illustrated with data on correct math solutions shown in Figure 4-5. The study begins with a baseline phase, which serves both to describe current performance and to predict future performance. When the rate of baseline responding has stabilized, the treatment phase commences. In most applications of the changing criterion design, positive, negative, or both forms of consequences are made contingent upon some specified rate of appropriate responding. The rate chosen for the initial criterion, as well as subsequent criteria, should represent a level of performance that the target child is very likely to meet, that is a meaningful improvement in the child's performance, and that will be detectable from a visual analysis of the graphed data. The first criterion in Figure 4-5, Criterion I, is established at two completed problems. This level of performance is clearly within the child's capability, as performance this good or better was accomplished on two of five baseline trials. Two problems also clearly represent an improvement over the stabilized baseline rate of zero completed problems; furthermore, this rate should be discernible from the rate of zero. The criterion of two problems is continued until performance stabilizes at, or near, this rate. Stability is required as the performance rate in Criterion I provides a new baseline for performance in Criterion II; furthermore, a match between performance rate and criterion is required for demonstration of control.

After the child performs consistently under one criterion, a new criterion is selected. In setting this, and subsequent criteria, also keep in mind your treatment goals and the length of time you have available to work with the child. These, as well as the previously mentioned considerations, play an important role in determining the number and magnitude of criterion shifts. Be careful not to set criteria too high, since excessively high criteria might result in unmet performance goals. That, in turn, may demoralize your child-subject and may also endanger your ability to demonstrate experimental control. Criteria also can be set too low. If this happens, responding may exceed the criterion, and again may jeopardize your ability to provide a compelling demonstration of control. Criterion II, set at three problems, appears

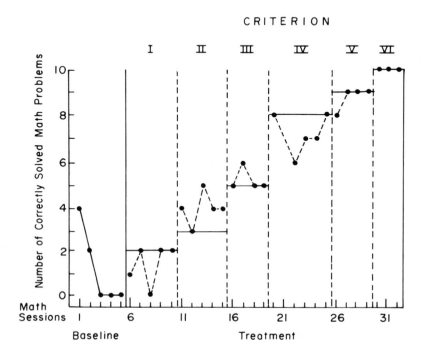

**Figure 4-5.** Data on number of math problems correctly solved demonstrating the changing criterion design. Solid horizontal line segments indicate the criterion for each treatment subphase. Modified from Hartmann and Hall (1976, Figure 1).

too low, and performance during this treatment subphase does not provide strong evidence of control. Criterion III, five problems, seems about right as the child-client's performance exactly matches the criterion on three of four treatment sessions. Criterion IV, eight problems, appears to be too high, as the child had some difficulty in meeting the criterion consistently. If practical considerations did not dictate otherwise, Criterion IV should have been extended as neither stability nor a criterion-performance match was achieved within five sessions. The final two criteria, set at nine and ten problems respectively, seem suitably chosen as performance matched these criteria in six of seven opportunities.

Of the six criteria established, three provide strong evidence of control (Criteria III, V, and VI). One provides modest evidence of control (Criterion I) and two provide weak or no evidence of control (Criteria II and IV). Considering the child's performance in all six treatment subphases, the evidence of control seems compelling. However, if the proportion of criteria falling into the "strong" category and into the "weak or no evidence" category were reversed, additional criteria or subphases would have had to be added if a compelling case were to be made.

We can see from a discussion of these data that practical, clinical, and experimental considerations must all be considered in establishing a changing criterion design's dimensions, including the number and magnitude of criteria, and the length of time each criterion is in effect. Further discussions of these issues can be found in the references previously cited.

*Advantages and disadvantages of the changing criterion design.* Unlike more popular individual subject designs, the changing criterion design requires neither the temporary worsening of desired behavior nor prolonged withholding of treatment. In fact, treatment is instituted quickly following an initial baseline phase, and continues until the child's performance goals are achieved. A sometimes equally important advantage of the changing criterion design is that it requires incremental changes in performance. For many changeworthy behaviors, gradual achievement of performance goals is desirable. Thus, in the changing criterion design we find a favorable correspondence between experimental and clinical requirements.

The changing criterion design has one serious limitation, and that occurs when performance changes do not match criterion changes. When this occurs, demonstration of control may be impossible. Lack of correspondence between behavior and criterion can occur in three ways: Performance changes may be so great that they overshoot the criterion; performance may be highly variable, sometimes overshooting and at other times undershooting the criterion; and criteria can be set too high so that they are not achieved. If your changing criterion design has gone awry because criteria and behavior do not match, two solutions might be considered. Both solutions involve adding additional treatment subphases or criteria, but differ in the nature of the criteria added. The first approach is simply to add more criteria of the type you have been using. This approach is particularly suitable if the later criteria have been more closely matched by the child's performance than have earlier ones. The second approach is to add criteria, some of which represent a *relaxing* of performance requirements. Thus, if the last three criteria in an exercise program originally had been 20 min., 25 min., and 30 min. of exercise, two additional criteria might be added — 25 min. and 30 min. The second 25 min. exercise criterion is a relaxation from the previous 30 min. criterion, and represents a mini-reversal phase. A criterion requiring a directional *change* in behavior rather than merely further improvements in behavior, may substantially aid in demonstrating control with a changing criterion design (e.g., Kazdin, 1982b).

## *Selecting an Experimental Design for Your Project*

The checklists in Tables 4-2 through 4-5 are for your use in determining which method of demonstrating control is most advisable for your project. After you have made a tentative decision based on the list, check with your instructor and get her or his approval. Whichever design you finally decide upon, remember the data gathering requirements of that design.

**Table 4-2.** Checklist for Determining Whether the ABAB Design is Suitable for Demonstrating Experimental Control in Your Project

---

*Necessary Requirements Include*:

_____     Target behavior relatively innocuous (undesirable behavior can occur without dire results).

_____     Caretaker approval obtained for temporarily worsening problem behavior.

_____     Baseline conditions under your direct or indirect control and so can be reinstituted.

_____     Control of the target behavior not likely to be lost to factors outside of the treatment context.

---

Unless you can meet each of the requirements listed in Table 4-2, do not use an ABAB design. Evaluate the possibility of a multiple baseline, alternating treatments, or changing criterion designs.

**Table 4-3.** Checklist for Determining Whether the Multiple Baseline Design is Suitable for Demonstrating Experimental Control in Your Project

---

*Necessary Requirements Include*:

_____     Time available to take baseline and continuous data on multiple responses.

_____     Two or more target responses for a single child, or a single target response in either two or more settings or for two or more children, are available.

_____     The rates of all target responses are likely to be independent.

_____     Treatment can be delayed for some responses, in some settings, or for some children.

---

Unless you have answered yes to each of Table 4-3's requirements, do not use a multiple baseline design. If neither the ABAB or multiple baseline technique is applicable to your problem, evaluate the possibility of alternating treatments, or changing criterion designs.

**Table 4-4.** Checklist for Determining Whether the Alternating-Treatments Design is Suitable for Demonstrating Experimental Control in Your Project

*Necessary Requirements Include:*

_____ Two or more treatments, or a control condition and one or more treatments to be directly compared.

_____ Treatments likely to affect responding quickly and briefly.

_____ Child can discriminate between treatments.*

_____ Child's performance not substantially different across times of day, class periods, teachers, or other conditions associated with treatment administration.

*May not be necessary for certain projects, including those investigating the differential effects of drugs.

Unless you have answered yes to each of the requirements listed in Table 4-4, do not use an alternating treatments design. If neither the ABAB, multiple baseline, or alternating treatments design is suitable for your problem, evaluate the possibility of a changing criterion design.

**Table 4-5.** Checklist for Determining Whether the Changing Criterion Design is Suitable for Demonstrating Experimental Control in Your Project

*Necessary Requirements Include:*

_____ Desirable to change behavior gradually and in step-like increments.

_____ Difficulty of behavior for child easily determined so that criterion changes can be correctly gauged.

_____ Target responding unlikely to display substantial variability during treatment.

Unless you have answered yes to each of these requirements given in Table 4-5, do not use a changing criterion design. If none of the four designs is suitable for your project, check with your instructor. Another form of the multiple treatment design, a recently described design such as the random stimulus design (Matson & Ollendick, 1981), or a patchwork design may be appropriate. Alternatively, you may have to switch treatments, target behaviors, or be willing to use a quasi-experimental (e.g., AB) design.

## Probe Questions for Chapter 4, Section 5

*1. What characteristics do the changing criterion and multiple baseline designs share?*

*2. What kind of problem behaviors seem particularly well-suited for study using the changing criterion design?*

3. Name those factors that should determine the number and magnitude of criterion shifts in a changing criterion design?

4. What is the single serious limitation of the changing criterion design?

5. What are the primary reasons for choosing each of the four individual subject designs?

6. Which design is unusually well adapted for target behaviors which are best modified in an incremental manner?

# Chapter 5
# INCREASING DEFICIT BEHAVIOR

## Behavioral Objectives for Chapter 5, Section 1

*When you have read Section 1 of this chapter, you should be able to:*

1. *Select the modification agent most appropriate for the situation, and justify your choice of agent.*

2. *Become acquainted with the child to set the stage for the treatment intervention.*

3. *Arrange a favorable learning environment, or know how to cope with a less than favorable treatment setting.*

4. *Describe stimulus control procedures and when to use them.*

## SECTION 1. GENERAL CONSIDERATIONS IN INITIATING A TREATMENT PROGRAM

### *Choice of Modification Agent*

It may not be easy to decide which person is best equipped to carry out a behavior therapy program with a child. The child's ordinary caretakers, such as his parents and teachers, have some obvious advantages as modification agents, primarily because they are the child's usual instructors in many academic and social skills. Consequently, they often have a valuable store of experience in the methods that are most effective with that particular child. They have established a relationship with the child, most often a generally positive one. Thus, they are important models, instructors, and disciplinarians.

In addition, caretakers are with the child for many hours every day, so that, unlike most therapists, they can observe bothersome low rate behaviors (Gordon & Davidson, 1981), and can conduct the intervention continually, rather than in brief sessions in unfamiliar settings, as is the rule for most programs administered by professional therapists. The caretakers can continue to administer the treatment program long after the student therapist has terminated his/her relationship with the child. As discussed in Chapter 7, adult caregivers may promote the durability and generalization of treatment effects (but see Atkeson & Forehand, 1978, regarding limited generalization of parent- and teacher-administered interventions). Many programs for children are managed by parents under the direction of professional therapists (Blechman, 1980; Clark, Greene, Macrae, McNees, Davis, & Risley, 1977; Cone & Sloop, 1974; Forehand & McMahon, 1981; Gordon & Davidson, 1981; Graziano, 1977; Tavormina, 1974). Parents' general success in managing their children constitutes a powerful reason to use parents as a treatment resource.

Nevertheless, there are several disadvantages in employing caretakers as therapists or trainers. Sometimes they oppose the philosophy of a behavior therapy program, or find it foreign or uncongenial. Some caretakers consider it undesirable, if not actually sinful, to materially reward or even to praise children for "things they should be doing anyway." It might prove easier to alter such a view through the demonstration of improved child behavior than through appeals to science or logic (but remember to seek informed parental consent when appropriate). Although they may not resist your doing so, caretakers may not themselves knowingly choose to reinforce the child for good behavior, at least not initially. If this is the case, your program might stand little chance of implementation by parents or teachers.

Even though some caretakers may agree with the *philosophy* of your program, they may not succeed as therapists. Many of the principles of behavior therapy are relatively simple and can be mastered and applied by people with little formal education (Bernal, Williams, Miller, & Reagor, 1972). However, mastery of the principles does *not* ensure that caretakers can carry out the procedures correctly and consistently. It is nearly a sure bet that they cannot do so without considerable training and supervision from you, which is a very time-consuming operation. Treatment program requirements pose particular problems if the caretaker is already very busy. Even with the best of intentions, a classroom teacher with 40 youngsters to manage, including several with behavioral problems or learning disabilities, may find it too taxing to carry out a behavior modification program with one particular child. There are too many competing demands on the teacher's time. Similarly, impoverished, overburdened, and socially isolated mothers may not continue to carry out programs that have markedly improved their children's behavior (Wahler, Breland, Coe, & Leske, 1977). They simply may lack the physical and psychological fortitude to do so.

Also remember that when instructing caretakers, you will be attempting to teach them complex new procedures but will lack powerful inducements for them to do so. Your unsubstantiated promise that the procedures you recommend will improve the situation may be insufficient if the procedures in question prove distasteful, time consuming, or dull, which is sometimes the case. It is easy to forget that behavior principles apply in work with parents and teachers as well as with children. If you are a stranger to the teacher or parents, and can offer them no appealing incentive to cooperate, you may have to spend more time than you can spare in trying to ensure that they carry out the program. If you are too demanding, they may simply withdraw their cooperation; if you are too ready to compromise, the diluted modification program may fail.

Another good candidate for the post of therapist is the child himself. No one else is as favorably situated to monitor the child's behavior throughout the day, to carry out treatment procedures continuously, and to employ newly acquired skills on other appropriate occasions. Consequently, you should consider involving the child in the behavior observations and in the implementation of the treatment program whenever feasible. Self-regulation programs and how to conduct them receive detailed consideration in a later section of this book (see Chapter 7, Section 2). Be aware, however, that self-administered programs may prove difficult for children younger than about 9 years of age, those who are extremely aggressive, the mentally retarded, and youngsters who are seriously emotionally disturbed. In general, self-administered interventions are newer and less thoroughly tested than are more conventional forms of treatment. There are fewer empirically based guidelines for the development and delivery of self-regulation programs, and consequently it might be wiser to choose another type of program for your first effort. Whatever treatment approach you adopt, in most cases the child must be your ally if the treatment is to succeed.

By now it probably is apparent that we are advising you to act as the treatment agent yourself. You have a knowledge of basic therapeutic principles upon which to base an effective treatment strategy, you are aware of the importance of consistency in program administration, and you will develop skills which allow you to accurately observe and record the child's behavior. If the caretakers and the child are at loggerheads over the child's conduct, the more objective, less emotionally involved student therapist can treat the situation calmly and allow the others to withdraw from the field of combat with some semblance of dignity. And it is crucial to avoid an embarrassing loss of face on the part of the child and the caretakers.

By acting as treatment agent, you have better control of program application than if you must depend on others to carry out the treatment plan. You will gain experience in basic behavior modification skills such as behavioral assessment, data collection, rapport-building, verbal instruction, modeling, and shaping, to name just a few. In addition, you will learn the many practical skills involved in dealing with school personnel, parents, and the children themselves. You are in a position to revise an ineffective procedure relatively quickly and easily, and you will not have to rely on the sometimes inaccurate reports of others. It is instructive to act as the modification agent yourself, particularly if you are a beginner.

## Arrange a Favorable Learning Situation

You can make the learning task easier for yourself and for the child by setting up an environment conducive to learning. Basically, this means that the setting should be as convenient and pleasant as possible, and, initially, at least, non-distracting.

## Get Acquainted with the Child

Most children become wary, uncommunicative, and unresponsive if unfamiliar therapists attempt to initiate a treatment program without prior acquaintance with the child. Consequently, you must first establish yourself as a friendly, rewarding person and the training situation as a non-threatening one. Otherwise, the child may be afraid of you and consequently may resist accompanying and remaining with you. Such an encounter is devastating for the child and the inexperienced therapist alike. And remember that the child and caretakers are free to withdraw from participation at any time, which makes it absolutely necessary to enlist their willing cooperation.

To avoid intimidating the child, you should approach him in his customary environment. Simply being in the classroom and acting as the teacher's assistant for a while may help to break the ice. Chatting with the child about his school work, his family, his pets or hobbies, or other interests or activities can prove informative as well as helpful in establishing you as a warm and caring adult. Teachers and parents can offer useful advice on how to approach the child. If you are unfamiliar with the ways of children and don't know how best to approach them, observe the teachers and others who work well with the child and ask them for suggestions. Unlike most adults, children often become shy, embarrassed, and withdrawn if an unfamiliar adult attempts to question them. Children respond better when the conversation takes place in a familiar and entertaining play context. The play materials need not be elaborate, and in fact it is better if they are not so attractive that they claim the child's rapt attention. Some simple dolls, puppets, construction or art materials, or the like provide convenient and effective contexts for interviewing children. When you and the child become fairly comfortable with each other, it is time for your therapeutic program to begin.

## *Explain the Program to the Child*

Honesty is the best policy. We recommend the fullest possible disclosure to the child of the purposes and procedures of your program. If your goal is to help the child reduce the number of fights and arguments he engages in, tell him so. But try not to appear accusatory or condescending; make every attempt to preserve his dignity and autonomy. A resentful, sullen child has many means of sabotaging the treatment program. Many therapists point out to the child the potential benefits to be derived from changing his behavior so that other children and adults will seek him out and treat him better. Some therapists set up an atmosphere in which children become eager to alter their behavior by presenting the treatment in a game-like context which is appealing to the children. For example, the "good behavior game" (Barrish, Saunders, & Wolf, 1969; Fishbein & Wasik, 1981) has proved popular and effective in improving elementary school children's classroom behavior.

Because such explanations require tact and social skill in dealing with children, some therapists avoid offering the child any explanation of their presence or their activities. Such evasions make the whole process appear unnecessarily enigmatic and arbitrary, and make it difficult for the child to comprehend and assist in the therapeutic process. We feel that you should explain as much about the program as is consistent with the child's developmental level and with the goals of the treatment intervention.

## *A Partner Aids in Assessment and Training*

As was pointed out in Chapter 1, a partner who can assist you in your data collection and treatment administration is a significant asset. It is very difficult to chat with the child, observe his behavior, find the stimulus materials, administer the program, and record data all at the same time, particularly when you are new to all of these activities. A partner can significantly decrease your burden during these early sessions and allow you to concentrate on the child and the program. It is like juggling three oranges; the feat can be learned best by starting with one orange, then adding another, and finally working up to managing all three. You can make your work easier and considerably more pleasant by not overloading yourself at first.

A partner also serves as a friendly critic. Being unimpeded by the demands of carrying out the program while you are acting as therapist, your partner can also note the quality of your general interactions with the child, and let you know whether you appear friendly or intimidating, whether your program administration is too rapid or too slow, whether you are performing consistently, and whether you follow the program script.

In case unforeseen difficulties arise, and they nearly always do, you can work together in formulating the best way to deal with them. Since both of you may have encountered the same problem, you will be better able to develop a successful plan for its resolution.

It also is easier to standardize your training procedures if both of you can be present at the initial sessions, at least. Otherwise you might each devise separate and different procedures, which could complicate and hinder your modification efforts. In order to relieve the burden on the beginning behavior modifier and to standardize procedures, it is best for both partners to attend treatment sessions and to share in the initial treatment efforts.

However, the most convincing argument for working in pairs is that it benefits the child-client. With two people administering the treatment program, the child can receive more treatment sessions than would be the case with only one therapist. This is so because some of the sessions can be conducted by each of the therapists working alone. Thus, the child can be treated on all or most weekdays, increasing the probability of treatment success.

## Location for Individual Sessions

If you will be engaging in one-to-one tutoring with the child, find a location that will maximize his attending to the learning task. Ideally, the location should be convenient, well-illuminated, and as quiet as possible. Realistically, you probably will be conducting your sessions in a corner of the child's classroom, in a resource room, or even in a busy corridor. Do not despair — it is inconvenient, but quite possible to carry out your project under less-than-ideal circumstances. In any event, you will want to end the training effort by teaching the child in his normal classroom setting to ensure that new-found skills will be exhibited in the child's usual routine (see Chapter 7, Section 1 regarding generalization and durability of treatment effects). Training can take place nearly anywhere if you are well-prepared, sensitive to the child's reactions, and well-organized.

Have your stimulus materials ready for presentation, and your system for awarding points or tangible reinforcers prepared before escorting the child to the tutoring location. The child may learn to be inattentive to you if you spend too much time fumbling. If you are using material reinforcers, it may be best to keep them out of sight so the child doesn't concentrate on them rather than on the task. And you certainly do not want to get into an unseemly wrestling match with the child over possession of the reinforcers.

## Projects Conducted in Homes and Classrooms

You will have somewhat less control over the situation if the modification program is to be conducted during the child's customary home or school activities rather than in a specially prepared tutoring setting. Nevertheless, the same principles hold. Try to ensure that no one else is attempting to conduct a competing program, and that there is no dissimilar program in effect to modify the target behavior, either of which could confuse the child. Your attempts to reduce a schoolboy's aggressive attacks on classmates may be hampered if his father is threatening to spank him if he doesn't stop menacing his younger brother, or, worse yet, the father may be actively encouraging his son to use his fists, not his wit, in confrontations with others. Similarly, if the teacher continues an ineffectual reasoning tactic with the child while you are trying to increase his attending to his schoolwork, your program will suffer. You must make sure that everyone knows about and has agreed to your plan for improving the child's performance. To accomplish this goal may well require all of the tact and persuasiveness that you can muster.

*Timing.* Accentuate the positive. Hold your treatment sessions at a time during which the child usually is alert and ready to learn, not when she is overly excited, hungry, tired, or cranky. A child who is eager to go to recess with her friends will be a distracted and inattentive learner. If your program uses food reinforcers, do not attempt to deliver them when the child has just finished a meal. One popular solution is to administer points or tokens which the child later can exchange for snack items, special play privileges, or other attractive reinforcers.

Timing considerations will affect your relationship with teachers and parents also. Try to minimize your intrusion on their routines. This means that you should not hold training sessions during times when the teacher wants all of the children to be in class, and that you should not try to compete with the child's and the parents' favorite TV programs or other types of eagerly anticipated recreation. Being deprived of such events is punishing. Insofar as possible, schedule around competing attractive activities, and eliminate tempting alternative activities whenever and wherever your sessions are scheduled.

Remember that fatigue, impatience, anxiety, and hunger will affect your performance as well as that of the child. If possible, select a schedule that does not put undue stress on you. Since you are a student, no doubt this sage advice will be impossible for you to follow, given the rigors of most academic programs. So if your current work schedule makes this advice laughable, remember that we and our students seldom abide by it either.

## Stimulus Control

You may be fortunate enough to encounter a child and situation that allow you to promote a beneficial change in the child's behavior simply by providing stimulus events that serve as prompts or discriminative stimuli for appropriate responding. Stimulus control procedures may represent the simplest, most economical, and most effective means of promoting desirable child conduct. Something as simple as pausing before assisting a child may suffice to increase the child's appropriate verbal requests and other productive language. For example, Halle, Baer, and Spradlin (1981) increased retarded children's language use through the *multiple stimulus control procedure* of delaying responding to the children's nonverbal requests for a 5-sec. period, and briefly delaying giving them the food or play materials they had requested nonverbally through pointing and other gestures. At the end of the 5-sec. delay period, the teachers modeled an appropriate verbal request (e.g., "Juice, please," or "Push [the scooter] please"), and then waited for the child to imitate the request before fulfilling the child's demands. This procedure dramatically increased the retarded children's verbal initiations directed toward adults. Similarly, nursery schoolchildren's use of speech rather than gestures to make requests was increased through the simple expedient of placing play materials in view but out of the children's reach so that it was necessary for the child to ask for them (Hart & Risley, 1975). Naturally, in such programs nonverbal requests are placed on an extinction schedule by the adults ignoring them. And programs of this type will succeed only when the child already has the relevant language production skills, but fails to use them consistently.

In other academic situations implied performance expectations have improved children's academic work. Students' math performances can be improved simply by requiring them to verbally describe the problems before writing the answers (Lovitt & Curtiss, 1968). Similarly, introduction of a timer set for the average amount of time required by a group of first-grade children to complete a predetermined amount of schoolwork sufficed to improve the speed and accuracy of their work (Rainwater & Ayllon, 1976). No other special feedback or reward was needed; however, the children's performance might decline over a longer period of time if no particular rewards are associated with fast and accurate performance.

Because interventions such as these are easy to implement and may be highly effective, we recommend that readers consider them before turning to more complex, and potentially more risky programs. However, it is advisable to read the articles we have cited in order to glean the details on how to implement stimulus control and modeling procedures. More complicated stimulus control procedures have been described by Etzel and LeBlanc (1979), and by Etzel, LeBlanc, Schilmoeller, and Stella (1981).

## Probe Questions for Chapter 5, Section 1

1. *What are the advantages and disadvantages of using parents and teachers as modification agents?*

2. *How do you explain treatment goals and the treatment program to a 10-year-old girl who frequently hits people and destroys furniture when she becomes angry?*

3. What problems might be encountered in conducting treatment programs in the child's home, school, or clinic?

4. Describe your ideal partner in administering a child treatment program.

5. What is stimulus control, and how can it be used in treatment?

## Behavioral Objectives for Chapter 5, Section 2

*Studying Section 2 of this chapter should enable you to:*

1. *Decide when it would be beneficial to include modeling in a treatment program.*

2. *Define guided participation and devise a guided participation program.*

3. *State the five components of successful modeling sequences.*

## SECTION 2.
## MODELING AND GUIDED PARTICIPATION

Modeling procedures are noncoercive and efficient providers of information, and are highly effective, especially in the alleviation of specific fears or phobias. If modeling programs fail, then the therapist can always turn to more cumbersome shaping procedures to build desirable behavior or can use response suppression techniques to reduce inappropriate responding. Modeling is a particularly effective means of teaching complex performances which are not easily acquired through shaping of individual components, such as the proper use of grammatical rules (Rosenthal & Bandura, 1978; Rosenthal & Zimmerman, 1978). Moreover, modeling has proved among the most effective methods of combating fear-produced avoidance behavior and teaching appropriate behavioral alternatives (Bandura, 1969; Gelfand, 1978; Rosenthal, 1974). Modeling techniques have been used to overcome fears of animals, insects, entering the water, approaching high places, interpersonal encounters, medical and dental treatment, and the dread school exam (see Bandura, Grusec, & Menlove, 1967; Davis, Rosenthal, & Kelley, 1981; Lewis, 1974; Mann & Rosenthal, 1969; Melamed & Siegel, 1973; O'Connor, 1969; Peterson & Shigetomi, 1981; and Ritter, 1968, 1969). Thus, many of the specific fears which are common during childhood can be treated through some form of modeling therapy, usually in only six to eight modeling treatment sessions when administered by experienced therapists (Gelfand, 1978; Kirkland & Thelen, 1977; Ross, 1981).

### *Guided Participation*

Models have proven effective both in live performances and in filmed or videotaped demonstrations. Although modeling alone can reduce clients' fearful avoidance behavior, *guided participation* in fear-provoking situations has been particularly effective (Blanchard, 1970; Rosenthal & Bandura, 1978). In guided participation, the client first watches models engage in approach behavior and then gradually imitates the models' performances. The client is gently induced to participate with the assistance of whatever *performance aids* are necessary. For example, the snake phobic child might first watch several child and adult models fearlessly approaching and handling harmless snakes. The use of several different models is more effective than confining demonstrations to a single one (Bandura, 1977). After witnessing the demonstration the client is asked to place his gloved hand on the hand of a model who is touching a snake. Next, the client might be instructed to touch the snake with a gloved hand. In successive and gradual phases the child-client is asked to behave increasingly boldly until finally he handles the snake just as the model did (Ritter, 1968). Bandura (1977) believes that such successful experiences are particularly helpful in building *self-efficacy expectations*, or feeling that one can successfully complete a task. Self-efficacy expectations, in turn, promote further performance gains. Efficacy expectations and performance skills are built hand-in-hand.

## Disadvantages of Modeling

Like other therapeutic techniques, modeling has drawbacks. It might be quite difficult to devise appropriate modeling scenarios involving safe, controlled exposure to feared stimuli such as imaginary creatures, and even to deal with fears of spiders, snakes, and taunting by schoolmates. Credible models must be trained and presented, preferably ones who resemble the client in age, gender, and appearance, and thus are more convincing to the client than are models who appear too old or too young, too capable, and generally dissimilar to the learner. Of course, great care must be taken to prevent the child's fears from appearing to be well founded. The feared animals must be prevented from turning surly, the models must not seem terrified, and certainly models must not get hurt. These unfortunate occurrences would only augment the child's fear.

Some children do not learn spontaneously through observation, so they must be taught to do so, which is a lengthy and demanding enterprise. We recommend that you avoid attempts to teach general imitation skills to children who do not imitate spontaneously. This would be an overly ambitious behavior therapy project (although simpler projects such as teaching them to attend to you or to the teaching materials usually are not difficult). Also, we recommend that you avoid attempts to teach subtle social skills to withdrawn, socially inept children. To do so successfully requires gathering data on appropriate conduct in the child's play group, analyzing the exact nature of the child's social deficit, arranging for peer models to enact various types of interactions, and perhaps introducing guided participation and contingent reinforcement. The best course is to confine the choice of target behaviors to specific fears, and the treatment procedures to replications of successful modeling programs described in journal articles. Leave novel modeling and guided participation interventions to the experts.

## Guidelines

Successful imitation of modeled routines depends on many factors. The child's developmental level and individual capabilities must be considered. For example, older children profit from modeling displays of bravery and cooperation, while preschoolers who must have surgery may become highly anxious if coping and modeling procedures overwhelm them with too much information too far in advance of their hospitalization (Ferguson, 1979; Melamed, Klingman, & Siegel, 1982). The child's relevant history is important too. Demonstrations of how they will be treated during dental or surgical procedures will help prepare novices, but not children who already have undergone the treatments. The experienced patients know what to expect and modeling neither provides them new information nor allays their fears (Klorman, Hilpert, Michael, LaGana, & Sveen, 1980; Melamed et al., 1982). Providing children the wrong modeling procedure could have paradoxical effects and accentuate their fears.

As Bandura (1969, 1977) has concluded, successful imitation requires the client's attending to the demonstration, retaining a memory of the modeled performance, being able to reproduce the model's behavior, and having the motivation to do so. In this section, we will deal with each of these components in turn.

1. *Attention.* Demonstrations not attended to are wasted. You must make every effort to ensure that the child attends to the model's behavior. This may require prompting through verbal instructions (e.g., "Now watch me,") or through manual tactics such as the trainer's holding a piece of candy near his mouth where the child must look to see the modeled language performance. In looking at the treat, the child sees how the model produces the sound. It also may be necessary to reinforce the child's attending to the model to ensure continued vigilance.

Additional efforts to promote observer attention might include using attractive and relevant peer models, presenting many demonstrations rather than just one, and avoiding highly anxiety-producing displays which might frighten the child and lead him to avoid watching the model (Rosenthal & Bandura, 1978).

Attention to the most important components of the demonstrations is enhanced by providing narrative explanations of the model's conduct and by asking the child to describe what the model is doing. Sequences which the child has failed to notice or has interpreted incorrectly can be repeated by the model as necessary.

2. *Retention.* To help the child remember the demonstration, it may be necessary to provide capsule labels characterizing the model's actions or the rules to be followed (e.g., "Just act calm when you get near the dog; don't jump around or shout."). Then the child can rehearse the desired actions mentally, physically, or both.

3. *Motoric reproduction.* The child must be physically as well as psychologically capable of replicating the model's behavior. This may require teaching the child new skills or refining old ones, such as how to pet a dog, pick up an insect, enter a swimming pool, and so on. These motor skills themselves may be taught through modeling, practice, and feedback or reinforcement. This process requires careful analysis of the child's actual and potential skill level.

4. *Motivation.* Is the child motivated to imitate the model? If not, modeling undoubtedly will fail. One way to increase the child's motivation is to use popular and attractive peer models whom the child naturally wants to emulate. Verbal encouragement and praise for the child's attempts at imitation may prove helpful also (Lewis, 1974), as will other types of reinforcers.

5. *Guided practice and corrective feedback.* First, have the child shadow the model's movements, where appropriate, just imitating them at a tolerable distance. In gradual steps, have the child touch the model who is engaging in the desired activity, gradually easing into a closer approximation of the modeled routine. Use whatever performance aids are necessary to convey a sense of safety — gloves, sticks or pointers, safety-lines or leashes, pens, or other restraints for the feared animals. Fade out the performance aids as quickly as possible lest the child become dependent on them. The child must attribute success to her own abilities rather than to the gauntlets, muzzles, safety-lines, or other protective devices. Give credit when due, but do not falsely reassure the child that she has completely overcome her fears when she knows she has not. This would reduce your credibility and hence your effectiveness as a therapist.

Give the child corrective feedback. If he makes a mistake such as screaming at the dog or jumping anxiously and waving his arms, quickly and calmly demonstrate the correct approach behavior and instruct the child to imitate it. If the child becomes noticeably fearful during guided practice, drop back to a less-demanding previous step. Establish the child's success at the previous step, then increase the performance requirements again, perhaps in smaller increments. If you confine yourself to replicating successful modeling treatments which are described in published articles, then you too should be able to help a child overcome a debilitating fear.

# Probe Questions for Chapter 5, Section 2

1. Describe a guided participation treatment for a child's fear of psychologists.

2. If modeling and guided participation are so successful in treating fears, why are other types of treatment necessary?

3. Describe the properties of a successful modeling treatment program.

4. What is self-efficacy, and what is its role in therapy?

## Behavioral Objectives for Chapter 5, Section 3

*Studying Section 3 of this chapter should enable you to:*

1. *Define and identify reinforcing events.*

2. *Distinguish between useful reinforcers and those you should avoid in treatment interventions.*

3. *Know what conditioned reinforcers are and when to use them.*

4. *Know how and when to fade reinforcement administration.*

5. *Describe the problems that may accompany the use of extrinsic reinforcement, and what can be done to counteract them.*

## SECTION 3. IDENTIFYING OR ESTABLISHING REINFORCING EVENTS

The treatment of many behavioral deficits involves the administration of reinforcers, so we will provide a detailed description of their selection and of the establishment and use of conditioned and generalized reinforcers. In later sections we will provide instructions on shaping, token reinforcement programs, and contingency contracting techniques used in treatment programs for teaching children new behavioral skills.

### Reinforcing Events

Students often incorrectly assume that the task of selecting a reinforcer is an easy one. "Don't you just give the child a piece of candy and say, 'Good?'" they ask. Alas, the process is rarely that simple. By definition, reinforcing events are identified behaviorally rather than rationally, so reliable observational or interview data are needed. Moreover, even for a particular child, different stimulus events may serve as reinforcers at different times. The child's states of satiation and deprivation play important roles in determining the momentary strength of a potential reinforcing event. Thus, the same play activity a child works toward eagerly at 9:00 a.m. he may view with disdain at 10:30 after returning from recess. Highly idiosyncratic preferences and particular setting events sometimes render reinforcer identification difficult.

### Premack's Principle

The task of selecting reinforcers is aided by acquaintance with Premack's Differential Probability Principle (Premack, 1959). This simple principle holds that for any two behaviors emitted by an organism, the rate of the less frequent behavior can be increased by making access to the (presumably more attractive) higher rate behavior contingent upon the emission of the lower rate behavior. So if a child rarely engages in solving his math problems, but often talks to classmates, you can increase his rate of solving math problems by reinforcing his work with free time during which the child can visit with his friends. In one such program Wasik (1970) increased the amount of time second-graders spent in appropriate schoolroom activities by making access to toys and games contingent upon their desirable behavior during specified intervals. Desirable behavior included following the teacher's instructions, seeking or giving help on assignments, working independently, and directing others to act appropriately. Similarly, access to play activities has been used to reinforce kindergarten children's attempts at printing (Salzberg, Wheeler, Devar, & Hopkins, 1971). In short, children can be led to engage in tasks they should complete, but do not complete spontaneously, by making access to preferred activities contingent on finishing the nonpreferred ones. It often proves inconvenient or impossible to provide the preferred activities immediately after the children's performance of nonpreferred ones. So points, tokens, or praise can be used to provide immediate feedback and then back-up reinforcers can be administered later at a more convenient time.

## *How to Identify Reinforcers*

Interviews with caretakers and with the child often provide clues regarding useful reinforcers. Appendix B provides a checklist that caretakers or children can complete to indicate the child's preferences. Other suggestions regarding reinforcers for children are available in papers by Clement and Richard (1976) and Madsen and Madsen (1972). Cautela and Kostenbaum (1967) have presented a checklist of reinforcers for use with adolescents and adults. Table 5-1 presents some unusual but effective reinforcers used in past studies.

Sometimes a brief interview will provide all of the information necessary regarding potential reinforcers. To conduct an interview, you might ask questions such as these:

- What are the child's favorite foods or snacks?
- Favorite drinks and candies? Any food allergies? Any foods prohibited by parents or bad for the child's health (such as sweets for an obese child)?
- Favorite indoor games? Favorite books, radio, or TV shows?
- Favorite electronic arcade games?
- Could videotapes of trips to movie theaters be used as reinforcers?
- Who are the child's favorite companions? List both children and adults.

**Table 5-1.** Novel Reinforcers Used with Children

| Reinforcer | Target Behavior | Reference |
| --- | --- | --- |
| 1. Publicly posting special education child's photo | Participation in singing with class | Gross & Drabman (1981) |
| 2. Publicly posting retarded child's photo | Making own bed | Bacon-Prue, Blount, Hosey, & Drabman (1981) |
| 3. Performance feedback, public posting child's photo, and praise | Appropriate social interactions with peers | Van Houten, Hill, & Parsons (1975) |
| 4. Showing videotape of first grade child to the class | Improving phonics performance | Gross, Thurman, & Drabman (1981) |
| 5. Individual tutoring session with peer or college student | Reducing non-disruptive classroom behavior | Robertson, DeReus, & Drabman (1976) |
| 6. Lever pressing vibration by profoundly retarded child | Decreasing self-injurious behavior | Bailey & Meyerson (1969) |

- What field trips does the child like? Ask about city parks, amusement parks, zoos, aquariums, shops, museums, hikes, fishing, etc.

- Does the child like to play with or care for pets? Would working toward owning a pet be reinforcing for the child?

- What are the child's athletic skills and preferences? Athletic equipment and activities serve as good reinforcers, as do hobby materials.

## Characteristics of a Useful Reinforcer

You will probably discover a number of different stimulus events that you could use as reinforcers. But some are more useful than others. The reinforcers most easily utilized in treatment programs possess the following characteristics:

1. *Reinforcers should be resistant to satiation.* Reinforcer satiation presents one of the greatest problems associated with the use of tangible reinforcers in modification programs. Whether they take place in the classroom, the home, or in another setting, programs are usually devised so that the child is presented with many learning trials in each treatment session. If he rapidly becomes satiated with the presumed reinforcer, the potential number of learning trials is significantly decreased as is the rate of his behavior change. Therefore, it is essential to combat satiation effects. There are several ways to do this.

First, *use a variety of reinforcers.* You could use some combination of edible treats, play opportunities, and praise and affection. Variety helps to counteract both momentary satiation and longer-term preference changes. One useful method for presenting a selection of potential reinforcers is the Reinforcing Event Menu (Addison & Homme, 1966; Dineen, Clark, & Risley, 1977). Young children can be shown a cardboard card similar to a restaurant menu that features pictures of the various stimulus events you are offering as reinforcers. The child makes his choice and you contract with him concerning exactly how much and what type of work he must complete to earn that reward. Older children can simply read or hear descriptions of the reinforcers available. An inventive reinforcement system is the chart move and grab bag procedure described by Jenson and Sloane (1979). A large follow-the-dots or Monopoly-type chart is posted and the child can earn chart moves which advance him toward selecting a prize from a grab bag. Children usually enjoy these types of reinforcement systems, and are slow to tire of them.

Second, *keep your training sessions relatively brief if the child's task is repetitive.* To teach specific skills, it is often more effective to hold daily 10-minute training sessions than one weekly one-hour session. The former schedule's superiority is probably due to the daily practice plus the accompanying minimal satiation effects. Brief and frequent sessions also allow you to change tactics more readily if you discover that your procedures require changes.

A third, and highly effective method for preventing satiation involves the use of *conditioned generalized reinforcers and signs of performance achievements* such as tokens, points, money, and verbal approval. Since these types of reinforcers are so frequently used in therapy programs, they will be discussed at length later in this section. Readers interested in information on these and additional methods for avoiding reinforcer satiation are referred to Bijou and Baer (1966) and to Kazdin (1977b).

2. *Reinforcers should be administered in small units.* Reinforcers should be administered frequently and in small units. It is better to reinforce a young or severely handicapped child frequently with small sips of fruit juice than to offer him a giant glass of juice but only at long intervals. Some therapists have found a plastic squirt dispenser a handy means of dispensing juice. The dispenser's spout is placed very close to or inside the child's mouth, and a small amount of juice is delivered. Offering a copious amount of a reinforcer, but infrequently and for large units of work can result in ratio strain and consequent disruption or collapse of performance. So be stingy and your program will prosper as long as the child is not being underpaid for his efforts.

3. *Reinforcers should be administered immediately after occurrence of the desired behavior — at least initially.* If you use infrequently available reinforcers, such a long time intervenes between the child's desirable performance and the reinforcing event that you cannot tell which of the child's responses are being effectively reinforced. Suppose he had just hit his little brother immediately prior to the TV show he had been working toward view-

ing. If he gets to see the show, he might be reinforced for hitting his brother. If he does not get to see the show because of his misbehavior, you have broken your agreement with him and have failed to reinforce his previous desirable performance. What should you do? Reinforce as quickly as possible after the desirable performance. This is particularly important early in the training program. Later, the duration of the interval between performance and reinforcement can gradually be increased. When you do use a delay, be sure to tell the child for what he is being reinforced. In at least some instances, you can remind him, and then reinforce him for his past performance. An additional option is to fine the brother-beater for attacks on his sibling (see Chapter 6 for techniques for eliminating undesirable behavior).

4. *Reinforcer administration should be exclusively under the treatment agent's control.* Suppose that you are using something pleasant like candy-coated bubble gum as a reinforcer. Now suppose that the child's favorite aunt has given him a toy bubble-gum dispenser for his birthday (which may be why she is his favorite aunt). The reinforcers you had hoped to use are now old hat to him, and won't likely be effective. You should arrange to have the child's caretakers limit access to the reinforcers for the duration of the treatment program or at least to inform you if something like the favorite aunt incident occurs. This is not to say that you should attempt to deny the child her favorite activities for the duration of your project. If possible, select reinforcers that are additional to those she can expect on an everyday basis. Otherwise the child may correctly perceive you as denying her customary pleasures — a situation not likely to promote cooperation.

During the training sessions, you must make sure that you, and not the child, control the administration of the reinforcers. Hold on to the trinkets, tokens, candies, etc.; do not put them on the table near the child and expect him to refrain from helping himself. You must establish early on that you, and you alone, control the administration of the goodies and that the child must *earn* them. However, a stray unearned reinforcer doesn't hurt anything as long as it happens only occasionally.

5. *Reinforcers should be compatible with the overall treatment program.* Do not use a reinforcer that will compete with the very behavior you are trying to teach the child. For example, do not use aggressive play with toy weapons to reinforce the class bully. Do not use fattening foods or sedentary activities to treat an obese child. Do not let kids lie, cheat, threaten others, avoid reasonable duties, or engage in other undesirable activities even though they are effective reinforcers. Choose instructive and potentially useful reinforcing activities whenever possible.

6. *Reinforcers must be practical.* Choose reinforcers that are imaginative and not too costly. Also, they should have no obvious undesirable side effects, should be easily administered, and be readily available in sufficient supply.

## Praise and Tokens

Whenever possible, you should use generalized reinforcers, such as praise or points which are exchangeable for back-up reinforcers, rather than primary reinforcers such as food. Generalized reinforcers need not depend upon momentary deprivation states for their effectiveness. Thus, they are relatively resistant to satiation, and can be administered in small units immediately after the desired behavior. Moreover, all but the youngest and most disturbed children can understand and will work for praise, money, or points which can be exchanged for opportunities to engage in desirable activities.

Generalized reinforcers also: (a) serve to bridge a delay between a performance and delivery of the back-up reinforcement, (b) can be administered flexibly and continuously throughout the day, and (c) may even acquire greater incentive value than would a single primary reinforcer because of the generalized reinforcers' association with a number of different back-up reinforcers (Kazdin & Bootzin, 1972).

Praise is a particularly useful reinforcer because it is used frequently in everyday life, and thus seems natural to both adult and child. Further, praise is greatly valued by most young children, and rarely is viewed as coercive. In fact, children tend to view praise as descriptive of their good behavior and exemplary motivation rather than as a means of modifying their behavior (Cohen, Gelfand, & Hartmann, 1981; Smith, Gelfand, Hartmann, & Partlow, 1979). Although many children and adults view material rewards as influencing and accounting for the recipient's good behavior, few consider praise to constitute an influence attempt. Consequently, many children believe that they behave well in order to win material rewards, and that any praise they receive does not influence their behavior. Praise is a particularly socially acceptable type of reinforcement. You should accompany material reinforcement with praise, since the combination may lead children to conclude that the motivation for their performing well lies in their own intrinsic goodness rather than in their desire to obtain the material rewards (Smith et al., 1979). Under some conditions, such attributions may encourage children to engage in socially desirable behavior (Grusec, Kuczynski, Rushton, & Simutis, 1978).

Avoid praise statements that are trite or very repetitious. This means you shouldn't say, "That's a good one!" or any single comment every time the child has earned reinforcement. The child will quickly become habituated to such praise, and praise may lose its reinforcing properties. Instead, you should vary your comments in a believable way. You might say, in succession: "What a super job you're doing on those homework problems"; "You did that like a big kid"; "I'm proud of you for doing a hard job so well"; "Incredible! You got every answer right"; and other statements in a similar vein.

Whenever possible, use praise statements that describe the desired performance as these statements aid children in identifying and responding to the reinforcement contingency. Such *descriptive praise* is especially useful when complex performances are required, such as novelty and creativity in composition or in art. For example, Goetz and her associates (Goetz & Baer, 1973; Goetz & Salmonson, 1972) used descriptive praise to increase young children's innovative constructions with building blocks. In these studies, adult caretakers made comments such as, "That's good! That's a new one," contingent upon the children's new and different uses of the blocks. Without a description of the contingency in the praise statement, the children probably would have required a long time to detect and respond to the reinforcement contingency. *We recommend using descriptive praise in reinforcement programs with children whenever possible.* Improvement often is more rapid when participants are informed of the contingencies in operation (Walker & Hops, 1973). Note, however, that it is unnecessary to describe the contingency in each and every praise statement — that could sound stupid. Occasional repetition will usually suffice.

*Guidelines for establishing praise or tokens as reinforcers.* Suppose that no matter what you say, the child finds your praise unreinforcing, an unfortunate state of affairs. If this should be the case, it is especially important to combine praise with effective reinforcers. In this way, praise acquires reinforcing properties. Perhaps you could pair your praise statements with an opportunity for the child to engage in highly preferred play activities. Your plan would be to offer praise as soon as possible after the child engages in the desired behavior. For example, in teaching a child to follow instructions, you would first praise the child in as genuine and enthusiastic a fashion as you can muster, then say, "You are doing so well at (whatever the child is supposed to do) today, that you can play another game of Pan Galactic Gargle Blaster." Then you allow the child to play the game. Present the paired praise and play opportunities several times — just how many times are required will vary with the child's age and intelligence. Eventually you will want to fade out the back-up reinforcers, and maintain the child's desirable behavior by intermittent praise alone.

Training is more difficult with severely impaired children when (a) it is inconvenient to administer the back-up reinforcer such as access to the food or play activity at the time the child performs as desired, and (b) your praise lacks reinforcing properties for the child. In such circumstances, you may need to establish points or tokens as reinforcers, and allow the child to exchange them for back-up reinforcers at a later time. If the child has the requisite communication skills, remember to tell him precisely how to earn the points, and to test his knowledge somewhat later to ascertain whether he remembers the contingency. When in doubt about his recall of the contingency, restate it. Reinforcement contingencies should not be matters of conjecture, but should be explicitly communicated to the child.

With a very developmentally delayed child, it may be an arduous task training the child so that her target behavior is sustained by presenting the conditioned reinforcers, and only later presenting the back-up reinforcers. First, you must establish the token as valuable by giving the child a token and immediately allowing her to exchange it for a play privilege, a treat, or some other reinforcer. Do this several times, each time telling her, "You can play with the markers a while (or whatever reinforcing event is being used) if you have a chip." Next give her an opportunity to earn a token and allow her to exchange her token for the back-up reinforcer. Repeat this process until the token itself functions as a reinforcer.

The object in using a token reinforcer is to initiate the desired performance, not to keep the child on the token program permanently. Consequently, you must immediately begin establishing praise as a reinforcing event, as it is for most normal children. The first time and every time that you present the child with a token, precede it with a smile and some remark about how well the child is doing, how smart or big she is, or some other positive comment. At first, you may want to exaggerate your praise and smiling so that the child will be more likely to attend to them. Eventually, your aim is to reduce and finally to eliminate the use of the token reinforcers, as was mentioned previously. Occasional praise is the consequence for most naturally occurring prosocial behavior, so the child should be helped to become accustomed to such a contingency if her behavior is to be maintained in everyday life. Further details on fading from the artificial treatment setting to the child's customary surroundings are presented in Chapter 7, Section 1.

Sometimes the child's caretakers and companions do not provide sufficient reinforcement to maintain the child's desirable behavior regardless of how carefully the therapeutic program is phased out. For example, a harrassed teacher with 40 students to attend to may simply overlook those occasions on which a behaviorally disturbed student deserves praise. In this circumstance, a therapist might consider implementing a self-regulation program in which the student observes, evaluates, and reinforces his own academic work (see Chapter 7, Section 2). Or he might be trained to bring his completed papers to the teacher at particular times when there is a high probability of the teacher's attending to and reinforcing his work. In addition, the teacher might be trained in reinforcement techniques, which might, in the long run, decrease the need for reprimands. These are all difficult training programs, which require skill in public relations as well as in behavior therapy. Consequently, they are better left to experienced therapists.

The elimination of the artificial reinforcement procedure proceeds by gradual stages. For target behaviors of long duration, such as the number of minutes remaining seated during classroom instruction, the child might initially be reinforced with tokens on the average of once each minute for staying seated. This variable interval of one minute schedule (VI 1'), varies the time between one reinforcement opportunity to the next from about 15 sec. to a maximum of 85 sec. The average duration of this interval schedule could be progressively increased in increments not readily detected by the child, until at last she receives no tokens. Experienced therapists can help you determine just when to fade to leaner schedules, but the rule is to reduce the reinforcement frequency after the child is meeting the criterion, but before the child's performance becomes so stable that further reinforcement thinning of any type results in performance collapse.

A similar procedure of thinning reinforcement schedules can be used with training tasks involving discrete trials such as occur in many language instruction programs. Initially the tokens, points, or whatever are administered for each correct response on a continuous reinforcement schedule (CRF). When the child is responding correctly on 80% or more of the training trials for two or three consecutive days, reinforcement can be administered for every other correct response (an FR2 schedule). When the intermittent schedule is first used, there may be a decrement in the child's performance. If necessary, stable correct responding should be re-established; then the therapist should introduce greater variability and intermittency by reinforcing the child on the average of every third or every fourth correct responses (a VR3 or VR4 schedule). Reinforcement intermittency can be increased gradually until tokens are no longer needed to maintain the target behavior.

## Problems with Extrinsic Reinforcement

In recent years researchers and nonprofessionals alike have questioned the use of extrinsic reinforcement in certain situations (Deci, 1975; Lepper, 1981). In particular, there has been widespread concern about the possibility of undermining children's intrinsic interest in activities by providing extrinsic reinforcement, such as tangible rewards, for engaging in the activities. In an often cited experiment, Lepper, Greene, and Nisbett (1973) found that young children who were initially attracted to playing with colored felt-tipped markers greatly reduced their subsequent use of the markers after having been offered and receiving a "Good Player Award" for drawing with the pens during a brief play period. In contrast, children who didn't receive such awards or who unexpectedly received them after the play period did not reduce their later use of the markers. Apparently the reward contingency led children to lose interest in the rewarded activity.

Such findings have been used to question the wisdom of using extrinsic reinforcers in children's therapy. Indeed, it would be foolish to offer unnecessary inducements to children if they find the activities intrinsically interesting. However, in the therapy situation children more typically are offered reinforcers for engaging in tasks they *don't* find intrinsically enjoyable. Furthermore, in treatment situations children usually are rewarded for accomplishments such as number of problems solved correctly rather than for merely engaging in an activity regardless of performance quality. When rewarded for accomplishments, children appear to gain rather than lose interest in their work (Reiss & Sushinsky, 1975; Ross, 1976). Some type of extrinsic reinforcement may be essential when much effort is required over a long time period. It is difficult for many children to find activities such as washing their ears, taking out the garbage, or memorizing the multiplication tables as inherently reinforcing, at least initially. In such circumstances (and they are fairly frequent), contingency management is a powerful and effective training technique. Like any other tactic, the contingent use of positive reinforcement can be misused. However, the possibilities of misuse are slight when compared with punishment. The next sections provide suggestions for the proper use of contingency management techniques.

## Probe Questions for Chapter 5, Section 3

1. *A therapist has used inexpensive toys successfully as a reinforcer for Larry. Will they be a useful reinforcer for Charles? Why or why not?*

2. *How could a therapist use Premack's Principle in treating a child?*

3. *Why might points earned be better reinforcers than candies?*

4. *Suppose a parent told you that she objected to bribing children to improve their behavior. How would you reply?*

5. *Describe the characteristics of useful reinforcers.*

## Behavioral Objectives for Chapter 5, Section 4

*After studying Section 4, you should be able to:*

1. *Devise a program to shape some new behavior for a child.*

2. *Cope with extraneous behavior and performance cessation.*

3. *Detect the likely causes for a low rate of desired performance and devise a program to remedy it.*

## SECTION 4. SHAPING AND STRENGTHENING LOW-RATE PERFORMANCES

Suppose that a clinician faces the task of increasing the rate of some deficit behavior that the child has never before exhibited. What training methods are available? The therapist might choose to employ techniques such as demonstrating the desired performance and verbally instructing the child to imitate his example. If the child cannot do so because his present performance is only a remote approximation to the desired one, and some extrinsic reinforcement is necessary, a shaping procedure may be required. Shaping will be described in this section. Then in the following section we will consider the procedures used in remediating behavioral deficits which stem from failure to cue the child that a performance is required. The type of intervention to be used depends upon the source of the child's behavior deficit.

### Shaping

Shaping consists of the therapist's requesting and reinforcing successive approximations to the final behavior. The child's behavior might initially be too infrequent or overly brief, as in the number of study sessions he engages in and the length of each session. A 10-minute study session twice a week will not suffice for the child to learn multiplication tables. The child's behavior might be too delayed — perhaps the child dawdles in complying with adults' instructions. Then again, the response may be too low in intensity; for example, some children mumble or whisper when they should speak loudly. Finally, a performance's form may be inappropriate and require change, as when a child eats with his hands rather than using utensils. In all of these situations shaping can be used to teach the child more appropriate response patterns.

In order to shape a new performance, it is necessary to utilize a powerful reinforcer that can be administered immediately after the desired approximation. Timing is crucial, and a delay may cause some other intervening behavior to be strengthened. To illustrate, if you are teaching a shy child to speak more loudly, reinforce him quickly after he does so and before his voice intensity drops once more. Praise, tally marks, or tokens are useful reinforcers because they can be administered quickly and do not distract the child or disrupt the learning process.

## Example of Shaping

Let us consider the case in which the desired terminal performance for a young child is dressing himself in the morning. It might be necessary initially to place his legs in his underpants and only require him to draw the pants up to his waist, and then to give him praise and a hug. The second step in the shaping process might involve placing one of his legs in a pant leg and requiring him to insert the other leg before pulling up the pants and receiving reinforcement. When this performance has stabilized, the requirement might be for the child to complete the entire procedure by himself (see the sample program in Table 5-2).

**Table 5-2.** Sample Program Including a Shaping Procedure: Training a Child to Dress Himself

| | |
|---|---|
| Step 1. | Child's legs are inserted into his underpants. Underpants are drawn up to his knees. Contingency: Child must draw underpants up into wearing position in order to receive hug and praise (probably conditioned reinforcers). He is verbally requested to do so (prompt). |
| Step 2. | Child performs Step 1 consistently (nearly 100%) upon request. Now only one of child's legs is inserted into underpants. Contingency: Child must insert other leg, then draw pants up to receive a hug and praise. |
| Step 3. | Child performs Step 2 consistently upon request. Now he is required to pick up underpants, insert both legs, and draw pants up to receive positive consequation (hug and praise). |
| Step 4. | Child consistently puts on underpants upon request. Now he is required also to put on slacks. [Note: In this and in each succeeding step, positive consequation follows successful performance.] |
| Step 5. | Putting on a pullover shirt. The shirt is put over child's head; he must locate the sleeves, insert his arms, and pull down the shirt. |
| Step 6. | Child picks up pullover shirt, pulls it over his head, locates sleeves, inserts arms, and pulls shirt into place. |
| Step 7. | Putting on socks. Socks are placed over child's toes. He must pull them up over his ankles. Shoes are put on him. |
| Step 8. | Child must pick up socks, gather each one together, put it over his toes, and pull it up over his ankle. Shoes are put on him. |
| Step 9. | Putting on shoes. Child puts on socks, shoes are placed before him in correct arrangement, right shoe in front of right foot. He must slip his foot into the shoe. Shoes are buckled or tied for him. |
| Step 10. | Shoes are not placed before child. He finds shoes and puts them on the correct foot.* |

*Note*: If this sounds like a difficult and tedious process, the description is correct. Winter weather in a cold climate further complicates matters by requiring boots, hats, mittens, and snowsuits. Even adults may have difficulty in outfitting themselves for excursions in subfreezing weather.

## Guidelines for Shaping

The motto to adopt in shaping is to think small. Set your requirements at each stage at just what the child can master without too much strain. It is best to keep reinforcement density high; our experience is that the child should be earning reinforcement on 80% or more of his attempts to perform the desired behavior. Avoid long intervals during which the child receives no reinforcement, because this will place many of his behaviors on an extinction schedule and he may cease trying. One way to avoid this possibility is to give the child some unearned reinforcers to help keep him working during the early phases of the program. An unearned reinforcer is one for which the performance requirements are either very minimal or absent. Its function is to maintain an activity level sufficient for shaping at a time when, for some reason, the child continues to emit incorrect, unreinforceable performances. Because they are not made contingent upon an acceptable approximation, unearned reinforcers must be used sparingly, but they occasionally prove very helpful.

The timing of closer approximations to the final performance is also critical to the success of a shaping program. Do not progress to a more stringent performance requirement until the child can consistently perform the behavior required at the preceding step. It is pointless to attempt to require the child to pick up his underpants and insert both legs if, having accomplished this, he only pulls the pants up to his waist successfully 50% of the time.

It is necessary to consider all possible reasons for a child's failure to meet a performance requirement. Perhaps he did not initially learn the easiest way to insert his leg into the underclothing. It may be that he was trying to do this while standing unsteadily on one leg. If so, you might suggest that he sit down to get his leg into his underpants, then have him stand up in order to pull them on. You might also have to demonstrate this operation for him yourself and give him considerable verbal instruction when he attempts it. Or you might offer him some physical assistance, such as helping him keep his balance, and guide his hand or leg (physical prompts). Finally, you can ask him to put his foot into the leg hole and pull up the garment in order to earn his reinforcer. These prompts are useful only if the child is compliant, and not if he is resisting or pulling away.

*Set specific criteria for reinforcement.* Develop specific criteria for reinforcement for each step in the shaping program (see example in Table 5-2). Detailed criteria enable you to remember the precise nature of the reinforceable response at each stage in the program so that the child does not get reinforced for more distant approximations. If you reinforce indiscriminately, he will respond indiscriminately. Unless the performance is deteriorating and you need to drop back to and restabilize an earlier performance, do not reinforce a poorer performance than that called for at the step at which the child is working. Panyan's (1980) booklet provides useful information regarding shaping procedures.

*How to deal with backsliding.* In the example just mentioned, suppose that the child is consistently pulling up his underclothes. You then increase the requirement to Step 2: Only one of the child's legs is inserted into the pant leg. He is required to insert the other leg, then draw the pants up. But upon contacting this new contingency, his behavior breaks down, and you find that he neither puts his leg in nor pulls the pants on. What should you do? Return to the earlier requirement of his only pulling the pants on; stabilize this performance once again, then reintroduce the leg insertion requirement.

In general, if a performance breaks down upon introduction of a particular contingency (e.g., Step 3), return to the preceding step (Step 2), and restabilize that performance. Then (a) introduce special cueing or prompting if that seems necessary or, (b) reduce the requirements at the next step (Step 3) so that the child can meet them more easily. Demanding too great an increment in performance can result in extinction not only of the required performance but also of preceding performances. Just remain flexible and let the child's behavior dictate the contingencies you set for him.

*Performance cessation.* If the child suddenly stops emitting correct responses, even though no new requirement has been introduced:

1. Go back to an approximation the child can emit without error, stabilize his performance, then increase your criteria more gradually and in smaller steps.

2. If this does not work, the child may have become fatigued or satiated on the reinforcer. Go back to a response the child can make successfully, reinforce him, and conclude that training session. Do not conclude a session with the child's repeated failure to perform correctly. End with a reinforced response so that the sessions themselves do not become aversive.

*Extraneous behavior.* In order to begin quickly shaping the desired behavior, it may be necessary incidentally to reinforce another, perhaps somewhat undesirable response if it occurs at a high rate and concurrently with the desired response. Perhaps a child is kicking the table strenuously and repeatedly while he is saying the required "puh." At the inception of training, it may be preferable to ignore the kicking, since it does not actively interfere with the desired vocalization. By not dealing specifically with the kicking, you will actually be reinforcing it because it occurs at the same time as the reinforceable verbal response. The kicking can be overlooked initially and dealt with, if necessary, at some later time when the child's verbal behavior has improved. Note that you would not want to reinforce highly undesirable acts that actually compete or interfere with the desired response. (In the example just cited, it might be best simply to move the table out of kicking range if that is possible.) The following chapter on excess behaviors will describe several procedures for reducing persistent disruptive behavior that interferes with the shaping process.

## Strengthening Low-rate Performances

Sometimes a behavioral deficit consists not of the total absence of a particular desired behavior but of its occurrence at an abnormally low rate. Suppose the child has at some time engaged in the desired behavior — for example, washing the dishes — but that he does so only very rarely. Probably no lengthy and complex shaping process is required in this instance, but the situation must be analyzed to determine the reasons for his low performance rate. Consider the components of a functional analysis of behavior — setting events, antecedent stimulus events, the target behavior itself, and consequent events. The reason for a low rate of performance may lie in any one or more of these factors. Since the child in our example actually does display the target behavior on occasion, a shaping process appears unnecessary. Perhaps setting events make the desired performances unlikely. It could be that the boy is tired at dishwashing time after a day of schoolwork, active play, and a large dinner. Perhaps the dishwashing chore deprives him of the opportunity to watch his favorite television program or to play with his friends who are having a noisy ballgame outside the window. If these are the reasons for his failure to help with the dishes, a possible solution might be to change his chore time. The dishes could just be stacked in the kitchen after dinner to be washed at some later, more convenient time. Or the family's dinner time might be changed to an earlier hour to avoid scheduling conflicts with his favorite pastimes. Possibly his work assignment might be changed from dishwashing to setting the table and helping with food preparation so that he would be free after dinner. Good behavior therapists can typically generate a number of different possible solutions; if one intervention proves unprofitable or not feasible, another can be tried.

Concerning antecedent events, perhaps no clear signal is given to the child regarding the proper time to start washing the dishes. Sometimes he is expected to begin before laggards have finished their dinners, but on other occasions he must wait until all have finished. Sometimes the completion of the dessert course is the cue, but at other times he is allowed to leave the table and watch television for a while until his mother's insistent instructions signal him to begin cleaning up. Under such circumstances, no one event reliably sets the occasion for the child to begin his work, and his performance is understandably unreliable. His work routine might be more easily established if the last diner's putting his napkin on the table were the stimulus event that nearly always preceded dishwashing time.

The youngster's cleaning work also might be facilitated by the provision of models, such as another family member's beginning to clear the table or wipe down the kitchen work surfaces. His father might offer a prompt such as, "Let's get these things off the table and washed up so that we can all go out for an ice cream cone," and might begin handing the dirty dishes to his son to aid in the cleanup.

Let us suppose that the setting events and antecedent events all favor the successful completion of the desired act. The child is neither overly fatigued nor deprived of some attractive competing activity. The cues to engage in the target behavior are clear, reliable, and unequivocal. The physical circumstances may place limits on the child's performance. He might be too short to reach the sink easily, or the work space might be otherwise very inconvenient for him, requiring undue exertion on his part. A simple rearrangement of the work area or provision of a step stool may solve a major portion of the problem. Another source of the deficit may be motivational. What reinforcers are available to strengthen and maintain the child's performance? Perhaps members of his family all go their separate ways, gratefully, while he is left alone with a pile of dirty dishes — an unattractive prospect. The reason for a low performance rate, then, may lie in inadequate reinforcement. The reinforcers offered may be too small in magnitude (just an occasional smile from mother), too infrequent (once or twice a month), or both, so that naturally the child does not respond positively to his parents' requests. To remedy this situation, the parents might come into the kitchen with him to chat, play guessing games, read poems and stories, or otherwise entertain and reinforce him while he does his work. If this is not feasible, the child might be paid for finishing the dishwashing, or he might receive both money and parental attention for his efforts.

As we have seen, a child's behavioral deficits can spring from a variety of possible sources. Modification programs that employ several types of interventions are more likely to be successful than are attempts that focus only upon any one set of possible determinants such as reinforcing events. It is, of course, much more difficult to identify the effective components of such complex interventions (see Chapter 4), but they do have the advantage of being more likely to produce dramatic improvement than programs that manipulate only the reinforcement schedule.

Since your primary goal is to produce beneficial change, you will probably choose effectiveness over elegance of analysis. As long as there remains some way of assessing the effectiveness of the particular treatment program employed, however complex that program is, one can satisfy both the evaluational and the therapeutic requirements of applied child behavior analysis.

## Probe Questions for Chapter 5, Section 4

1. *Explain why a therapist who is using a shaping procedure must act quickly.*

2. *How should a therapist deal with extraneous behavior while conducting a shaping program?*

3. *Why must therapists consider setting events and antecedent events in planning treatment programs?*

## Behavioral Objectives for Chapter 5, Section 5

*When you have studied Section 5, you should be able to:*

1. *Devise effective instructions and physical prompts for use in a treatment program.*

2. *Detect and remedy problems in verbal instructions given to a child.*

3. *Know how and when to fade prompts.*

## SECTION 5.
## VERBAL INSTRUCTIONS AND PHYSICAL PROMPTS

Suppose that the child never or only very rarely engages in the desired behavior. If this low performance rate stems from the child's unfamiliarity with the behavior rather than with inadequate incentives, then instructions or physical guidance may be required.

As an example of a prompt, therapists who wish to teach a child to maintain eye contact with them and who are using food as a reinforcer frequently employ the following procedure. The therapist holds a spoonful of food up to her face near her eyes and instructs the child, "Jenny, look at me." Since the food is attractive to the child, she looks at it and, in the process, looks the therapist in the eye. As soon as the child responds correctly to the command, "Look at me," the prompt of holding the spoon up is faded, and the performance is under appropriate verbal control.

Similarly, you might use prompting to teach a child to say a "puh" sound. You would demonstrate the initial approximation by saying, "Listen, Jimmy, say puh," several times. Then you might prompt him by holding his lips together while he attempts to spit or blow, and then reinforce each appropriate attempt. When the child says "puh" reliably with the aid of the prompt, you should begin fading the prompt. You no longer hold his lips in place, but just touch his lips. When he has mastered this stage, just hold your fingers to his chin. Finally, you can take your hand away and he is still successfully saying "puh."

The same procedures are required whether you are giving instructions or making requests of a child.

First, be sure that you have his attention by saying his name, and then wait for him to look toward you.

Second, make sure that he is capable of doing what you ask. You must judge this by becoming well-acquainted with the child's typical behavior, perhaps by making classroom or home observations, or by asking the child's teacher or parents about his behavior.

Third, make sure that you are using directions and vocabulary that the child understands. Listening to teachers and parents speaking with the child will help you to gear your verbal instructions to his level of comprehension.

Fourth, either reinforce the child's compliance with your instruction, or repeat the instruction, but slightly differently phrased. You might begin by saying, "David, pick out the yellow clown," and then if this is not effective, a few seconds later say, "David, show me the yellow one." Allow enough time between your requests so that you aren't interrupting any attempt to comply. Some children have slower response tempos than others, so you must tailor your instructions to the child's natural style of responding, but without tolerating inordinate delays.

## Trouble Shooting

But what should you do if repeated verbal instructions prove fruitless? In that case, it may be necessary to use gentle physical prompting. So you might take the child's hand and put it on the yellow clown, saying, "That's right, he's the yellow one." Then immediately ask the child to show you the yellow clown once more, using manual guidance if necessary. Remember to fade the physical prompting as soon as possible, so the child's reponding does not become dependent on it.

The prompts you use should *not* be negative or coercive; their sole purpose is to initiate appropriate responding. Just gentle touching, guiding the child's hand or lips or direction of his gaze (by moving his head), or direction of movement should be sufficient. As an example of a positive prompt, one can use a popsicle stick or tongue depressor dipped in something tasty such as chocolate fudge or honey to prompt a child to say "Mmmm." Simply pop the coated stick into the child's mouth while asking him to say "Mmmm." Now there's a pleasant prompt.

## Fading Prompts

Withdraw the prompts in small steps and as quickly as possible while still maintaining correct responding. If you fade too slowly, the child may perseverate at some step and you might have to introduce some quite different task in order to get him learning again. For example, perhaps you have been trying to teach the child to say "Mama," and despite your best efforts to teach him to say the whole word, he continues to say "Maaa." You might have to drop the training of "Mama" temporarily and begin to work on another word such as "Hi," and then return to the original task some time later. This strategy provides a way out of an instructional impasse.

Alternatively, fading prompts too quickly may lead to performance breakdown. In that case you must quickly return to an approximation the child can perform and start building once more.

# Probe Questions for Chapter 5, Section 5

1. Give examples of physical prompts that might be useful in teaching a child to attend to the teacher, to sit down when instructed to do so, and to brush his teeth.

2. How can a therapist prevent a child from becoming overreliant on physical prompts?

3. What procedures should a therapist follow in order to give appropriate verbal instructions to a 5-year-old child?

4. When might verbal instructions prove counterproductive?

## Behavioral Objectives for Chapter 5, Section 6

*Studying Section 6 should enable you to:*

*1. Construct a simple contingency contract.*

*2. Detect and remedy problems in the contract.*

*3. Write a complete treatment script.*

## SECTION 6.
## CONTINGENCY CONTRACTING AND
## PREPARING A TREATMENT PROGRAM SCRIPT

Throughout this book we argue for involving the child in the treatment process as much as possible, on the assumption that children who are engaged in generating and applying the therapeutic intervention are more likely to change their behavior than are unwilling or uninvolved participants. A good way of engaging a child in the behavior change project and to ensure his cooperation is by means of a reinforcement contingency contract between the child and the therapist or parent. The contract spells out clearly and concisely the amount and type of work required of the child, and the amount and type of reinforcer he will obtain for his work. Sometimes it is useful to formalize the contract by negotiating the work and the reinforcers with both parties, and then writing up an agreement to be signed by both. In this way the reinforcement contingencies to be employed are clearly understood and agreed to both by the child and the adult. A sample contract appears in Table 5-3. The written contract provides greater specificity and clarity than do spoken contingency agreements, and thus lessens the chances of disagreement over whether or not a task was completed by the child or whether or not the child was given the promised reinforcement. Note that in preparing contracts, as in coding behavior observations, the target behaviors or tasks required of the child must be specified exactly so there is no question about whether the homework was completed, the dishes dried, the lawn mowed, or the bed made. This means that each task must be analyzed in detail so that all components can be recognized and their completion can be verified. For example, if the desired child behavior is homework completion, then it may be necessary to require the child to obtain a note from the teacher indicating whether the work was done on time or late, and, if it was completed, up to what standard. Without such verification, the child may be tempted to lie, and inadvertently could be reinforced for doing so.

In addition to its other merits, the written contract provides a means of transition from behavior management by adults to self-contingency management or self-regulation by the child. For example, Homme, Csanyi, Gonzales,

**Table 5-3.** A Sample Contingency Contract to Increase Studying

---

I,    (child's name)   , agree that I will do the following work, for which I will get the rewards specified:

1. Study the subject(s)    (math and spelling)    in    (my bedroom)    and no other place.

2. Begin studying at    (7:00 p.m.)    and stop studying at    (7:30 p.m.)    and (do at least 2 pages of math problems and study my spelling list once).

3. Report accurately the amount of schoolwork I do at home each day.

4. Study these subjects each day assigned:    (Mon., Tues., Wed., Thurs., Sun.)   .

5. For my work, I will get the following rewards:

    a.    (A dessert of my choice at 8:00 p.m.)

    b.    (To select the television program the family watches at 8:00–9:00 p.m.)

    c.    (To attend a Saturday afternoon movie of my choice.)

    d. _____

    e. _____

6. I will also receive    (5¢)    for (each problem sheet returned by the teacher with 80% correct) and    (50¢)    for each (spelling test on which I get at least 90% correct).

7. For each week I do all the work described, I will also    (be allowed to invite a friend to Saturday lunch and movie).

8. But if I claim one of my rewards without having earned it, I will be fined    (75¢)   .

_____(Child's Signature)

_____(Manager's Signature)

---

and Rechs (1970) suggested a succession of steps proceeding from complete adult control of work requirements and reinforcement contingencies to complete client self-control of contingencies. After the child has come to abide by the initial contract, the transfer to self-control can begin. First, the child is given some say in determining the type and amount of required performance and payoff. The child and adult may jointly determine the amount of task performance required and the child alone determines the reinforcer. Alternatively, the child alone decides the work requirement and they jointly determine the amount and type of reinforcement. In this manner, the child is given systematic practice in specifying work requirements and reinforcer allocation, and she receives additional reinforcement for doing so. The adult manager's role fades as the child becomes more accomplished in setting up her own reinforcement contingencies, until at last the child has assumed sole control. Other aspects of self-regulation training are presented in Chapter 7, Section 2, so you should read that portion of the book if you are considering including self-regulation training in your treatment program.

## Limitations

Obviously, very young children or very disturbed ones cannot participate in contingency contracting, so some other approach, such as simple contingency management, probably should be used to alter their behavior. Some other situations make contracting desirable, but pose challenges for the beginning-level therapist. For example, some of the first applications of contingency contracting were with pre-delinquent youths and their parents (Stuart, 1971; Tharp & Wetzel, 1969). The adolescents and their parents engaged in a great deal of sulking and shouting or were not on speaking terms, so experienced and resourceful therapists were required to work out the contract provisions and supervise the participants' behavior. Our conclusions are that contracting with the very young, the developmentally delayed, and with antisocial youngsters is usually beyond the skills of new therapists. As Ross (1981) has observed, the therapist must be able to create a climate of compromise so that no one appears to be the loser. The therapist's skill as a mediator may be more important to the intervention's success than the particular structure or content of the contract. There is one more, very important, limitation on the use of contingency contracting, namely, that very few searching research analyses have been conducted on this treatment approach. Usually, the available research has been on clinical case studies, and has lacked rigor. However, even when controlled studies have been conducted, very complex interventions have been applied. Consequently, it has proved impossible to determine how much of any treatment success was attributable to contracting as opposed to other therapy procedures.

## Guidelines

The following rules for contingency management have been drawn from various sources, including Homme et al. (1970), Stuart (1971), and Tharp and Wetzel (1969). Readers who wish more information about contracting should read those reports and the discussions of behavioral contracting by Ollendick and Cerny (1981) and Ross (1981). If a contract fails or is of only limited effectiveness, it is advisable to check to determine whether *each* of the following rules is being observed. Often, it is necessary to alter contracts from time to time as one or the other party becomes dissatisfied or unmotivated. The overriding rule is that the participants must be satisfied that the contract is fair and is being followed.

*Rule 1.* The contract payoff should be as specified and should initially be administered immediately following the task performance.

*Rule 2.* Initial contracts should call for and reward small approximations to the desired performance. Asking too much has predictably poor results. This means that you should maximize the chances of the initial contract's succeeding, so both parties are encouraged to attempt more demanding requirements in future contracts.

*Rule 3.* Reward frequently with small amounts. Being allowed to work toward purchase of a bicycle at Christmas is not particularly rewarding in June. However, earning the right to more time spent bicycling each day could be an appropriate and effective reward.

*Rule 4.* Remember to reward the performance *after* it occurs, not prior to the child's completing it.

*Rule 5.* The contract must be fair. This is difficult to achieve, since it is probable that the parents' initial position is that the child should perform the specified tasks without repeated instructions and with no need of extrinsic reinforcement, and the child's initial position is that reinforcement should be noncontingent. To achieve fairness in the contract, both sides should participate in its construction and agree to abide by the contract. Here is where the therapist must guard against unfair dominance by either side. Both adult and child must feel fairly treated, and not be intimidated.

*Rule 6.* The terms of the contract must be clear. That is, both parties should know what is expected of them and what they can expect in return. To achieve this state of affairs, the contract must specify the performances and reinforcers in behavioral terms. For example, a girl might earn the privilege of staying at a friend's house for two hours after school if she sets the table for dinner with silverware, china, folded napkins, sets out butter in a small dish, puts salt and pepper shakers on the table, and places the chairs in their proper positions. The task required of the girl is specified in detail so that her work can be assessed objectively, and her reward is equally specified, so the adults cannot capriciously change the time or type of privilege promised.

*Rule 7.* If making the promised rewards contingent upon misbehavior does not suffice to reduce misbehavior rates, then the therapist must add contractual provisions for additional privilege losses, fines, or other sanctions. However, you must take care not to over-punish, lest the child's incentives be reduced to zero.

*Rule 8.* Include a bonus in the contract for the child's near-perfect compliance with the contract for some specified period of time. The availability of the extra incentive may help outweigh the reinforcers which the child might gain by violating the agreement. Bonuses could include a parentally financed trip to an amusement park, funding and transportation for the child to play video games in an arcade, the opportunity to attend a movie, permission to hold a party for friends, or any other safe and legal activity the child enjoys.

*Rule 9*. The adult should keep an ongoing record of the child's compliance performance and the rewards given to the child. This record should be posted in a prominent location for both parties to see. When the child is performing well, the mere sight of the record is rewarding. Also, without the record, the child's compliance may go unrewarded, or the child's failure to comply may be reinforced, due to the adult's memory errors. Thus the record encourages the systematic use of contracting.

A written contingency contract of the type just described can play a useful role in managing children's behavior problems in that it increases the commitment of the participants, it clearly specifies the obligations and the advantages to all, and it does not lend itself to misunderstanding, capriciousness, or distortion due to faulty memory as much as does an informal, conversational agreement. These benefits are more presumed than proven, however, since the evaluative research basis of contracting is lacking. Whether or not you decide to use a written contract involving the child, you will need to prepare a script describing your treatment program, a topic we consider next.

## The Program Script

Behavior therapists succeed to the extent that their programs are precise and consistent. Therefore, it is important to prepare a written script describing each detail of the setting, the equipment and data collection procedures, and the treatment procedures. If therapists work in pairs, then the script helps ensure that both are following the same procedures in their work with the child. The script helps remind therapists of the materials needed for each treatment session, and allows supervisors to take a look at the plan and advise the student therapists of any procedural changes that might improve the treatment program. One final advantage is that the written program can serve as the Procedure section in the final project report.

Table 5-4 offers a format you might use in writing up your treatment program. The table presents the information needed to describe the major treatment intervention, but does not include generalization or self-regulation training procedures, which are discussed in Chapter 7. If you are planning to use either of these training procedures, they also should be described in your script. In addition, it might be advisable to include your plans for phasing out and concluding your work with the child, and for transferring the treatment effort to a new therapist, if appropriate. Many treatment agencies appreciate receiving a copy of your treatment program so that they can continue the training effort after you have left the treatment center. Leaving a copy of the program is helpful to the agency and the child, especially if the program was effective.

**Table 5-4.** Treatment Script Format

---

I.      *Introduction.* Use a fictitious name for your target child, and describe her briefly. Include in your description how the child was selected, as well as her problem behavior and diagnosis, age, sex, institutional affiliation, and other information that may be important in evaluating the remainder of this treatment script.

II.      *Objectives.* This portion of the written program describes the anticipated terminal behavior produced by the treatment intervention. Example: At the completion of this program, Alice will engage in a normal amount of interactive play with other children. Specifically, at least 60% of her play time will be spent in interaction with children. (The required percentage would be based upon observations of the percentage of interactive play engaged in by peers.)

III.      *Acquaintance Procedures.* Describe how you will become acquainted with the child prior to initiation of the treatment program. Example: The therapist will have lunch with the child two times and will take the child for a walk through the park. Solicit teachers' or parents' suggestions on how best to do this.

IV.      *Setting.* Describe the location and times at which the modification program will be carried out. Example: The training sessions will occur in an individual tutoring booth at 10:00 a.m. each weekday morning.

V.      *Materials.* Provide a list of materials that the therapist should have on hand for each session. Example: Teaching stimuli, paper tissues, card for recording points earned, cereal and soft drink reinforcers, data recording materials including clipboard, data sheets, pencil, stopwatch.

VI.      *Data Collection.* Describe how the behavior will be scored and recorded. Example: On the prepared data sheet, the observer will enter a check mark in the proper box for each 10 sec. interval Johnny spent in studying. For each training session, the observer will calculate the percentage of intervals during which Johnny studied. This figure will be entered on Johnny's graph.

         The baseline data collection procedures should also be described here. Example: Johnny and his teacher were instructed to follow their usual procedures for his schoolwork. An observer recorded his study behavior in the classroom during the reading period at 10:00 to 10:45 a.m. each morning.

         Moreover, a schedule for the collection of reliability data throughout the program should be included in the script. Example: Interobserver reliability checks will take place on the first and third session during each phase of the program.

VII.      *Modification Program.* This is the script the therapist will follow in conducting training sessions with the child; it should be complete enough to allow some other person to carry out the same program independently.

         a. *Session Length.* State how long each session will last and how often sessions will occur. State criteria for concluding a session (e.g., if the child begins making errors on material previously mastered, if he appears very bored or restless after having been eager and attentive). Include instructions on how to conclude the session (e.g., return to a performance the child emits successfully, reinforce that performance, and conclude on this positive note).

         b. *Instructions.* Describe verbatim what you will say to the child about how and when she should behave, and what she will receive for behaving correctly.

         c. *Reinforcers.* Identify and gain control over reinforcers. If necessary, establish conditioned reinforcers (describe how this will be accomplished). For token reinforcers, specify where and when they will be exchanged for back-up reinforcers and describe the back-up reinforcers.

         d. *Reinforcer Delivery.* Specify when the reinforcers are to be delivered to the child, and by whom. Example: After each vocalization that follows the therapist's vocalization within 5 sec., the therapist will praise the child and give him one poker chip token.

Also state the reinforcement schedule to be employed and the criteria to be used in thinning the reinforcement schedule. Example: Reinforce every correct response until the child reaches a criterion of 90% correct responses (or some other near-perfect level) for at least two consecutive training sessions.

e. *Modeling and Prompting.* Specify the modeling and physical prompting methods to be used, if any. Example: The therapist instructs the child, "Do what I do. Now clap your hands." The therapist demonstrates, then takes the child's hands and claps them together." You must also describe when and how the prompts will be faded.

f. *Shaping.* If you are using a shaping procedure, describe the steps to be used in performance requirements and the criteria for proceeding to each closer approximation. Example: When Billy pulls on his shoes successfully 90% of the time when requested to do so, require him to pull the straps through the buckles.

g. *Reviews.* Describe the schedule to be followed in reviewing previously mastered performances. Example: Review all previously mastered performances at least once during each session. Intersperse review trials with new tasks so that the child has just successfully completed a review item prior to the introduction of a new requirement.

h. *Competing and Disruptive Behaviors.* State the procedures to be used in dealing with the child's disruptive behaviors. Example: Whenever the child begins to get up from his chair or look around the room or squeal, the therapist will sit quietly looking away from the child until the child sits down and attends to the therapist. Then the therapist begins the next training trial.

---

# Probe Questions for Chapter 5, Section 6

*1. Describe the advantages of formal, written contracts as compared with informal conversational agreements.*

*2. What types of information are included in contingency contracts?*

*3. Under what circumstances should contracts not be used?*

*4. Why should a treatment script be prepared?*

*5. What types of information should be included in the treatment script?*

# Chapter 6
# REDUCING EXCESS BEHAVIOR

## Behavioral Objectives for Chapter 6, Section 1

*After you have finished reading this section, you should:*

1. *Be aware of the professional ethical principles governing the use of aversive behavior control techniques.*

2. *Know the considerations governing the choice of a response reduction technique.*

## SECTION 1. CONSIDERATIONS IN SELECTING DECELERATION TECHNIQUES: THE LEAST COERCIVE METHOD

In selecting among the many different deceleration methods available, a therapist must consider the child's circumstances and age or developmental status. For example, isolation timeout might be a good procedure to use with a preschool child who is closely supervised, but not with a non-institutionalized, highly aggressive teenager. The teenager could put the therapist in timeout or worse, which presents a convincing argument for considering clients' capabilities when deciding how to treat them. As another example, young children might thrive under the combined use of teacher attention for good work and the teacher's ignoring disruptive behavior. Older children who are more responsive to peers than to teachers may fail to react positively to the same type of teacher intervention. Thus, to choose the best treatment program, one should know something about developmental psychology and should have identified the reinforcers maintaining the child's excessive rate of misbehavior.

If you know or have a very strong suspicion of the identity of the maintaining reinforcers, you can use an extinction technique on unwanted behaviors or can systematically reinforce alternative behaviors and put the deviant behavior on an extinction schedule. The latter is called differential reinforcement of other behaviors, or DRO. If you do not know exactly what factors control the target behavior, it may be necessary to use a punishment procedure such as response cost, which withdraws generalized conditioned reinforcers such as points, tokens, or cash when the undesirable target response occurs.

Another consideration is the acceptability of the deceleration technique to whoever must administer it, to the child, and to significant others such as parents, siblings, and friends. Don't forget that schools, treatment agencies, governments, and society as a whole all determine the appropriateness of treatment procedures. Generally speaking, interventions based on positive reinforcement of behavior incompatible with the problem behavior represent the most widely accepted interventions, followed by timeout from reinforcement, positive practice overcorrection, and psychoactive medication (Kazdin, 1980, 1981b). Not surprisingly, the less coercive methods are favored over those that restrict the client's freedom or those that cause pain. For example, timeout procedures involving no physical isolation are more acceptable than isolation timeout (Kazdin, 1980). And those with no or few side effects are preferred to those with unpleasant or dangerous concomitants (Kazdin, 1981b). Electric shock is the least acceptable deceleration technique, since it can be dangerous, unpleasant, painful, and coercive (Kazdin, 1980). Thus, the use of electric shock is not recommended in these pages. An intervention's appeal to users, recipients, and observers is a major determinant of the choice of therapeutic techniques to be employed.

## Probe Questions for Chapter 6, Section 1

1. *What deceleration techniques can be used if the maintaining reinforcers are known? If they are unknown?*

2. *Which types of interventions are generally most and least acceptable?*

## Behavioral Objectives for Chapter 6, Section 2
*After studying this section, you should be able to:*

1. State the conditions under which an extinction procedure will be most and least effective.

2. Describe the possible side effects of extinction procedures.

3. Describe similarities and differences between DRO and extinction procedures.

4. State the guidelines for using DRO.


## SECTION 2. EXTINCTION AND DRO

In the following sections we will describe some of the most commonly used deceleration techniques and will weigh the advantages and disadvantages of each one. Some considerations in the choice of deceleration techniques are summarized in Figure 6-1.


### *Extinction*

The term extinction is applied to a procedure in which reinforcement that previously followed an operant behavior is discontinued. No punishment is involved; instead, a formerly available reinforcer is no longer provided when the target response occurs. Compared with other procedures, extinction less rapidly produces behavior cessation, and may even cause a brief increase in the emission of the previously reinforced behavior (an extinction burst).

It is easy in principle but difficult in practice to identify and *consistently* withhold reinforcement for the particular target behavior. Moreover, to be most effective extinction should be used with behaviors that have been continuously rather than intermittently reinforced. As you might expect, such situations are relatively rare, and some attempted extinction programs paradoxically have produced stable increases in the rate of the undesirable behavior. For example, adult attention for desired responding and ignoring of misbehavior (attempted extinction) have sometimes *increased* the misbehavior's frequency (Herbert, Pinkston, Hayden, Sajwaj, Pinkston, Cordua, & Jackson, 1973; O'Leary, Becker, Evans, & Saudargas, 1969; Sajwaj, Twardosz, & Burke, 1972; Wahler, 1969). As the preceding, long list of references indicates, attempts at extinction fail with some regularity. However, in none of those studies was adult attention demonstrated to act as a reinforcing event for the oppositional, disruptive children treated. If parental attention was not acting as a reinforcer, then withholding it for misbehavior did *not* constitute extinction. In consequence, true extinction and reinforce-

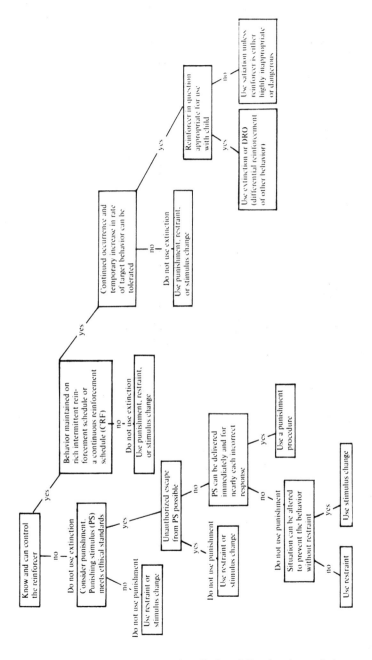

**Figure 6-1.** Conditions Governing Choice of Deceleration techniques.

ment procedures may not have been administered. These studies do, however, dramatically illustrate the necessity of attempting to identify the reinforcing events operating on the child's behavior.

*Applications.* In a classic case study, Williams (1959) eliminated a toddler's intense bedtime protests through extinction by arranging to remove the adult attention which had been reinforcing the boy's crying and tantrums. Also, withholding reinforcing teacher attention effectively controlled aggressive interactions in a nursery-school class (Brown & Elliott, 1965). Whenever caretaker attention acts as a reinforcer, as it nearly always does for preschoolage children, withholding attention constitutes extinction.

Also, self-stimulatory behavior and compulsive-like rituals of severely developmentally disabled children have been controlled through *sensory extinction procedures* (Rincover, 1978; Rincover, Cook, Peoples, & Packard, 1979). Sensory extinction removes the reinforcing auditory, visual, or proprioceptive feedback produced by the self-stimulation or the ritualized responding. As an example, Rincover (1978) carpeted a table top to reduce the auditory feedback produced by one boy's plate-spinning ritual, which greatly decreased the boy's plate manipulation. Other examples include masking proprioceptive feedback through use of a vibrator, and reducing reinforcing visual feedback of repetitious, inappropriate responding by contingently decreasing room illumination or by briefly blindfolding the children. Note that these sensory extinction procedures require close analysis of the child's target behavior, are relatively new, and consequently have been little tested in clinical practice. Student therapists should use other deceleration techniques of proven effectiveness in their initial attempts to control clients' excessive inappropriate responding.

## DRO

It is harsh and often counterproductive to decrease the amount of reinforcement children customarily receive, so DRO procedures (differential reinforcement of other behavior) often are useful. DRO consists of differentially reinforcing the child's behaviors *except* one specific target behavior. Thus, the target behavior is placed on an extinction schedule while behavioral alternatives are reinforced (see Homer & Peterson, 1980 for reviews of DRO). Omission training, a similar procedure, involves reinforcing the child for failing to emit the objectionable behavior during a specified time period. Alternatively, one might reinforce behaviors that are physically incompatible with the undesirable response (this is DRI or differential reinforcement of incompatible responding). For example, a child might receive reinforcement for speaking in a soft voice, which is incompatible with ear-piercing screaming, or for cooperation, which is incompatible with aggressive attacks.

In one more variant of DRO the target behavior might be tolerable, or even appropriate at a low rate, but troublesome when very frequent, as in a child's bidding for the teacher's attention. Lower rates of responding are reinforced in such situations, which is referred to as DRL (differential reinforcement of low rates of behavior). For convenience, we will limit our discussion to DRO procedures, the most general case.

*Applications.* DRO has been used primarily in classrooms, most often with retarded persons. The types of behavior successfully decreased or eliminated through DRO contingencies include disruptive or otherwise inappropriate classroom behavior (Deitz, 1977; Deitz, Slack, Schwarzmueller, Wilander, Weatherly, & Hilliard, 1978) and self-injurious behavior (Frankel, Moss, Schofield, & Simmons, 1976; Luiselli, Helfen, Colozzi, Donellon, & Pemberton, 1978). To treat an inattentive child who moved about excessively during instruction periods, Luiselli, Colozzi, and O'Toole (1980) awarded stickers for good behavior, using a DRO schedule. The stickers were later traded for free time, which allowed the child access to a number of interesting activities.

DRO programs are reported to have both beneficial and undesirable side effects. On the positive side, DRO schedules have been reported to produce durable and generalized response reduction (Homer & Peterson, 1980). Moreover, the teacher who administers the DRO program may acquire reinforcing properties (Frankel, Moss, Schofield, & Simmons, 1976). However, a DRO contingency may result in the inadvertent reinforcement of inappropriate behavior *other* than the target behavior. To prevent this untoward result, therapists might specify in advance that no highly undesirable behavior will be reinforced even during intervals in which the child fails to emit the inappropriate target behavior. Alternatively, therapists might make one or more negative events contingent upon the child's misbehavior of any type. For example, Luiselli and Krause (1981) displayed a tangible reward to a child during training, but removed it contingent upon the child's misbehavior. In addition, the child was required to sit with his hands at his sides for 5 sec. following each instance of misbehavior.

*Guidelines for Use of DRO.* To optimize the results of DRO programs, therapists should:

1. Specify the length of the DRO interval, depending upon the rate of the target behavior's occurrence. With behaviors of high frequency, one might use a 5–10 sec. interval; with moderate rate behaviors, use 1–10 min., and perhaps use as long as 30 min. for low rate, but highly undesirable ones. Do not use an FI schedule, which can easily be discriminated. VI schedules are less detectable and may result in more stable decrements in rates of responding.

2. Use a timer with an audible signal indicating the elapse of each time interval. Otherwise, you might forget to reinforce the child at the appropriate time.

3. Decide what to do if the "other" behavior includes some form of disruptive or uncooperative behavior lest you unintentionally reinforce the wrong thing.

4. Decide whether to simply recycle the interval if the child emits the undesirable target behavior or to use a changeover delay procedure which adds a penalty for the child's responding incorrectly, such as screaming, destroying property, and kicking you. Use a changeover delay contingency if the misbehavior is very frequent or if the disruptive behavior does not respond to the DRO program.

5. Set criteria for lengthening and fading the DRO contingency without reducing the child's net reinforcement level. You should fairly quickly increase the length of the DRO intervals, perhaps after as few as two or three reinforced intervals. Otherwise the child may resist your increasing demands for better behavior over progressively longer intervals.

6. Inform the child of the DRO contingency. Knowledge of the rules will hasten the child's learning (Hartmann, Gelfand, Smith, Paul, Cromer, Page, & LaBenta, 1976), and children who understand instructions can sustain low rates of reinforcement from the very beginning of the intervention (Martin & Pear, 1978).

## Probe Questions for Chapter 6, Section 2

1. *Explain why attempts at extinction might fail.*

2. *What are the problems in using DRO procedures?*

3. *Ten-year-old Jeff disrupts his class frequently by talking out-of-turn, making faces, and laughing and making noises. Would it be better to use DRO or extinction procedures in treating the problem, and why?*

4. *Describe the guidelines for the therapeutic use of DRO.*

## Behavioral Objectives for Chapter 6, Section 3

*Study of this section should enable you to:*

1. *Define punishment and describe instances of the appropriate use of punishment procedures.*

2. *State the possible negative effects associated with the use of punishment.*

3. *Describe conditions that will maximize the effectiveness of punishment, while protecting the child's rights.*

## SECTION 3.
## PHYSICAL PUNISHMENT AND REPRIMANDS: ETHICS AND PRECAUTIONS

Punishment consists of decreasing the rate of a particular response by applying an aversive stimulus or event contingent upon the emission of that response. Punishment can consist of the contingent presentation of an aversive stimulus (as in fines, reprimands, or physical punishment) or of the contingent withholding of positive reinforcement (as in time-out procedures). Unlike extinction and DRO procedures, punishment can be used even if you have failed to identify the reinforcers maintaining the child's misbehavior. However, since engaging in the punished behavior may previously have been reinforced, it is important to reduce the child's motivation to misbehave. This is achieved by accompanying punishment procedures with systematic positive reinforcement of desired alternative behaviors. The latter procedure also increases the effectiveness of mild punishment (Costello & Ferrer, 1976; Kircher, Pear, & Martin, 1971; O'Brien, Azrin, & Bugle, 1972). *Punishment should not be used without concomitant efforts to reinforce appropriate behaviors* because punishment may only suppress inappropriate behaviors, but not teach new, more desirable ones. In this section of the book, we will describe various punishment procedures and offer guidelines for their ethical and successful use.

*When to consider using punishment.* Punishment should be used as a last resort after positive reinforcement, extinction, and DRO programs have failed to alter the child's behavior. Great care should be exercised to protect the rights and welfare of the child-client. It is tempting to overuse punishment because of its immediate suppressive effects on child behavior. Consequently, therapists must guard against the temptation to rely on punishment rather than on slower, but more humane and informative verbal instruction, modeling, guided rehearsal, and reward procedures.

*Alternatives to harsh physical punishment.* In recent years a number of new punishment procedures have been devised as effective alternatives to more severe and dangerous physical punishment procedures such as electric shock. For example, although in the past shock punishment has controlled life-threatening ruminative vomiting — self-induced vomiting unaccompanied with nausea (Kohlenberg, 1970; Lang & Melamed, 1969), more recent studies have demonstrated that the presentation of undiluted lemon juice contingent upon ruminative vomiting effectively and quickly treated this condition (Apolito & Sulzer-Azaroff, 1981). The administration of disagreeable-tasting substances such as lemon juice and hot-pepper sauce can produce skin and mouth irritation, and so must be used with extreme caution. Nevertheless, their acceptability and safety far exceed those of electric shock and other types of severe physical punishment, and even of the punishing stimuli in everyday use by parents and other adult caretakers (Gelles, 1978). Punishment and alternative strategies have been reviewed by Harris and Ersner-Hershfield (1978), by Hobbs and Goswick (1977), and by Parke (1977). Table 6-1 summarizes some of the many recently developed alternatives to severe corporal punishment.

## Reprimands

Reprimands, criticism, and just plain screaming are the punishment procedures most commonly used by parents and teachers. In the interest of generalizing positive behavior changes from therapeutic situations to everyday life, therapists should give serious consideration to the use of reprimands to suppress children's undesirable behavior following the failure of positive reinforcement contingencies to increase the rate of alternative responses. In addition to being used frequently, reprimands are simpler to apply than most other punishment procedures such as timeout or response cost. Moreover, reprimands are not physically painful, so are less objectionable than most other forms of punishment. Reprimands can serve as a mild but effective response suppression technique if used systematically and thoughtfully.

Reprimands may be combined with other punishing events such as timeout. The objective in such combinations is to enhance the suppressive power of the reprimands. Later, when reprimands are used alone, perhaps in the classroom or in other public places, they may suffice to reduce the rate of undesired behavior (Kazdin, 1980).

In normal classroom settings, a reprimand such as saying, "No," has been found to suppress students' disruptive behavior relatively quickly (Hall, Axelrod, Foundopoulos, Shellman, Campbell, & Cranston, 1971). However, the manner in which reprimands are voiced may affect their impact on children's behavior. Reprimands delivered softly to the disruptive child have been found to be more effective than those stated loudly and overheard by

**Table 6-1.** Alternatives to Painful Physical Punishment

| Child's Target Behavior | Treatment Procedure | Authors' Names |
|---|---|---|
| Noncompliance | Paced instructions and commands from teacher every 1 min. until child complies. | Plummer, Baer, & LeBlanc (1977) |
| Aggressive physical attacks | 1. Teacher ignores attacker, sympathizes with victim. | Pinkston, Reese, LeBlanc, & Baer (1973) |
| | 2. Teacher gives paced instructions and paced reprimands every 10 sec. until child complies. | Goldstein, Cooper, Ruggles, & LeBlanc (1979) |
| Self-stimulation, aggression, and inappropriate speech | Contingent exercise (10 physically and verbally prompted stand-up and sit-down alternations). | Luce, Delquadri, & Hall (1980) |
| Chronic ruminative vomiting (self-induced vomiting without nausea) | Feeding child undiluted lemon juice contingent upon vomiting (this is mild physical punishment). The acidic juice can irritate tissues, and should be used very carefully under medical supervision. | Sajwaj, Libet, & Agras (1974) Apolito & Sulzer-Azaroff (1981) |
| Self-injurious behavior | Facial screening, consisting of briefly covering child's face with a loose-fitting terrycloth bib contingent upon the occurrence of self-injury. | Zegiob, Jenkins, Becker, & Bristow (1976) |
| Self-stimulatory behavior | Immobilization—15 sec. in which adult seated behind the child grasps child's forearms and gently holds the child's hands at his sides. | Bitgood, Crowe, Suarez, & Peters (1980) |

*Note*: Many of these procedures are restrictive and are used only as a last resort. This table does not include procedures discussed in the following sections, e.g., overcorrection, time out, DRO, response cost.

other children in the classroom (O'Leary, Kauffman, Kass, & Drabman, 1970). The loud reprimands may draw the reinforcing attention of classmates to the antics of the misbehaving child, and thus increase rather than decrease disruptive behavior (Madsen, Becker, Thomas, Koser, & Plager, 1968). However, in small groups of mentally retarded children, loud reprimands accompanied by a glare have proved more effective in reducing noncompliance than have other punishment techniques including timeout and positive practice (Doleys, Wells, Hobbs, Roberts, & Cartelli, 1976). Thus, the reactions of the other children must be considered in the determination of whether and how to use reprimands.

We believe that reprimands should be the first punishment technique tried, because of their relative acceptability and potential utility. If reprimands suffice to suppress the undesirable behavior, there is no need to consider using more punitive and potentially more ethically questionable interventions. On the other hand, if the target behavior unexpectedly escalates when followed by reprimands, the therapist has discovered useful information regarding the probable origin and the maintenance of the child's unacceptable behavior. This information could be used in planning positive reinforcement and extinction contingencies for the child. There is little to be lost and possibly much to be gained by using reprimands to attempt to suppress children's inappropriate actions.

## Probe Questions for Chapter 6, Section 3

1. *Define punishment, and give one ethically acceptable example of the use of a punishment technique in child therapy.*

2. *When, if ever, is it legitimate to use physical punishment in child treatment?*

3. *Why are reprimands recommended as a first behavior reduction procedure, and how effective are they?*

## Behavioral Objectives for Chapter 6, Section 4

*Study of this section should enable you to:*

1. *Describe a response cost contingency, the conditions governing its effectiveness, and its merits relative to physical punishment, extinction, and DRO.*

2. *Identify the limitations and undesired effects associated with response cost.*

## SECTION 4. RESPONSE COST

The concept of response cost is familiar to anyone who has ever received a library fine, a traffic ticket, or some similar penalty. In a response cost (RC) contingency, engaging in a specified prohibited behavior produces a loss of reinforcing stimuli and events. Most often, points, tokens, or money are removed contingent upon the child's making an incorrect response. Response cost penalties are employed most often in situations in which the child is earning points or money for desirable performances (see Chapter 5, Section 3). For instance, parents may institute a home program in which their children earn specified numbers of points for completing assigned household chores. The children also may lose a portion of their earnings for failing to complete their jobs, and for fighting, or throwing their clothing on the floor, under their beds, in dark recesses of their closets, or in other imaginative locations. Response cost procedures often are included in token economy programs (e.g., Atthowe & Krasner, 1968; Kazdin, 1980; Phillips, Phillips, Fixsen, & Wolf, 1971), and in individual contingency contracts (e.g., Patterson, Reid, Jones, & Conger, 1975).

Deprivation of privileges is another common, but relatively little researched response cost procedure. In everyday life teachers may deprive errant pupils of free time, or parents may refuse to permit their disobedient children to watch television, or may restrict them to the house for various transgressions. Table 6-2 indicates the variety of effective response cost procedures in current use.

It is easy and useful to include RC fines for misbehavior in programs in which children earn points for engaging in desirable activities (but see McLaughlin & Malaby, 1972, for an exception). Researchers have reported that RC contingencies can effectively reduce misbehavior even if children are presented with unearned conditioned reinforcers (Iwata & Bailey, 1974; Rapport, Murphy, & Bailey, 1978) or are given noncontingent points after having lost all of their points from accrued fines (Hall, Axelrod, Tyler, Grief, Jones, & Robertson, 1972). When employed correctly, response cost is a mild and useful deterrent to misconduct, especially if combined with positive reinforcement for behaving appropriately.

**Table 6-2.** Examples of Response-Cost Procedures: Fines and Deprivation of Privileges

*Fines*

1. Fines taken from tokens given to or earned by children improved their attending to their work and their academic performances (e.g., Hundert, 1976; Iwata & Bailey, 1974).

2. A 12-year-old retarded boy who severely bit his nails and fingertips earned 20–30 tokens a day for compliance, but was fined 1 token each time his hands or fingers touched his mouth. RC was much more effective than extinction or DRO programs tried (Myers, 1975).

3. In a laboratory problem-solving study, children were given 12 pennies, but fined 1 penny for each impulsive error (Arnold & Forehand, 1978).

4. On shopping trips, children received 50¢ for good behavior and were fined 5¢ for each incident of disruptive behavior (e.g., touching merchandise, roughhousing, fighting, wandering away) (Clark, Greene, Macrae, McNees, Davis, & Risley, 1977).

5. In the treatment of children's obesity, their parents were therapists, and were fined for failure to record their children's weight regularly or if their children failed to comply with the program. Some parents also were instructed in the use of positive reinforcement contingencies with their children (Aragona, Cassady, & Drabman, 1975).

6. One million customers' use of telephone directory assistance decreased after they began being charged 20¢ for overusing local directory assistance (McSweeny, 1978).

*Deprivation of Privileges*

1. A classroom teacher posted a booklet with pages numbered zero to 30, corresponding to minutes of free time the class could have. The teacher looked up periodically and turned the booklet page to remove 1 min. of free time for any off-task student behavior. The target child also did so on a small cardholder on his own desk (Rapport, Murphy, & Bailey, 1978). This method also was used in a program in which the entire class lost free time for disruptive behavior (Sulzbacher & Houser, 1968).

2. Institutionalized predelinquents all were given an earlier-than-usual curfew for any individual's curfew violations or failure to attend class. This group contingency effectively reduced curfew violations and was easy for the staff to administer (Alexander, Corbett, & Smigel, 1976).

## Limitations and Undesired Effects

Like other disciplinary measures, response cost can be abused. Overwrought and untrained users can assess so many fines that fines lose their effectiveness (Kazdin, 1980). When they are in debt, children don't receive positive reinforcement for their good behavior. Overly heavy reliance on response cost procedures to maintain discipline has been reported in poorly supervised programs in correctional institutions (Bassett & Blanchard, 1977). Even if not abused by the children's caretakers, fines levied on an entire group because of the inappropriate behavior of a single group member can have unintended negative effects. For example, Axelrod (1973) reported a sharp increase in classmates' verbal threats toward children whose misbehavior would lose free time for the whole class.

One must be something of an economist in order to use response cost tactics effectively. How should the magnitude of the fine or loss of privileges be determined? Generally, the economy should be adjusted so that children who perform well most of the time receive most or all of the available back-up reinforcers (Phillips et al., 1971). However, fine-tuning a token economy is not easy for novices, and requires some trial-and-error experimentation, which could appear capricious to children and their caretakers.

## Implementation

1. Introduce RC contingencies only *after* sole reliance on positive reinforcement contingencies has been given a fair trial and failed. Determine whether the use of verbal criticism alone would solve the problem.

2. Ensure that some positive reinforcement is available to the child for desired behavior incompatible with the designated misbehavior. Do not overuse fines or loss of privileges that deprive the child of customary privileges and positive experiences.

3. Do not apply RC contingencies to new forms of misbehavior on-the-spot while you are angry. Decide on the magnitude of penalties when you are calm and capable of objective thinking and can warn the child in advance of the RC contingency. Should other problems arise, such as the child's going deeply into debt, take time to formulate a recovery plan. Don't respond impulsively, or you may demonstrate responses that you don't want the child to learn.

4. Phase out the RC contingencies gradually as desirable alternative behaviors become habitual. It's always possible to reinstate the contingencies should the undesired responding reappear.

5. If you are advising the child's caretakers in the administration of RC contingencies, provide consultation and supervision to ensure proper use of response cost. It is always wise to role-play the administration of therapeutic techniques until the responsible adults become confident in their ability to administer response consequences.

In conclusion, perhaps the best precaution is to imagine yourself in the child's position. Would you want to receive the same types of contingencies that you are applying or advising others to apply to the child? If not, perhaps the program is unfair or unduly harsh.

# Probe Questions for Chapter 6, Section 4

1. *What is response cost, and when should it be used?*

2. *What information should a therapist use to decide on the magnitude of fines used in a treatment program? When should rates be readjusted?*

3. *In a fit of anger, Mary's mother fined Mary her entire monthly allowance. How would you expect Mary to respond to her mother's response cost tactic?*

## Behavioral Objectives for Chapter 6, Section 5

*After studying this section, you should be able to:*

1. *Define and give examples of time-out contingencies.*

2. *Devise a response reduction program using a time-out procedure.*

3. *State why it is desirable to use brief time-out periods.*


## SECTION 5. TIME-OUT FROM POSITIVE REINFORCEMENT

Time-out from positive reinforcement is a mild form of punishment in which an undesired response is followed by a short period during which customary, ongoing reinforcement is withheld. For example, a youngster may be removed briefly from view of a favorite TV cartoon after hitting a companion viewer. As the name implies, time-out from positive reinforcement (henceforth termed TO) derives its effect from a contrast with a rich positive reinforcement schedule for the child's desirable actions. Otherwise, there is nothing to withhold and the TO contingency is undetectable or perhaps even positively reinforcing to the child. Consequently, the TO procedure nearly invariably is accompanied by positive contingency management programs. TO often is a preferred punishment procedure because it involves shaping and maintaining desirable behavior, and suppresses unwanted behavior without the presentation of physically painful stimulation (Johnston, 1972).

### *Effectiveness of TO*

In their helpful pamphlet on how to use TO, Hall and Hall (1980) claim that, if used correctly, TO *always* results in a decrease in the target behavior's rate. However, if used incorrectly, a seeming TO procedure can cause problem behavior rates to increase, as Plummer, Baer, and LeBlanc (1977) have demonstrated. Therefore, therapists must make careful, detailed observations of the child's behavior in everyday settings before, during, and after applying a TO procedure designed to improve a child's conduct.

The typical form of TO, in which the misbehaving child is removed from the fray, has advantages over physical punishment: the angry caretaker and angry child do not continue to interact with each other and perhaps escalate their conflict. TO usually can be administered calmly and objectively, and, in fact, is most effective when applied in that manner. Informative reviews of TO are those by Gast and Nelson (1977), Hobbs and Forehand (1977), and Lahey and Drabman (1981).

TO procedures have been used successfully with clients ranging in age from 1½ years to adulthood, especially for profoundly retarded and psychotic adults. Moreover, TO procedures have successfully reduced clients' rates of inappropriate behaviors such as throwing tantrums, primitive foraging at the dinner table, food theft, severely disruptive and aggressive conduct, and negativism and noncompliance (Baer, 1962; Barton, Guess, Garcia, & Baer, 1970; Bostow & Bailey, 1969; Burchard & Barrera, 1972; Hobbs, Forehand, & Murray, 1978; LeBlanc, Busby, & Thomson, 1974; Roberts, Hatzenbuehler, & Bean, 1981; Sachs, 1973; White, Nielson, & Johnson, 1972).

## Limitations of TO

Isolation TO, whereby the offending child is deprived of the usual companionship and diversion for a brief interval, may be nearly impossible to administer in crowded homes and schools, or when the miscreant is large and potentially assaultive. Moreover, earning many TOs may increase a youngster's reputation for courage and toughness among groups of delinquents (Kendall, Nay, & Jeffers, 1975). In general, TO is easier to administer to younger children than to older ones. It is more socially appropriate for younger children, and often is more effective with them, perhaps because they are less resourceful at entertaining themselves during supposed TOs and less able to recruit peer accomplices in treatment plan subversion.

TO procedures have not been particularly effective in reducing some undesirable behaviors such as self-stimulation, possibly because TO periods allow the child to practice uninterrupted self-stimulation (Solnick, Rincover, & Peterson, 1977). Ross (1981) has sensibly recommended that therapists identify the reinforcers for a child's misbehavior before embarking on a TO program which otherwise might prove futile.

Isolation TO can result in decreased training time and lost learning opportunities if the child amasses many TOs. Fortunately, there are effective alternatives to isolation TO, for instance, having the child wear a special TO ribbon (Foxx & Shapiro, 1978) or display a brightly colored card which can be removed to indicate that the child is receiving a TO and should not be reinforced (Spitalnik & Drabman, 1976). Other TO methods also let children remain in their ordinary surroundings. For example, the TO can occur within the classroom at a desk removed from the other children (LeBlanc, Busby, & Thomson, 1974; Scarboro & Forehand, 1975). Porterfield, Herbert-Jackson, and Risley (1976) have developed a useful alternative to isolation TO for use with preschool children. In the *contingent observation* procedure, the teacher places disruptive children on the sidelines, and tells them how to act more appropriately (e.g., "No, don't take toys from other children. Ask for the toy you want.") They are told to stand aside and watch the other children who are acting appropriately. After less than a minute, the children are asked whether they are ready to rejoin the group and behave more appropriately. This method is very useful in preschool settings.

In another variant of TO, Mansdorf (1977) has removed reinforcing items and has withdrawn sources of entertainment (such as TV sets) from the client's vicinity rather than removing the client to a TO room. There are many ways to achieve the temporary response contingent removal of reinforcing events, which is the essence of TO.

## Guidelines for the Use of TO

1. TO is a somewhat restrictive procedure, so you must try less coercive methods first, such as differentially reinforcing desired behavior and using a DRO schedule. In any case, the child must receive copious reinforcement for desirable behavior.

2. For this and for the preceding step, you must identify the stimuli and events which the child finds reinforcing. Some initial shaping and modeling may be required to ensure that the child can perform the desired responses and that he knows that such behavior is valued by adults.

3. Then try the mildest forms of aversive control. Will the child comply with simple rule statements ("We don't hit other people") or mild reprimands (Doleys et al., 1976)? As with other forms of punishment, TO should be employed only after less restrictive methods have failed.

4. Put only the selected target behavior on a TO schedule. Using TO too freely is unnecessarily aversive and is confusing for the child (Hall & Hall, 1980).

5. Be consistent; apply TO even if the child initially complains, resists, or promises to reform (Hammer & Drabman, 1981). Such behavior does not usually persist. Once you have stated the TO contingency to the child, abide by it as invariably as possible (i.e., on a continuous schedule if possible). However, TO often retains its effectiveness on a fairly rich intermittent schedule (Calhoun & Lima, 1977; Clark, Rowbury, Baer, & Baer, 1973; Jackson & Calhoun, 1977).

6. Employ a moderate TO duration of about 4 min. (Hobbs & Forehand, 1977) or no more than 1 min. per year of the child's age (Hall & Hall, 1980). The TO duration can be increased if it is too short initially, but employment of longer TO durations often precludes the later effective use of shorter ones (White, Nielson, & Johnson, 1972). Use a timer to ensure that you do not forget to release the child from TO at the end of the predetermined interval.

7. Use a pre-TO warning to indicate that the child must cease misbehaving immediately in order to avoid a TO. Nonverbal signals, such as the hand signal used by basketball officials to indicate an impending technical foul (see Figure 6-2), are useful in avoiding prolonged quarreling and haggling with the child.

**Figure 6-2.** Line drawing of arms and hands signaling a technical foul warning.

8. Employ a release contingency for terminating TOs. For example, the TO ends after 4 min. if the child behaves appropriately during the last 15 sec. The child must behave quietly for at least 15 consecutive seconds to earn release from TO. Without such a release contingency, the child's disruptive responding would be (negatively) reinforced by the removal of an aversive stimulus, the TO. The child must not be released from TO until she has ceased crying, breaking things, kicking, howling, or hurling imprecations. If the child has damaged or messed up the room, she must repair and clean it as well as possible prior to release from TO. Therapists and caretakers must be resolute if they are to use TO successfully.

9. If you use isolation TO in a school or treatment agency, the child's parents must have agreed in writing to your doing so. Certain state and federal laws and judicial rulings apply (see Public Law 94-142). If isolation TO is used, the TO cubicle must be safe, comfortable, and well-ventilated, and must be at least 6 ft x 6 ft in size. The door must be unlocked so that the child

can escape in case of fire, and someone must monitor the child continuously during the TO to ensure the child's safety. A reasonable TO duration must be used, no more than necessary to ensure that the child has become calm and that the TO is effective. As Ross (1981, p. 185) put it, "Solitary confinement is not made acceptable by renaming it time-out!" If a TO interval exceeds 1 hr., a supervisory staff member must be notified and must decide on a course of action. Further, the incident should be described in detail in the client's case folder (Gast & Nelson, 1977).

10. Plan a back-up contingency for use if your TO procedure fails. For example, an isolation TO could be used if a nonexclusionary TO is unsuccessful; alternatively, deprivation of privileges could be employed.

11. TO can still be used If the child seriously misbehaves while outside his home, school, or treatment agency. For example, the child's hand can be marked with a nontoxic felt-tipped pen to indicate TO periods to be administered later (see Drabman & Creedon, 1979, for details). Also, a teacher or aide can defer a pupil's TO until recess, as long as the child is not deprived of most or all recess time.

If this lengthy list of guidelines is used, you have a very good chance of reducing a child's severely disruptive and inappropriate behavior through the application of TO procedures.

## Probe Questions for Chapter 6, Section 5

1. *What criteria can be used to determine whether a particular TO contingency is ethical and appropriate or not?*

2. *Describe the advantages and disadvantages of using TO.*

3. *Suppose that a child whom you have put in the bathroom for a 3-min. time-out has sprayed water all over the walls and floor. What would you do and why?*

4. *Suppose that someone protests that use of TO with children is inhumane. How would you reply, and what evidence could you offer?*

## Behavioral Objectives for Chapter 6, Section 6

*When you have completed Section 6, you should be able to:*

1. *Define and recognize instances of restitutional and positive practice overcorrection.*

2. *Compare overcorrection and other response rate reduction procedures on restrictiveness, effectiveness, and professional and general acceptability.*

3. *State when use of overcorrection would be justified and unjustified.*

## SECTION 6. OVERCORRECTION

It is not easy to choose an appropriate response reduction technique. As previously stated, extinction and reinforcement of alternative behaviors may prove ineffective. Response cost may be effective, but is used mostly in the context of some systematic, established reinforcement program rather than as a single intervention tactic. And the use of physical punishment is distasteful, potentially damaging, and, in some cases, prohibited. Yet dangerous and highly disruptive behavior must be controlled. In response to this need, Foxx and Azrin (1972, 1973) developed a method called *overcorrection* (OC). OC is a complex procedure that is not easily defined. Typically, OC consists of a reprimand ("Don't bite your hand"), a description of the unacceptable behavior ("You are tearing up papers again"), or a rule statement ("We don't hit people."). Then the child is administered restitutional or positive practice OC, or both.

### Restitutional Overcorrection

As the name implies, restitutional OC requires the child to make amends for any damage he has done and to overcorrect or improve on the original state of affairs. Thus, the child who has persisted in defecating on the floor might be required to change his soiled clothing and deposit it in a laundry hamper and clean the floor in and beyond the area of the accident (see Azrin & Foxx, 1974; Matson & Ollendick, 1977). For hitting someone a child might be required to pat the injured area gently for 30 sec. and then to apologize 10 times ("I'm sorry") after each hitting incident (Ollendick & Matson, 1976). A good rule of thumb is to require the child to perform the OC response 10 times.

In restitutional OC the child is required to compensate for whatever harm she has done. In either type of OC, if instructions do not suffice to induce the child to practice the OC, gentle, but firm physical guidance is used (graduated guidance). That is, you must be willing and able to require that an unwilling child carries out the OC routine.

## Positive Practice Overcorrection

Some troublesome behaviors do not harm other people or things, so restitution is impossible. Positive practice OC has been used for such behaviors as facial tics, self-stimulation, and other socially inappropriate behaviors. Typically, positive practice OC consists of repetitive practice of more appropriate behaviors which are physically incompatible with the undesired acts. For example, Foxx and Azrin (1973) controlled a retarded girl's self-stimulatory head rotation by having her repeat three exercises (holding her head up, level, and down) for 20 min. following each head-weaving occurrence. In another study, positive practice of arm movements reduced a retarded boy's masturbation in the classroom (Luiselli, Helfen, Pemberton, & Reisman, 1977). Positive practice consisted of a sequence of raising his arms over his head, extending them in front of and beside his body, and crossing his arms across his chest repeated four times. Table 6-3 presents some of the more frequently used OC procedures.

## Effectiveness of Overcorrection

OC is a popular response reduction method which has proved effective in the rapid reduction of self-stimulation in psychotic and retarded children, and in the control of aggressive and disruptive behaviors (see reviews by Azrin & Besalel, 1980; Luiselli, 1980; Marholin, Luiselli, & Townsend, 1980; and Ollendick & Matson, 1978, for more information). OC appears to be somewhat less effective in eliminating self-injurious behavior, but often is a more humane alternative than shock punishment or continuous physical restraint. OC has successfully reduced self-injurious behaviors such as head-banging, nail-picking, and eye-poking (see Azrin, Gottlieb, Highart, Wesolowski, & Rehn, 1975; Harris & Romanczyk, 1976; Kelly & Drabman, 1977; Webster & Azrin, 1973, respectively). However, in at least one instance OC *increased* a child's rate of head banging (Measel & Alfieri, 1976).

Sometimes, but not always, OC has produced behavioral improvement for as long as a year (Freeman, Moss, Somerset, & Ritvo, 1977; Luiselli, Helfen, Pemberton, & Reisman, 1977). Treatment effects seem to be more enduring with children than adults, perhaps because adults have engaged in disordered behavior for longer periods (Marholin, Luiselli, & Townsend, 1980).

**Table 6-3.** Frequently Used Overcorrection Procedures*

| Overcorrection Procedure | Description |
| --- | --- |
| 1. Oral Hygiene Training | Oral Hygiene Training is applied to behaviors which involve the inappropriate use of the mouth; e.g., biting, swearing, and pica. The child brushes his teeth repeatedly with a toothbrush soaked in antiseptic. Duration of each incident is 2–3 minutes. |
| 2. Functional Movement Training | The most frequently used procedure, Functional Movement Training is used to reduce self-stimulatory and self-injurious behavior. The child is instructed to move the related body part through tedious positions; for example, with head-banging, the child moves his head first down onto the chest, then directly out in front, and lastly straight up. Each position is held for 10–15 seconds. Manual guidance is used for uncooperative children. Duration of each OC incident is 5–20 minutes. |
| 3. Cleanliness Training | Cleanliness Training is used to toilet train normal and retarded children. For accidents, the child is required to change his clothes, clean up any mess, and repeatedly practice going to the bathroom, e.g., he walks to the restroom, pulls pants down, sits for 10 seconds, and pulls pants back up repeatedly. Duration of each routine is 20–30 minutes. |
| 4. Household Orderliness Training | Household Orderliness Training is used to reduce destructive and disruptive behaviors such as property damage and overturning chairs and tables. It requires the child to correct and vastly improve the situation; for example, for a few overturned tables, all tables are straightened and cleaned. OC duration ranges from 15–30 minutes. |
| 5. Social Reassurance Training | Social Reassurance Training is applied to aggressive or threatening behaviors which may upset others. The child is instructed to repeatedly apologize for his behavior (10–30 times) and offer additional condolences. In the case of aggressive attacks, the child may be required to practice touching the victim gently. |

*From Foxx, R. M. An overview of overcorrection. *Journal of Pediatric Psychology*, 1978, 3, 97–101.

## Limitations of Overcorrection

It is difficult to devise new forms of OC since there are no established guidelines for doing so. Foxx and Azrin (1972) advised that OC should: (a) be topographically related to the misbehavior (e.g., hand exercises for inappropriate use of the hands), (b) immediately follow the misbehavior, and (c) be actively performed so the work and effort serve as a deterrent to inappropriate behavior. However, effective OC procedures often fail to include many of the preceding features (Marholin, Luiselli, & Townsend, 1980; Ollendick & Matson, 1978). The effective components of the complex OC procedures remain largely unidentified (but see Libet & Forehand, 1979; Matson, Horne, Ollendick, & Ollendick, 1979; and Ollendick & Matson, 1976).

Practitioners cannot predict for how long each OC exercise must be engaged in, and durations have varied between a few seconds and 2 hours over a period of days or weeks. It appears that effective OC procedures dramatically change the client's behavior rapidly, within only a few sessions.

The OC procedure is a demanding one, since caretakers must monitor the child's behavior continuously and intervene to ensure that the child follows the prescribed OC exercises. As a result, even effective OC procedures may be abandoned by overburdened institutional staff members (Kelly & Drabman, 1977). Moreover, staff members may find it difficult and embarrassing to try to overpower children who refuse to engage in OC. And unfortunately the physical restraint feature of OC can lend itself to abuse by overenthusiastic practitioners. For these reasons we advise extreme care and caution in the use of OC.

## Guidelines for Use of Overcorrection

If you are considering using OC, we recommend that you do so in the following manner.

1. Thoroughly explore the use of treatment programs based on positive reinforcement (DRO and extinction) and on modeling prior to attempting an OC intervention. Only when more positive, less coercive methods clearly fail is it ethical to introduce OC.

2. In designing an OC program, use published, well-established procedures rather than developing your own method. This helps ensure that your procedure is, in fact, OC, and has passed professional ethical scrutiny. Always combine OC with a program of positive reinforcement of appropriate academic or social behavior.

3. Make sure that the child's parents or guardians understand and give written permission for the use of OC with their child. Describe the OC procedure to them thoroughly before seeking their consent.

4. Precede application of the OC exercises with a command not to engage in the undesirable behavior, a description of the incorrect behavior, or a rule statement. Such remarks themselves may suffice to suppress the target behavior.

5. Select an OC duration of moderate magnitude. Luiselli (1980) suggests starting with a duration of 3-4 min., which can be extended if it proves ineffective. However, if the OC duration has been increased to render it more effective, don't expect to decrease it later with positive results.

6. If possible, use positive practice OC which is related topographically to at least one of the child's undesirable behaviors, in order to enhance the educational aspect of the procedure. Try to teach behaviors that are useful to the child and are not themselves socially inappropriate.

7. Program OC across settings and caretakers, since generalization of treatment effects cannot be expected. In practice, this may require training the child's parents, teachers, and other caretakers to apply OC throughout the day and to employ it later if the troublesome behavior recurs.

8. Inform caretakers of potential difficulties in applying OC, and involve them in advance to plan overcoming foreseeable problems. They should be prepared for children to cry or protest, and for large, aggressive ones to scream at, hit, kick, and otherwise attack the trainer.

9. Check for indirect effects of OC; for example, increases or decreases in other appropriate or inappropriate behaviors when one target behavior is reduced through OC. Also, there may be vicariously produced suppression of similar undesirable behaviors in classmates.

If the preceding guidelines are adhered to, OC can be an effective, safe, and long-lasting treatment for highly problematic behavior excesses.

## Probe Questions for Chapter 6, Section 6

*1. Give examples of restitutional and positive practice OC.*

*2. Describe the guidelines for the effective and ethical use of OC.*

*3. Which types of treatments should be attempted prior to using OC?*

*4. Who is qualified to develop new forms of OC?*

# Chapter 7
# EXTENDING TREATMENT-INDUCED GAINS

## Behavioral Objectives for Chapter 7, Section 1
*Study of Section 1 of this chapter should prepare you to:*

1. *Enumerate procedures for enhancing treatment generalization.*

2. *Avoid inadvertently teaching the child to behave well only in your presence or only in the treatment setting.*

## SECTION 1. GENERALIZATION AND MAINTENANCE OF TREATMENT EFFECTS

The following is one of the best-known quotations in applied behavior analysis, and one well worth remembering: "In general, generalization should be programmed, rather than expected or lamented" (Baer, Wolf, & Risley, 1968). The production of appropriately generalized and durable treatment effects is one of the remaining, major challenges for behavior therapy. Many other treatment approaches have failed to meet this challenge, and it is only through careful planning that behavior therapists can hope to make clinically significant and enduring contributions to their clients' welfare. As Baer and his associates have long maintained (Baer et al., 1968), generalization must be planned, and not merely hoped for.

The technology for producing general and lasting treatment benefits is limited at present. Still, some tactics are known to promote generalization, and others might be expected to do so. This section will summarize what is known and surmised about programming to enhance generalization. Student projects of limited scope and brief duration may not be expected to accommodate many generalization training features. Nevertheless, we present these guidelines for your consideration and possible future use. Some good reviews of generalization techniques include Drabman, Hammer, and Rosenbaum (1979), Marholin and Siegel (1978), Stokes and Baer (1977), and

Wahler, Breland, and Coe (1979). In addition, Baer (1981) has prepared a helpful little monograph entitled, *How to plan for generalization.*

There are several types of generalization: Behavioral improvements might extend across physical and social settings, over time, when the client is with various persons; and to similar interaction patterns, rather than in just a single, narrowly defined target behavior. Thus, a child might be taught to behave cooperatively at home as well as at the clinic or in school, at various times of the day, in the company of many different people, and in many ways, both verbally and non-verbally. On the whole, the techniques used to enhance generalization across settings increase the durability or maintenance of treatment effects as well. Consequently, we will present a single set of procedures for attaining both goals (generalization across settings and over time). Readers can consult the relevant sections of Chapters 5 and 6 for techniques to increase the durability of behavior improvements achieved through application of each of the various intervention methods presented in those chapters.

## Guidelines

The following procedures for programming generalization are drawn largely from reviews by Stokes and Baer (1977) and Wahler, Breland, and Coe (1979). We advocate the blockbuster approach in generalization as well as in treatment: When in doubt, apply as many generalization aids as possible. At least some of them may be expected to work.

1. *Teach behaviors that customarily elicit reinforcement in everyday settings.* Examples are eye contact and adequate voice volume during social interactions, greeting people appropriately upon first seeing them, and cooperation with requests from peers and supervisors. Even when these socially appropriate actions are not specifically reinforced, they are seldom punished in normal social encounters, and consequently tend to persist (Baer, Rowbury, & Goetz, 1976). And in order to increase the probability that newly learned behaviors will receive support, children might be taught to cue others to attend to and approve of their efforts (Stokes & Baer, 1977). For example, children could be instructed to ask for evaluative feedback from adult caretakers once or twice a day. For example, a child might ask a teacher how well he is doing in reading.

2. *Check to verify that the child's family, teachers, peers, and others important to him all will at least tolerate the child's changed behavior* (Baer, 1981). If they won't, the program stands little chance of long-term success. Associates' commitment to the child's behavior changes is necessary for generalization as well as for initial treatment success.

3. *Use many and varied trainers.* To be useful, the newly learned behavior must be displayed in interactions with a variety of people, and not with just

one therapist. So use more than one trainer and test to ensure that the child's new skill will be used widely in diverse company. Sometimes as few as two trainers will suffice to produce the client's generalized responding in the presence of many different people (Baer, 1981).

4. *Diversify the training program.* Early in training, you should make the task as simple and discriminable as possible to produce rapid mastery, and to provide the child with many success experiences. However, after this initial phase, the primary consideration becomes to aid the child in generalizing his performance to other settings, other tasks, and other trainers. In this later phase, if the task is to train the child to identify dogs, don't limit yourself to presenting two pictures of dogs. Use many pictures and actual dogs, then vary your instructions so the child can answer appropriately if someone asks a question different from, "What is this?" Commands and inquiries such as: "Tell me what this is," and "Which one is this?" should also elicit appropriate replies, and will do so if various cueing questions are asked during training. Similarly, use a variety of social reinforcers ranging from, "That's right, you're doing fine," to a smile and caress in order to help sustain the child's performance across settings and people. You should use a variety of back-up reinforcers too. Variety is essential in stimulating the child's interest and motivation as well as in equipping him to handle the complexities of everyday life.

5. *Although immediate reinforcement is useful in initial training, delayed reinforcement may be necessary later.* Early in training reinforcement should follow correct performance as quickly as possible. However, this immediate reinforcement should be replaced by delays as the child achieves mastery of the therapy task. Introducing delayed reinforcement must be done gradually so as not to disrupt the child's performance.

Delayed reinforcement aids generalization by obscuring the boundaries between the training and the generalization contexts. Consequently, it may be better to withhold reinforcement for children's appropriate behavior during a morning training session, and reinforce them at the end of the day than to reinforce them during or immediately after the morning training session (Fowler & Baer, 1981). The answer to the children's question, "Do we have to be good all day?" is, "Yes, you do" (Fowler & Baer, 1981). In some cases, making the reinforcement contingencies ambiguous to the child helps to ensure continued good behavior.

6. *Make it difficult for the child to discriminate training from nontraining settings by incorporating common features in both.* If you are teaching the child skills she will later use in the company of other children, then peers should be introduced into the training setting, perhaps as tutors (Stokes & Baer, 1977). Teachers should be present if appropriate child-teacher interactions are the goal (Gross & Drabman, 1981), and they and other concerned adults can be instructed to implement the program in their day-to-day interactions with the child. Be sure to commend those adults for their work

— they like reinforcement, too (Greenwood, Hops, & Walker, 1977). In general, do not use novel stimuli or unfamiliar social settings throughout training if you want the training effects to generalize.

7. *Reinforce the child's spontaneous generalization of newly acquired skills, at least upon occasion*; that is, don't expect much untaught transfer of training to other settings. Baer (1981) has suggested listing all of the client's changeworthy behavior in all settings, and doing the same for everyone else who is involved. Then devise a realistic plan for altering the child's behavior and for maintaining the improvements. Remember to attempt to enlist the cooperation of the child's caretakers, siblings, and perhaps playmates who can provide support for the child's utilizing the trained behaviors at home, at school, and at play.

8. *Phase out the treatment program gradually and as undetectably as possible following stabilized behavioral improvements.* Introduce more intermittency into the child's reinforcement schedule, and raise reinforcement criteria until they match criteria normally encountered in schools and homes. Training should fade almost imperceptibly into follow-up.

9. *Plan follow-up sessions to assess the child's behavior and to provide "booster shots" of training if necessary.* Check on the child's progress every few weeks at first, and every few months later. If backsliding occurs, a retraining session or two may re-establish the treatment-produced gains.

In addition to the preceding methods, *self-regulation training* has been suggested as a method of enhancing treatment generalization and maintenance. The child-client may be the person best able to apply the treatment program where and when it is needed. Accordingly, we next consider the merits and techniques of training children in self-regulation.

## Probe Questions for Chapter 7, Section 1

*1. Identify and give examples of four types of generalization.*

*2. Why are two trainers usually better than one?*

*3. When is it advisable to use delayed reinforcement?*

*4. What should you teach to the child's significant caretakers to aid generalization of learned behavior? How can peers help in generalization?*

*5. Describe as many generalization aids as you can.*

## Behavioral Objectives for Chapter 7, Section 2

*After studying this section, you should be able to:*

1. *Identify and give examples of self-regulation and self-instructional training.*

2. *Name the components of self-regulation training.*

3. *Describe the current limitations of self-regulation training.*

## SECTION 2. SELF-REGULATION TRAINING

Wouldn't it be wonderful if children could be taught to regulate their own behavior! Then they could continuously monitor what they were doing, and could arrange appropriate antecedents and consequences for themselves. Effective self-regulation interventions might solve the recalcitrant problems of the limited durability and generalization of treatment effects. The child could simply use self-regulation tactics whenever and wherever needed, and thus gains made during treatment could be maintained, and perhaps even extended to new behaviors and settings. Although these ideal conditions have yet to be met, the past ten years have witnessed the proliferation of self-regulation training programs, some of them quite effective.

In self-regulation training, clients are taught to monitor, evaluate, and provide consequences for their own behavior in the form of reward, withholding reward, or punishment. There are two major types of self-regulation training — the *operant approach* as typified by Karoly and Kanfer (1982; Karoly, 1981), and the *self-instructional techniques* developed by Meichenbaum (1979), and by Kendall and his associates (Kendall & Finch, 1979; Kendall & Hollon, 1979). Let us consider the operant intervention first. The operant approach of Kanfer and Karoly (1972) involves four steps: (a) deciding to modify a certain behavior; (b) selecting a goal as defined by meeting a predetermined standard of behavior; (c) monitoring and evaluating one's own behavior as compared to the goal; and (d) selecting and delivering rewarding consequences for success and either no reward or punishment for failure to meet the standard.

The operant approach to self-control stresses the self-reinforcement contingencies; in contrast, the self-instructional procedure emphasizes the important mediating role of self-speech. Both approaches require the client's commitment to the prospect of behavior change because there is little likelihood of successfully completing a self-regulation program with a reluctant client. Also, both the operant and the self-instructional approaches advocate training in self-observation, self-evaluation, and the application of reinforcement contingencies to oneself. The operant treatment closely resembles other reinforcement contingency management programs, except that the contingency is self-imposed. In contrast, self-instructional training involves learning to generate and employ behavior control strategies, sometimes through the application of self-directed comments or self-talk (Meichenbaum, 1977).

Typically, all types of self-regulation strategies are taught through complex interventions including verbal instructions, the therapist's modeling the desired behavior, overt and covert rehearsal, prompting to initiate self-regulatory behavior, feedback on performance attempts, and reinforcement (e.g., self-directed praise in imitation of a self-praising model or self-reward through engaging in favorite activities). A therapist or caretaker first manages the child's behavior, but control is gradually shifted to the child, who eventually assumes primary responsibility. Self-regulation training has been used in efforts to cope with usually resistant problems such as impulsive and inadequate attempts to complete complex tasks, hyperactivity and inattention to school assignments, learning problems, verbal or physical aggression, delinquency, severe fears, and social withdrawal (see recent reviews by Cole & Kazdin, 1980; Karoly & Kanfer, 1982; Kendall, 1981; Meichenbaum, 1979; and S. O'Leary & Dubey, 1979).

## Components of Self-Regulation

Self-regulation training of any type usually commences with instruction in self-observation. The child who doesn't realize that she is biting her nails or that she interrupts others who are trying to work is in no position to improve her conduct. Habits, of which we are largely unaware, but which we may consider harmless or endearing, can be major nuisances to others. Thus, self-awareness is a vital first component in the self-directed change process. You can use the same recording techniques with clients that are usually used with therapists or observers (see Chapter 3), but remember that recording must be easy and unobtrusive or children will not do it!

Usually, self-monitoring is insufficient in itself to produce lasting behavioral improvements, so the child must also learn other behavior modification skills. In most instances the child will be helped to learn and self-apply the same skills that originally were taught by caretakers and therapists. In theory, any modification technique which can be used by others for treating clients can be used by the clients themselves. However, clients may be understandably reluctant to impose punishment contingencies on themselves, especially if they are children. Finally, the desirable, self-directed behavior changes must be made general and enduring. Here, again, proven behavior therapy methods must come into play (see Section 1 of this chapter).

The following self-instruction training package was originally described by Meichenbaum and Goodman (1971) for use with impulsive children who make many errors in their haste to complete problem-solving tasks. This approach, which has been adapted by others, is called *cognitive self-regulation training*, or self-instruction training, and begins with a trainer's modeling appropriate problem-solving strategies, and then instructing the child in their use. Usually modeling demonstrations and verbal instructions are used in the initial portion of self-regulation training.

1. *Modeling.* The trainer or some other model performs a problem-solving task while describing the strategy aloud to herself and the child-client. If the adult trainer proves ineffective or is inappropriate as a model for the client, another model may be used, such as a classmate or sibling. The model should be respected and liked by the child, and the child should consider himself capable of performing what the model does. Obviously, children don't find lion tamers appropriate models when learning to approach fearsome animals or aerialists as relevant models when learning to overcome a fear of heights. Therapists can employ other children, and especially those who experience some initial hesitation, as *coping models*. Their attempts to perform difficult tasks reassure the client that others share their apprehension, and the models' portrayal of difficulties and their successful solution provide both information and reassurance to the client.

In teaching a child how to employ a new problem-solving strategy, the model demonstrates self-directed instructions on how to approach the task ("I'm going to read the question carefully"), and how to monitor oneself and correct errors in a question-and-answer format ("Where did I read about that? Page 82; let's look it up. I'll write the answer. Is that right? Whoops, I didn't put down everything I needed. I've got to add some"). Finally, self-praise is modeled ("Another one done — I'm doing really well"). The self-talk script focuses on repeating the task instructions, formulating a plan of attack, and dealing with errors patiently and resourcefully.

2. *Instructions and prompting.* The trainer next gives the child instructions on how to perform the task while the child attempts to do so ("Stop and read the problem carefully. What does it say?. . . OK. Now do you know what to do?").

3. *Overt rehearsal.* Here the child performs the task while instructing herself aloud. For example, Snyder and White (1979) taught impulsive, aggressive adolescent girls appropriate self-talk. When their counselors awakened them early in the morning, the girls were instructed to use self-statements such as the following: "Already. Damn. Feels good to stay in bed, but if I get up I'll get the points I need for the movie. OK, just open my eyes; sit up. Good, I made it." Note that the girls were encouraged to use their customary speaking style while retaining the gist of the instructors' self-regulation message.

4. *Covert self-guidance.* To progress from overt to more socially appropriate covert self-talk, the child first whispers, then thinks the instruc-

tions to herself while performing the task. Unless the child is very young or self-talk is acceptable in the relevant setting, it is best to progress to covert self-guidance before encouraging the child to use self-regulation tactics in public. Stares or comments from onlookers could dissuade the child from using self-talk. Perhaps fortunately, improvement sometimes occurs despite clients' failures to use self-talk (Copeland, 1982). This suggests that self-talk may not be a necessary component of self-regulation in some situations.

5. *Reinforcement contingencies.* The type of self-instruction presented thus far relies on strong client motivation to effect behavioral change. Many children lack such motivation, and require extrinsic rewards for compliance and mild punishment for noncompliance with the self-instructional routine. Consider, for example, the following cognitive-behavioral therapy program by Kendall and his associates (Kendall, 1981). The program aims to treat children who exhibit impulsive, nonself-controlled behavior and requires about six weeks of treatment with two 45–50-minute sessions per week. The therapist uses modeling demonstrations to teach the child to use self-instructional procedures when working on a variety of problem-solving tasks, beginning with easy, impersonal problems such as completing incomplete sequences of forms and numbers, and concluding with hypothetical social quandries such as the following: "You are watching television and your little brother changes the channel," or "You say the wrong answer in class and the person behind you starts to laugh." Throughout training, the therapist provides verbal guidance and demonstrates the appropriate manner in which to deal with the problems. When performing each task, the child is taught to follow these procedures: "Find out what I'm supposed to do, look at all the possibilities, focus in on the task, choose my answer," and conclude either "I did a good job," or "I made a mistake; I can remember to be more careful next time." To motivate the children to perform these tasks, they are given praise and token reinforcement for correct responding and fines (response cost) for errors. Following an error, the therapist explains what the child did incorrectly and once more demonstrates what the child should do.

At the end of each treatment session, the child uses his accumulated tokens to buy a prize from a reward menu, which might include trinkets such as pencils, crayons, or he can save some tokens for larger, but delayed prizes such as ball point pens, and small books. In general, it would be wise to use incentives such as these, since much is required of the child, and naturally occurring rewards might be delayed or absent.

## Limitations

Despite a number of reports of successful self-regulation training efforts, little is known regarding which of the many training components are essential to success and which are unnecessary (Cole & Kazdin, 1980; Hobbs,

Moquin, Tyroler, & Lahey, 1980; Urbain & Kendall, 1980). In addition, there have been disturbing failures to replicate established self-regulation training programs (e.g., Combs & Lahey, 1981; Friedling & O'Leary, 1979; Sharp, 1981). And despite expectations that treatment effects would be very long-lasting, relapses are not uncommon (Hall, 1980). Many of the evaluation studies are laboratory analogues that have used nonclinical subject samples and have administered contrived measures with questionable external validity, such as speed and accuracy in recognizing line drawings in a matching-to-sample task.

Worse yet, self-talk has sometimes been found to interfere with performance on complex tasks by distracting the performer (Denney, 1975; Fox & Houston, 1981). Since audible self-instruction is almost never practiced in social and academic settings, children may resist engaging in it or in obvious self-monitoring and record-keeping. Their resistance represents a formidable problem for the trainer because the cooperation of the client is essential in self-regulation (Cole & Kazdin, 1980). As a result of these several limitations, the clinical utility of instructional or cognitive self-regulation training remains to be established (Karoly, 1982).

However, results have been somewhat more promising with operant self-control procedures, which train children in self-evaluation and self-reward. Such programs have been reported to remediate a wide range of problem behaviors (Ollendick & Cerny, 1981), and are particularly useful when they follow external contingency management. That is, after traditional behavior modification programs have substantially improved the child's behavior, instruction in self-monitoring and self-reward may help to maintain and generalize therapeutic gains. Consequently, it might be advisable for student therapists to confine themselves to therapist-administered guidance programs, and to use self-regulation training to enhance the durability and generality of positive behavior changes. Certainly there is ample evidence that children as young as five years can be taught to observe, record, or report, and even reward their own behavior (Gelfand, Jenson, & Drew, 1982; Karoly, 1977). In contrast, self-instruction training may pose formidable challenges to young children.

## Guidelines

Should you decide to attempt self-regulation training, the following suggestions may prove useful.

1. Determine whether the desired goal is developmentally and culturally appropriate for the child. To take an extreme example, it is probably inappropriate to aim to teach a 7-year-old child to sit and solve arithmetic problems for an hour at a time. Although such a goal is theoretically obtainable, the child's performance would be age- and socially inappropriate for anyone

other than a mathematical prodigy. So make sure that you are not exceeding age norms in your expectations for the child (Hartmann, Roper, & Bradford, 1979). Observations of the child's classmates can provide information on normative behavior patterns. Don't try to create a super-performer; usually average performance is sufficient.

2. Enlist the child's, the caretakers', and the child's peers' cooperation in the behavior change endeavor. As Karoly (1981) has stated:

> The boundaries of self-management assessment and training are set by the level of cooperativeness of the child, of significant others, and of the child's natural environment. Always try to ascertain early the degree to which the system is capable of sharing information and responding to feedback. Do not presume that clinical expertise can overcome a system that strongly rewards children's misbehavior. (p. 119)

The child's wholehearted participation is required if self-regulation is to prove successful (Friedling & O'Leary, 1979; Kendall, 1981). Contingency management might be necessary if the child does not find correctness itself sufficiently reinforcing. Meichenbaum (1977) has suggested attempting to increase the child's motivation to use self-regulation by introducing self-talk in a play setting and employing peer models, who may be more acceptable to the child than adult models. Peers can be useful tutors too, and can remind children when to engage in self-regulation (Cantor, 1980).

3. Don't attempt to remedy long-standing, overly difficult problems. For example, it is possible to teach self-control to antisocial, impulsive, or aggressive children, but to do so requires cleverness, persistence, tight contingency management, and close surveillance of the client. This far exceeds the scope of a student behavior analysis project. Some youngsters' defiance and hostility make it difficult to turn contingencies over to them, and doing so prematurely can result in self-reward for nonexistent desirable behaviors (Santogrossi, O'Leary, Romanczyk, & Kaufman, 1973). Consequently, such training efforts are best left to seasoned professionals. Table 7-1 provides suggestions on feasible student replication projects.

4. Try to select naturally occurring methods of self-control. Such methods may have a greater likelihood of success than highly artificial, rationally based ones. And there is some empirical information regarding naturally occurring and useful self-control methods. For example, overweight children who maintain diet-produced weight losses have been found to monitor their own food intake and weight change without directions to do so from others. They also counteract weight gain by increasing their exercise and decreasing their food consumption, and can state their plans for restraining their eating in tempting situations. The successful children praised themselves for weight control, and, in general, relied on themselves rather than on their parents

**Table 7-1.** Some Successful Self-Regulation Training Programs for Replication

| References | Clients and Goals | Program | Results |
|---|---|---|---|
| 1. Humphrey, Karoly, & Kirschenbaum (1978) | 7–9-yr.-olds; increase reading rate and accuracy | Self-reward or response-cost contingencies | Both methods successful, but reward slightly better. Both also decreased disruptive behavior |
| 2. Brownell, Colletti, Ersner-Herschfield, Herschfield, & Wilson (1977) | 8–9-yr.-olds, improve math problem-solving accuracy and persistence | Contingency (no. of points for each correct solution) either self- or externally imposed | Self-imposed enhanced time at task; both increased accuracy, especially stringent standards used |
| 3. Edgar & Clement (1980) | 8–9 yr.-old under-achievers | Self- or teacher controlled reinforcement | Self- more effective than teacher-control, and produced higher achievement test scores |
| 4. Fantuzzo & Clement (1981) | 8–9-yr.-old boys deficient in math and in sustained attention with behavior problems in school | Boys observed a peer self-reinforce for appropriate behavior and were given an opportunity to reinforce themselves | Produced improved academic and social behavior in observers and in peer models |
| 5. Ballard & Glynn (1975) | 8–11-yr.-olds; increase number of sentences, descriptive and action words, and rated story quality | Post rules and ideas to write about, self-awarded points toward activities time for each action and description word | All targeted behaviors increased, as did non-targeted on-task behavior |

*Note:* Replications should be confined to clients as similar as possible to those in the original study (e.g., same age, sex, grade, SES). Replication failures frequently stem from attempting treatments which are inappropriate for or unacceptable to another group of children.

to control their weight. Other children who had participated in the same successful weight loss program, but who became obese once more, exerted fewer self-control measures (Cohen, Gelfand, Dodd, Jensen, & Turner, 1980). Similar findings have been reported for adults. Untrained, but successful college students who wished to lose weight or quit smoking used more self-reinforcement procedures, and used a greater number of different self-control techniques for a longer period than did those who were less successful in self-management (Perri & Richards, 1977). Other than the previous two reports, little is known about naturally occurring, successful self-regulation practices. However, therapists might be wise to avoid artificial self-management tactics that rarely are used by people in their self-generated control efforts.

5. Identify the child's existing productive and counterproductive strategies and self-statements. If the child already has a useful task strategy, teaching him another one is unnecessary and may even cause performance deterioration (Carter, Patterson, & Quasebarth, 1979). Perhaps the child knows the task strategy, but fails to employ it when needed. In this case the child must be instructed to recognize the cues signaling the need for action. A review by Kendall and Williams (1982) offers some useful suggestions for assessing children's self-management deficits and skills.

6. Assess whether the child's existing skills are sufficient to solve the problem. It may be necessary to teach the child the relevant verbal assertion or academic skills if they are not in the child's repertoire. The skills under consideration here are not self-regulation skills, but nevertheless are necessary to the success of a self-regulation effort. If a child doesn't know how to add three-digit numbers, self-talk cannot save him. On the other hand, knowing how to add three-digit numbers, but acting impulsively and carelessly, calls for a different training strategy.

7. Train the child in self-observation. Check the child's data against yours or those of some other observer. Discuss differences in the various observers' data, and reward the child for accuracy. Without training in accuracy, children tend to assume that their behavior is nearly perfect, and merits copious rewards. Reserve the rewards for accurate observation records, and continue to check the accuracy of the child's self-reports at least occasionally and as surreptitiously as possible so the child cannot detect when he is being checked.

8. Reinforce the child for engaging in the desired behavior (review Chapter 5 for instructions in reinforcement contingency management). Gradually transfer contingency management to the child, checking periodically to ensure that the self-regulation program is succeeding.

9. Assess whether the child is using self-regulation tactics in all of the settings where they would be useful. For specific techniques to use see the discussion of generalization in Section 1 of this chapter.

Finally, remember that self-regulation skills are not easily learned. As Friedling and S. O'Leary (1979) have commented, "Teaching children why and when to use self-instruction, and ensuring that they do, may be as important as teaching them how to self-instruct." Ultimately, nearly every child is expected to exert some measure of self-regulation in daily life. A self-regulation training program aims to teach in a systematic way the self-management tactics used informally, but effectively, by older children and adults. And research on self-regulation promises to add to the repertoire of existing techniques for solving problems and resisting temptation.

## Probe Questions for Chapter 7, Section 2

1. How do self-regulation and self-instructional training differ, and how are they similar?

2. For which types of problems is self-regulation training appropriate and effective?

3. How do overt rehearsal and covert self-guidance differ? Why are both used together?

4. Describe the major limitations of self-regulation training.

5. Why is it so difficult to teach children self-regulation tactics?

# Chapter 8
# RELIABILITY

## Behavioral Objectives for Chapter 8, Section 1

*After studying Section 1 of this chapter, you should be able to state why:*

1. *It is important to obtain reliable data.*

2. *It is necessary to determine the reliability of your data during each phase of your study.*

3. *Your child-client should be informed of the reasons for the presence of an observer.*

4. *The data sheets from co-observers should be compared immediately after each reliability check.*

   *Finally, you should be able to:*

5. *State the three questions that require answering before you determine the reliability of your data.*


## SECTION 1: INTRODUCTION AND PRELIMINARIES

### Introduction

The technical meaning of reliability is not unlike the colloquial meaning. If friends or acquaintances are unreliable, they are inconsistent, hence little confidence can be placed in them. So it is with data. Behavioral data are reliable to the degree that independent measurements provide consistent data, or data that are in agreement. The sources of these data determine the type of reliability to be calculated. Data collected by two or more independent observers making simultaneous observations of samples of behavior allows us to determine *interobserver agreement* or reliability.[1] Data obtained from different time periods assess *temporal stability or reliability*, whereas data obtained from different settings index *cross-situational consistency* or reliability (e.g., Anastasi, 1976). The present chapter focuses on the reliability of observers; the following chapter addresses an equally important issue in applied behavioral studies — that of temporal stability.

Attainment of a high degree of observer reliability is a crucial requirement for your study. If your data are highly reliable, you will be able to detect small as well as large changes produced in the target behavior. The absence of change then can be attributed to inadequate treatment procedures and not to faulty measurement techniques. On the other hand, if your data have poor reliability, you may be unable to detect or demonstrate change no matter how dramatic the change actually might be.

In this chapter we will describe the steps you should follow in conducting interobserver reliability assessments. We will also introduce the distinction between the reliability of a session score and the reliability of smaller unit scores, such as trial scores within sessions. We will discuss the concept of observer bias and drift, and then describe for you the data gathering requirements and calculation formulas for quantifying these concepts.

## Collecting Data

Before you begin to collect formal baseline data (see Chapter 9), check the reliability of your observations. Recruit a second observer (or your partner) and repeat the reliability assessment procedures described in Chapter 2 substituting your new response definitions and observation tactics. *You will also want to include a reliability check at each successive phase of your project* to insure that you are not altering definitions or in some other way deteriorating as a data gathering instrument, a danger discussed at some length in Section 3 of this chapter.

Before you begin data collection, see that both you and your reliability checker are completely familiar with the behavior definitions, the data sheet, and the use of any timing devices you might need. A brief "dress rehearsal" quickly exposes improper preparation.

---

[1]A related term, observer accuracy, refers to comparisons between an observer and an established criterion. Various investigations have argued that applied researchers should focus on observer accuracy rather than on observer reliability (e.g., Cone, 1981, 1982; Johnston & Pennypacker, 1980). Accuracy may be assessed when a relatively permanent product measure of the target behavior, such as number of diapers soiled, is available (e.g., Boykin & Nelson, 1981; Nay, 1979). However, established criteria are not available for many of the behaviors included in observational systems. As a result, the adequacy of measurements of these behaviors must be determined by means of interobserver reliability assessments (Hartmann, 1982a).

If the observations are to be carried out in some quasi-private place, such as in a home or unused classroom, be certain that your fellow observer and the child have been introduced to one another. Needless to say, the unexpected appearance of even familiar persons can be disruptive, so provide your child-client with some understanding of the reason for the observer's presence. Even better, also have the reliability checker present during your initial observations, so that the target child can adjust or habituate to the presence of a second observer (Wells, McMahon, Forehand, & Griest, 1980).

While collecting data, position yourself and the reliability checker in such a way that you both will have an unimpeded view of the child. However, be certain that you are not so close together that you cannot collect the data independently. Interobserver reliability estimates are meaningless if one observer copies or is in some way influenced by the other observer's recordings. Ideally, you should not even be able to tell whether the other observer is writing anything down at any given time. When using wrist counters, the observers should not be able to hear the click of one another's counters.

Check one another's data sheets *immediately after* the observation period, while behavior incidents are still fresh in your mind. If disagreements occur, as they probably will, develop rules to resolve questionable incidents. For example, assume that tantrumming was the target behavior and duration data were being collected. One of the observers might click off his stopwatch when the child stopped kicking his mother's shins; the other observer might not click off his stopwatch until the child stopped both kicking and throwing tableware at his mother. A decision should then be made as to which criterion will be used.

More frequently, disagreements arise when a general class of behavior is being observed, such as appropriate classroom behavior, and the observers do not have an exhaustive list of what constitutes the general class. (Be sure you have a list if your target behavior is a response class.) When a behavior not previously considered occurs, the observers might then disagree concerning its classification. If this happens, the observers should decide how the behavior will be classified when it again occurs, and should add the new behavior to the appropriate list so that future occurrences will be reliably categorized.

## Preliminary Considerations

Assume that you and your reliability checker have obtained data in a format similar to that given in Table 8-1. Depending upon which of the four types of data acquisition systems you employed (see Chapter 3), the number of recording or observation intervals will vary from a minimum of eight (if you used event or duration recording) to some number much larger than that (if you used the interval method or momentary time sampling). The numerical values you obtain for these recording intervals will also vary depending upon which data acquisition method you used. For event or duration data, each recording interval will be scored either zero or some positive number, indicating the frequency or duration of the behavior. For interval or momentary time sampling data, each recording interval will be scored either zero (the behavior did not occur in that interval) or one (the behavior did occur in that interval).

**Table 8-1.** Example of a Two (Number of Observers) by k Number of Intervals) Table for Interobserver Trial Reliability Data

| | Recording Interval Number | | | | | | | | |
| | 1 | 2 | 3 | 4 | 5 | 6 | 7 | | k |
|---|---|---|---|---|---|---|---|---|---|
| Observer 1 | 0 | 1 | 1 | 1 | 0 | 0 | 0 | | 1 |
| Observer 2 | 0 | 1 | 1 | 0 | 1 | 0 | 1 | | 1 |

In order to assess the reliability of your data, you first make three basic decisions (Johnson & Bolstad, 1973, pp. 10–17).

1. The first decision requires specification of the *score unit* on which reliability will be assessed. If your target behavior is a single response, such as the number of dishes broken or the amount of time spent watching TV, the score units checked for reliability are simply the numbers noted in the recording intervals on your data sheets.

The problem is more complicated, however, if the target behavior is really a response class or category that includes a number of component behaviors. Consider the target response "physical aggression toward peers," which includes four component responses — hitting, kicking, scratching, and shoving. If data had been collected on each of these four separate behaviors, reliability could be calculated on either the sum of hits, kicks, scratches, and shoves (the total physical aggression scores) in each recording interval, or on each of the four separate component scores in each recording interval. Which of the two reliabilities (total score or component scores) should be calculated depends on the score unit that will be used in graphing and data analysis. If total physical aggression is the primary dependent variable, then these total scores should provide the basis of the reliability assessment. If, instead, each of the four "aggression" responses will be analyzed separately (for example, in a between-behavior multiple baseline design), then each of the four scores should be examined separately for reliability.

2. The second decision requires specification of the *time span* over which scores will be summed for purposes of reliability assessment. Reliability could be calculated on the scores in each of the eight or more recording intervals (see Table 8-1) for sessions in which two observers collected data. This is

referred to as *trial* reliability (Hartmann, 1977). Trial reliability primarily indicates the adequacy of behavior definitions and the thoroughness of observer training in the use of both these definitions and the observational equipment (such as coding sheets, recorders, and timers). Without a reasonable degree of interobserver reliability at the trial level, a study is uninterpretable because of the ambiguous meaning of the basic data.

Reliability also could be calculated on the total session scores for each of the two observers. Referring again to Table 8-1, an observer's total session score is obtained by adding together the scores for the recording intervals within a session. A reliability analysis performed on these session totals is referred to as *session reliability*. Session reliability indicates how much confidence you can have in a session score. Put another way, it indicates the smallest difference between session scores that is not due to observer error.

Which of the two reliabilities (trial or session) is more appropriate for your study again depends on the scores used in graphing and data analysis. While session totals (or averages) are typically analyzed in applied behavioral studies, most behavior therapists determine only trial reliability. Because of its frequent use, trial reliability will receive the majority of our attention. An additional reason for our focus on trial reliability is that in most cases it provides a lower bound or minimum estimate of session reliability (Hartmann, 1976). Therefore, you can assume with reasonable assurance that if your trial reliability is acceptable, your session reliability will be as good or better.

3. The third and final decision concerns the *statistical method* used to summarize trial reliability data, a topic to which we will next direct our attention.

## Probe Questions for Chapter 8, Section 1

1. *Why is it important to obtain reliable data?*

2. *State how reliability might be improved by attention to simple human engineering factors.*

3. *How can the requirement of independence of data be violated in subtle ways during reliability assessments?*

4. *Why might the positioning of observers during reliability assessments affect the reliability of their ratings?*

5. *Distinguish between trial and session reliability. What scores are used in the determination of these two kinds of reliability?*

# Behavioral Objectives for Chapter 8, Section 2
*After studying Section 2 of this chapter, you should be able to:*

1. *Summarize the data from a single session in a form that facilitates reliability computations.*

2. *Calculate the reliability of trial scores within a single session.*

3. *Overcome problems that contribute to poor reliability.*

4. *Determine whether your data are sufficiently reliable to begin your study.*

## SECTION 2. TRIAL RELIABILITY

### Calculating Trial Reliability

There are two general approaches in determining trial reliability: percentage agreement indexes and reliability coefficients or correlations. We will discuss both percentage and correlational indexes of reliability and will tell you how to calculate them for data collected by the various methods described in Chapter 3. You should consult those sections that pertain particularly to the data collection method you are using.

### Interval Recording and Momentary Time Sampling

If you have used the interval method or momentary time sampling, and hence have occurrence-nonoccurrence data, summarize your data by collapsing the two-by-*k* table (see Table 8-1 in Section 1 of this chapter) into a two-by-two table like the one shown in Table 8-2. This table will be used to summarize your observations — to indicate the number and kind of agreements and disagreements included in your observations.

To collapse your data, follow these steps.

1. Count the number of observation intervals for which both observers agreed that the target behavior occurred. Enter this number in cell *B*.

2. Count the number of observation intervals for which both observers agreed that the target behavior did *not* occur. Enter this number in cell *C*.

3. Count the number of observation intervals for which Observer 1 indicated that the target behavior occurred while Observer 2 indicated that the target behavior did *not* occur. Enter this number in cell *A*.

4. Finally, count the number of observation intervals for which Observer 1 indicated that the target behavior did *not* occur while Observer 2 indicated that the target behavior did occur. Enter this number in cell *D*.

Consider the data given in Table 8-1. The two-by-two summary table for these data is given in Table 8-2.

**Table 8-2.** A Two-by-Two Summary Table of the Data Contained in Table 8-1

Observer 2

|  | 0 | 1 |  |
|---|---|---|---|
|  | A | B |  |
| 1 | *1* (.13) | *3* (.37) | =*4* (.5) |
|  | C | D |  |
| 0 | *2* (.25) | *2* (.25) | =*4* (.5) |
|  | *3* (.38) | *5* (.62) | N=*8* |

Observer 1 (left margin, rows 1 and 0)

*Note:* Figures are given in italic; proportions are given in parentheses.

Be sure to check your entries in the summary table as follows: (a) Count the total frequencies included in the table; this number should be equal to the total number of intervals used on your data sheet. In the example above, these values should both be 8. (b) Compare the total number of "1"s and "0"s for each observer in the two-by-two table (see values given on the bottom and right margins) with the totals in the two-by-$k$ table given on your data sheets. For example, the total frequency of "1"s marked by Observer 1 in the two-by-two table is obtained by summarizing the frequencies in the first row of the two-by-two table; that is $A + B = 4$. Next, calculate one of the alternative measures of observer reliability. We will only describe two of the most popular and most frequently recommended methods; however, there are well over 20 different reliability statistics that could be used (e.g., Fleiss, 1975; House, House, & Campbell, 1981).

*Percentage agreement.* Percentage agreement is determined by multiplying the proportion of observed agreements ($p_o$) by 100. The proportion of observed agreements is obtained by adding the numbers in the agreement cells (cells *B* and *C*) and then dividing that value by the sum of the number of agreements plus the number of disagreements $(A + B + C + D)$. For example, for the two-by-two data given in Table 8-2, percentage agreement is 62.5% — i.e., $[(3 + 2)/(1 + 3 + 2 + 2)] = p_o$ and $p_o \times 100 = 62.5\%$. Thus, the observers agreed on 62.5% of the intervals scored.

Percentage agreement is the measure of reliability most commonly used in current behavior modification work (Kelly, 1977). It is simply calculated and readily understood. However, percentage agreement has certain undesirable characteristics (Hartmann, 1977), the most serious of which is overestimating the quality of the observers' performance, and hence the reliability of their data. The quality of observers' performance can be overestimated by failing to consider that some of their agreement (entries in cells *B* and *C* in Table 8-2) could have occurred by chance. Consider what would happen if each of two observers scored 100 intervals by tossing a coin. An interval would be scored an occurrence if the coin came up heads, and a nonoccurrence if the coin came up tails. If the coin was fair, on the average, each of the two observers would score one-half of the 100 intervals as occurrences, and the other one-half as nonoccurrences. Furthermore, their scoring would coincide on one-half of both the occurrences and nonoccurrences. Because the observers agreed in their scoring of 50% of the 100 intervals, we might be tempted to interpret their performance as being moderately good, whereas in fact their agreements were entirely due to chance.

A variety of statistical methods have been proposed to overcome the overestimation problem of percentage agreement. Perhaps the most adequate solution has been achieved by Cohen's kappa (Cohen, 1960; Fleiss, 1971).[2]

*Kappa.* The reliability statistic kappa deals with the problem of chance agreements by only including those agreements that are not likely due to chance. It does this by taking the formula for proportion agreement (for reasons that will become apparent in a moment, we will write it as $p_o/1.0$) and subtracting the proportion of agreements that could be expected by chance $(p_c)$ from both numerator and denominator. Thus, kappa $(k) = (p_o - p_c)/(1 - p_c)$.

---

[2]Two other popular reliability statistics that have been suggested for handling the problem of chance or expected agreements are *occurrence agreement* and *nonoccurrence agreement*. These variants of percentage agreement omit the entries in either cell *B* or cell *C* (see Table 8-2) in their calculation. Occurrence agreement employs only the intervals which one or both observers scored as occurrences (cells *A*, *B*, and *D*). Occurrence agreement is defined as $[B/(A + B + D)] \times 100$. It sometimes is used to evaluate interobserver agreement when the target behavior in an acceleration program has a very low initial rate of occurrence. Nonoccurrence agreement employs only those intervals which one or both observers scored as nonoccurrences (cells *A*, *C*, and *D*). Nonoccurrence agreement is defined as $[C/(A + C + D)] \times 100$. It sometimes is used when the target behavior has a very high rate of occurrence; e.g., during the beginning phase of a deceleration program.

The calculation of kappa is illustrated with the data given in Table 8-2. Based on the values given in parenthesis in this table, $p_o = .625$. Chance agreement must be found for both cell $B$ (occurrences) and cell $C$ (nonoccurrences), and summed to find $p_c$.

The proportion of chance agreements for cell $B$ is found by multiplying the column and row proportions — sometimes called marginal proportions or base rates — that intersect at cell $B$ (.5 for the top row and .62 for the right-hand column); this product is .31. The proportion of chance agreements for cell $C$, the other agreement cell, is similarly found by multiplying the row and column proportions that intersect at cell $C$ (.5 for the bottom row and .38 for the left-hand column); this product is .19. The sum of the expected agreements for cells $B$ and $C$ is .50; $p_c = (.31 + .19)$. This value is the chance or expected agreement value for a two-by-two table with marginal proportions of .5, .5, .38, and .62. Now that we have calculated both $p_o$ and $p_c$, we need merely to combine them to determine the value of kappa: $x = (.625 - .50)/(1 - .50) = .25$.

Kappa is interpreted as the chance-corrected proportion of agreements; it ordinarily varies from 1.0 (obtainable only if no disagreements are present) to .0 (when the proportion of obtained agreements equals the proportion of chance or expected agreements). If you should happen to obtain a negatively valued kappa, your observers have agreed less often than expected by chance!

For additional information on percentage agreement and kappa, as well as on other related reliability statistics, read the lively controversies published in two issues of the *Journal of Applied Behavior Analysis* (1977, *10*(1), pp. 97–150; and 1979, *12*(4), pp. 523–571).

A sample work sheet for determining the interobserver reliability of trial data is presented in Table 8-3. After you have completed the calculations, enter the occurrence totals for Observer 1 and Observer 2 and the reliability measure on the appropriate lines of the Summary Table, Table 8-4.

Examining Table 8-4 from left to right, the first four columns ask for simple information to identify the sessions. The next column entitled "duration of session or number of recording intervals" is included because occasionally you will have to deviate from your standard session length. When sessions vary in length, the scores must be adjusted in order to make all session scores comparable.

The adjustment is based on the ratio of the length of the atypical session to the length of a standard session. For example, assume that a standard observation session is 15 minutes long and contains 180 5-sec. intervals. If a session is shortened to 10 minutes, with 120 5-sec. intervals, the total for that session would have to be adjusted or prorated to make it comparable to other session totals. This adjusted total can be expressed as a percentage of the total intervals employed, in which case all totals should be expressed

**Table 8-3.** Sample Work Sheet for Trial Reliability Calculations
Using the Interval Recording Method

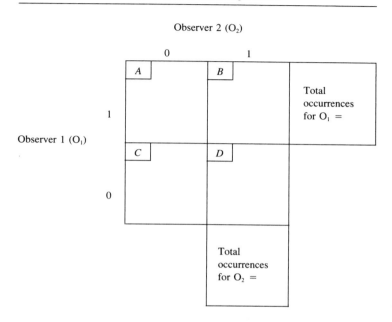

Observer 2 ($O_2$)

Formula for percentage agreement:

$$[(B+C) / (A+B+C+D)] \times 100 =$$

Formula for kappa:

$(p_o - p_c) / (1.0 - p_c)$
where
$p_o = (B+C) / N$ and
$p_c = [(A+B)(B+D) + (C+D)(A+C)] / N^2$

as percentages. Or the session total could be prorated. Proration of the 120 interval session total is accomplished by multiplying the obtained total by 180/120 or 1.5 (see Chapter 10 for further discussion of this problem).

Whenever an adjustment technique is used, the adjusted total should be entered in the "adjusted total" column. The "comments" section at the bottom should be used to note information that will be used to qualify certain of the scores in your final report. For example, if a session has to be terminated immediately after its inception, the reason should be entered in the comments section and this fact noted on the final summary graph.

**Table 8-4.** Data Summary Sheet

| Date | Time | Condition | Observer | Duration of Session or Number of Recording Intervals | Raw Total | Adjusted Total | Reliability |
|------|------|-----------|----------|------------------------------------------------------|-----------|----------------|-------------|
| ___ | ___ | ___ | ___ | ___ | ___ | ___ | ___ |
| ___ | ___ | ___ | ___ | ___ | ___ | ___ | ___ |
| ___ | ___ | ___ | ___ | ___ | ___ | ___ | ___ |
| ___ | ___ | ___ | ___ | ___ | ___ | ___ | ___ |
| ___ | ___ | ___ | ___ | ___ | ___ | ___ | ___ |
| ___ | ___ | ___ | ___ | ___ | ___ | ___ | ___ |
| ___ | ___ | ___ | ___ | ___ | ___ | ___ | ___ |
| ___ | ___ | ___ | ___ | ___ | ___ | ___ | ___ |
| ___ | ___ | ___ | ___ | ___ | ___ | ___ | ___ |
| ___ | ___ | ___ | ___ | ___ | ___ | ___ | ___ |
| ___ | ___ | ___ | ___ | ___ | ___ | ___ | ___ |
| ___ | ___ | ___ | ___ | ___ | ___ | ___ | ___ |
| ___ | ___ | ___ | ___ | ___ | ___ | ___ | ___ |
| ___ | ___ | ___ | ___ | ___ | ___ | ___ | ___ |
| ___ | ___ | ___ | ___ | ___ | ___ | ___ | ___ |
| ___ | ___ | ___ | ___ | ___ | ___ | ___ | ___ |
| ___ | ___ | ___ | ___ | ___ | ___ | ___ | ___ |
| ___ | ___ | ___ | ___ | ___ | ___ | ___ | ___ |
| ___ | ___ | ___ | ___ | ___ | ___ | ___ | ___ |

Comments:

**Note:** For each session in which two observers collected data, bracket the two row entries in this table.

## Event or Duration Recording

If you have used either event or duration recording in your observations, you should have between 8 and 12 pairs of scores for purposes of reliability assessment. That is, the total observation period has been divided into 8 to 12 discrete observation intervals, and each interval contains a score of zero or greater for each observer. If you have not divided your total observation interval into 8 to 12 smaller intervals as we suggested in the previous chapter, you may be limited to calculating a simple ratio measure of reliability.[3] If you slipped up this time, remedy the situation at the next opportunity, as most of the 20 or more methods of calculating trial reliability on continuous scores require multiple scores from each observer (see Berk, 1979). Two of these many methods seem particularly useful, the intraclass correlation and the product-moment correlation. As the former method requires familiarity with analysis of variance procedures, our discussion will be limited to the product-moment correlation coefficient approach to reliability.

*The product-moment correlation.* The formula for the product-moment correlation is given below.

$$r_{O_1 O_2} = \frac{N\Sigma O_1 O_2 - \Sigma O_1 O_2}{\sqrt{N\Sigma O_1^2 - (\Sigma O_1)^2} \sqrt{N\Sigma O_2^2 - (\Sigma O_2)^2}}$$

While this formula looks quite forbidding, it is really quite easy to calculate a correlation coefficient, especially if your hand calculator has a correlation key. An example of the calculations required for the data given in Table 8-5 using this formula is shown in Table 8-6.

**Table 8-5.** Sample Duration or Frequency Data Obtained by Two Observers

| | Observation Interval Number | | | | | | | |
|---|---|---|---|---|---|---|---|---|
| | 1 | 2 | 3 | 4 | 5 | 6 | 7 | 8 |
| Observer 1 | 5 | 0 | 17 | 0 | 0 | 8 | 7 | 1 |
| Observer 2 | 4 | 1 | 17 | 0 | 0 | 6 | 9 | 0 |

[3]This simple, and limited, measure of reliability is obtained by taking the ratio of the lower total to the higher total and multiplying by 100. If the total for $O_1$ = 90 and for $O_2$ = 80, the ratio is (70/90) × 100 = 78%. This percent reflects the fact that the totals obtained by the two observers differ from one another by 22%. See Hartmann (1977) and Kazdin (1982b) for discussions of this statistic.

After you have completed similar calculations for your own data, triumphantly enter the value of $r_{o_1 o_2}$, as well as the session totals in the Data Summary Table, Table 8-4.

The value of $r_{o_1 o_2}$ ordinarily will range from zero to 1.0. The value of zero indicates that the observers are so inconsistent that knowing all of one of the observer's scores gives us no more information about the other observer's scores than knowing only the first observer's average score. The value of 1.0, on the other hand, tells us that one of the observer's scores can be perfectly predicted from knowing the other observer's scores.[4] If $r_{o_1 o_2}$ was less than zero, it would mean that when one observer reported high scores, the other observer was more likely than not to report low scores, and vice versa. Thus, if you obtain a $r_{o_1 o_2}$ that is less than 0, but equal or greater than $-1.0$, your observers should be embarrassed. If you obtain a $r_{o_1 o_2}$ that is even more negative than $-1.0$, it is your statistician who should be embarrassed, as $r_{o_1 o_2}$ cannot take on values below $-1.0$.

**Table 8-6.** Illustration of the Calculation of $r_{o_1 o_2}$
Using the Data From Table 8-5

---

$N$ (number of recording intervals) $= 8$

$\Sigma O_1$ (total for observer 1) $= 5 + 0 + \ldots + 7 + 1 = 38$

$\Sigma O_2$ (total for observer 2) $= 4 + 1 + \ldots + 9 + 0 = 37$

$\Sigma O_1^2 = 5^2 + 0^2 + \ldots + 7^2 + 1^2 = 428$

$\Sigma O_2^2 = 4^2 + 1^2 + \ldots + 9^2 + 0^2 = 423$

$(\Sigma O_1)^2 = 38^2 = 1,444$

$(\Sigma O\ )^2 = 37^2 = 1,369$

$\Sigma O_1 O_2 = (5 \times 4) + (0 \times 1) + \ldots + (7 \times 9) + (1 \times 0) = 420$

$r_{o_1 o_2} = (N \Sigma O_1 O_2 - \Sigma O_1 \Sigma O_2) / \sqrt{N \Sigma O_1^2 - (\Sigma O_1)^2} \sqrt{N \Sigma O_2^2 (\Sigma O_2)^2}$

$\quad = (8 \times 420 - 38 \times 37) / \sqrt{8 \times 428 - 1,444} \sqrt{8 \times 423 - 1,369}$

$\quad = 1954 / \sqrt{1980} \sqrt{2015}$

$\quad = .98$

---

[4]A perfect correlation between the two observer's scores (i.e., $r_{o_1 o_2} = 1.0$) does not necessarily mean that they obtained exactly the same scores for each interval. However, if the two sets of scores are not exactly the same, they only differ by some constant, call it $c$. For example, if $O_1$'s scores were 5, 27, 42, and 18, $O_2$'s scores would be $5 + c$, $27 + c$, $42 + c$ and $18 + c$.

## *Interpreting and Evaluating Measures of Trial Interobserver Reliability*

It should be noted that the measure of reliability you have calculated is based on the scores obtained by dividing the data for a single session into a series of discrete intervals or trials. Thus, the measure of reliability indexes the consistency of the observers' ratings of the target behavior for these trials or intervals within a session.[5] You will have occasion to repeat this procedure on other single sessions at least once each week or two during your project to help insure adequate performance by your observers throughout the treatment program.

There is no generally acceptable level of reliability. As a general principle, the reliability necessary for your study is dependent upon the degree of change in the target behavior you want to be able to demonstrate. To detect small changes produced by your treatment manipulation, reliability must be high. Large changes, on the other hand, can be detected with even relatively unreliable measures. Those guidelines that have been suggested for acceptable levels of reliability range from .70 to .90 for percentage agreement, and from .60 to .75 for kappa and correlational reliability statistics (see Hartmann, 1982a, for a selective review of this literature).

If the values you obtain fall below the recommended minimum, your first step is to do some trouble-shooting. Are your calculations correct? Are your definitions clear? (Perhaps you need to add more examples of positive and negative instances of the target behavior.) Are all of your observers adequately trained? (Perhaps one observer consistently disagrees with whomever that observer is paired. If so, the observer should be retrained or assigned other responsibilities.) Were your timers synchronized? Was the child blocked from one of the observers' view for part of the time?

Review the observation procedures recommended in Chapter 2. Whatever the problem is, try to remedy it, and collect another set of practice reliability data. If you still have problems with the second set of data, check with your instructor before you begin to collect formal baseline data. Your instructor

---

[5]At the close of your project, after you have finished your last trial reliability check and you have completed the Data Summary Table (Table 8-4), you can, if you wish, determine session reliability. Session reliability coefficients indicate the consistency of observers' ratings for session scores, and thus indicate the degree of confidence one can place in session scores. Session reliability is particularly appropriate when analyses are conducted on session scores, as is the case in most applied behavioral studies. To calculate session reliability, you use session totals — e.g., total performance frequency, duration, or occurrences for each session that was observed by two or more observers. These are the total scores you included in the "adjusted totals" column of the Data Summary Table. You should have 8 to 12 of these sessions during which two observers collected data. These data can be used to assess the product-moment correlation reliability — in this case, session reliability — as described above.

may suggest that you use more than one observer to gather data, and then analyze the average of the observers' scores, which is more stable than the data from one observer alone (see Hartmann, 1982a, p. 61).

## Probe Questions for Chapter 8, Section 2

1. *How will your choice of method of collecting data determine the number of data points with which you have to work?*

2. *What kinds of agreements and disagreements do the four cells in a two-by-two table include?*

3. *What methods are available for determining the reliability of occurrence-nonoccurrence data? For determining the reliability of continuous (event or duration) data?*

4. *Describe the advantages and limitations of percentage agreement and kappa as measures of reliability for interval or momentary time-sampling data.*

5. *Why is it necessary to adjust data resulting from sessions of atypical length?*

6. *What action should be taken if your reliability estimates fall below acceptable standards?*

## Behavioral Objectives for Chapter 8, Section 3

*After studying Section 3 of this chapter, you should be able to:*

1. *State the primary problems with the use of human observers.*

2. *Assess and evaluate observer drift.*

3. *Detect consensual observer drift.*

## SECTION 3. OBSERVER EFFECTS

### *Overview of Observer Effects*

The reliability assessments discussed in Sections 1 and 2 of this chapter were intended to help you to maintain the quality of your data. Poor or decreasing reliability alerts you to problems with your data-collection method that should be remedied. These problems may include faulty behavioral definitions, inadequate attention to observational equipment, and undesirable observer effects. These latter observer problems can be serious and may not always be detected by ordinary reliability assessments. Hence they deserve additional consideration.

Observer effects refer to changes in the data produced by the observers rather than by the treatment manipulation or independent variable. A number of authors (Johnson & Bolstad, 1973; Kent & Foster, 1977; Wasik & Loven, 1980; Weick, 1968; Wildman & Erickson, 1977) have catalogued and discussed the potential dangers of a substantial number of these observer effects. The most widely recognized of them are discussed below.

### *Reactive Effects on the Child Being Observed*

The mere presence of an observer can produce changes in the child's behavior (Baum, Forehand, & Zegiob, 1979; Kazdin, 1982a). These changes most likely increase positive behaviors in older children and adults, and occur when observers are conspicuous (e.g., Haynes, 1978). Fortunately, these disruptive effects are most likely to occur during initial periods of observation and tend to dissipate with time as the child habituates to the observer's presence (Haynes & Horn, 1982; Medley & Mitzel, 1963); however, habituation is not uniformly observed (Mercatoris & Craighead, 1974). If these effects are present in your study (see Chapter 2 regarding how they might be limited), they would most likely affect the early baseline data. Therefore, you should compare your early and late baseline data to see if such effects are present. If the early and late baseline rates differ considerably, the observer's presence may have affected the child's behavior more at the inception of the study. Therefore, the later data points may be more representative of the child's baseline behavior rate than are those obtained earlier during this phase.

## Observer Bias

Observer bias is a term that refers to a variety of factors that produce systematic observer inaccuracies. These inaccuracies may be produced by observers' expectancies, prejudices, or information processing limitations (e.g., Hartmann & Wood, 1982). *Expectancy effects* refer to the unintentional selective misperception or miscoding of the target behavior because of the observer's hunches, guesses, or expectations about how the child should behave (e.g., Nay, 1979). *Prejudices* refer to more overt expectations resulting from knowledge of experimental hypotheses, subject characteristics, and the like. *Information processing* limitations refer to cognitively based distortions, such as imposing order on otherwise unruly data. Also included are consistent errors produced by other misapplications of the behavioral definitions, the coding system, the data sheets, or any other aspect of the data collection method.

Clearly the best strategy is to avoid or minimize these biases, for example, by having well-trained observers use codes that require few inferences (e.g., Redfield & Paul, 1976). If surefire prevention of errors is not possible, some detective work is required to identify the extent of their presence. For example, while not all instances of observer bias can be ferreted out of your data, consistent *differences* in the degree of bias displayed by your two observers often can be detected. To do so, compare the two observers' totals for the target behavior after *each* reliability assessment. If your totals disagree, work at trying to find out why. If you can't find the problem and you continue to disagree systematically on the totals (e.g., one observer regularly rates 10-15% more occurrences of the target behavior), it will be necessary to assign one observer the status of primary data gatherer; that observer will take data during each session while the remaining observer would be used only for reliability assessments.

Also check at the conclusion of your study to see whether the session totals for the two observers in Table 8-4 are approximately the same across all of the jointly observed sessions. If they differ by no more than a few points, no action need be taken. For larger discrepancies, the action required depends upon which of the following circumstances was in effect in your study.

1. If one observer has rated all sessions, that observer's data should be used in the primary data analysis.

2. If two observers are used and neither one rates all of the sessions, check with your instructor. Changes in the child's behavior across conditions may be confounded with differences between observers across conditions.

3. If two observers rated all sessions, analyze the average of the two observers' data. Using two observers and pooling their ratings not only produces more reliable data but also avoids another observer effect, which we consider next.

## Reactivity of the Observer to a Second Observer's Presence

Recent studies have shown that the occasional presence of a reliability checker can have reactive effects on the performance of the primary observer (see review by Kazdin, 1977a). That is, the quality of an observer's data improves, sometimes dramatically, with the presence of another person serving as a reliability checker, and deteriorates in that person's absence (e.g., O'Leary & Kent, 1973; Reid, 1970). While there are other experiments that question the generality of this phenomenon (e.g., Whelan, 1974), some precautions seem in order. It may be worthwhile to use two observers throughout the project, if you are able conveniently to do so. If not, it may be as useful if your observers believe that all of their data are being monitored by a second observer, even if they are not. Alternately, reliability should be unobtrusive, so that the observer cannot distinguish reliability check conditions from normal data gathering.

## Observer Drift

Observer drift refers to gradual changes in the definitions observers use for scoring responses. Like the other undesirable observer effects, observer drift is better avoided or limited, for example, by retraining observers, by assessing reliability frequently, and by changing the individuals who are paired for various data-gathering chores such as reliability assessments (e.g., Haynes, 1978). These preventive actions are not always possible, particularly the last one, in student projects such as yours. As a result, there is some danger from a form of observer drift (referred to as consensual observer drift) in which two or more observers gradually develop similar variations in scoring criteria (Johnson & Bolstad, 1973). Gradual changes in both observers' criteria are particularly likely with a response such as "speech intelligibility." As the observers become more acquainted with the child's speech, the rated intelligibility increases — although the objective quality of the child's speech has not improved. A method that we have used to help detect this kind of "deterioration" in observer performance is to record three or more tapes of the child's verbal behavior early in the study and have a third, trained observer rate these tapes. Then one tape is rated by the two usual observers at the beginning phases of the study, a second in the middle portion of the study, and a third at the end of the study. If the latter tapes are rated higher by the two regular observers in comparison with the ratings made by the third observer, there are grounds for concern about downward drifting of criteria. For additional information on this method, see Gelfand, Hartmann, Lamb, Smith, Mahan, and Paul (1974) and Patterson and Harris (1968).

While it is better to detect than not to detect observer drift, bias, etc., we want to emphasize again that it is better still to avoid these unwanted observer effects entirely. This is best accomplished by thorough and continuous training of the observers, maintenance of observers' interest in the task, attention to basic human engineering factors, and the other suggestions made in the sections devoted to separate observer effects.

## Conclusions

The reliability procedures recommended in this chapter are fairly complex. To help you from getting lost in this complexity, we have summarized these procedures in a series of steps in Table 8-7. If you are collecting data on more than one target behavior, these procedures should be followed for each behavior.

**Table 8-7.** Step-by-Step Summary of Reliability Procedures

1. Both observers collect data during an observation session prior to formal baseline data collection. Check trial reliability and observer bias for each target behavior.
   (a) If summary data are unacceptable, troubleshoot problems and repeat Step 1.
   (b) If summary data are adequate, begin formal baseline data collection.
2. If necessary, construct material to assess observer drift.
3. Include trial reliability assessments once each week or two, and at least once during each phase of the study. Check trial reliability and observer bias; resolve disagreements immediately following each reliability assessment.
4. Summarize trial reliability data in Table 8-4.
5. Check for observer bias and drift over the entire course of the study.

To learn more about the intricacies of observer effects, see Rosenthal and Rosnow (1969) and Weick (1968). Additional information on reliability theory can be found in Nunnally's (1978) excellent text. If you are specifically interested in the problems of reliability in behavior modification, check the recent papers by Hartmann (1982a), House et al. (1981), and Wallace and Elder (1980). Reliability methods based on the analysis of variance, and related to the correlation approach described in this chapter, are described in Brennan (1983), in Cronbach, Gleser, Nanda, and Rajaratnam (1972), in Medley and Mitzel (1963), and in Wiggins (1973).

# Probe Questions for Chapter 8, Section 3

1. *Distinguish between the two types of reactive effects (on the child and on the observer in the presence of a second observer) discussed in this section.*

2. *What is observer bias? How might observer bias pose a problem in interpreting your results?*

3. *How might failure to detect consensual observer drift affect the evaluation of the effectiveness of a treatment program?*

4. *Describe two methods for limiting each of the four types of observer effects discussed in this section.*

# Chapter 9
# FORMAL DATA COLLECTION

## Behavioral Objectives for Chapter 9, Section 1

*After studying Section 1 of this chapter, you should be able to:*

1. *State the advantages of keeping up-to-date graphs of the target behavior's rate.*

2. *Describe the three functions of baseline data.*

3. *Determine the length of the baseline phase of your study.*

4. *State the solution to problems that commonly occur during the baseline phase of treatment studies.*

## SECTION 1: COLLECTING BASELINE DATA

### *Introduction*

You should have now completed all the steps leading up to formal data collection. Your definitions have been refined, a smoothly functioning data collection method has been developed and tested, and minor reliability problems have been resolved. Now use your observation and recording techniques to collect a record of the child's rate of responding. As your study passes from one phase to the next, continue to collect data on the target behavior. Before you begin collecting data each day, review the Data Collection Checklist presented in Table 9-1; it may help you avoid some errors. When you have completed your daily observations, summarize them by tabulating occurrences of the target behavior in the Data Summary Sheet (see Table 8-4) as well as on a working graph. (Specific details on the construction of graphs are found in Chapter 10.) We found that a daily graphic record of the rate of the target behavior has a number of advantages. First, a well-constructed graph will allow you to determine at a glance whether program changes should be made. It is the behavior of your child-subject that should control the pace and flexibility of your program, including the appropriate time for modifying treatment procedures and changing design phases. The child's behavior can only become controlling when it is continuously available to you through daily entries on a graph. Second, a simple, easily interpreted graph can be used to provide feedback and reinforcement to the child's caretakers, perhaps to the child him- or herself, and of course to you and your partner (also see Chapter 3, Section 1 and Parsonson & Baer, 1978).

**Table 9-1.** Data Collection Checklist

1. _____ Have you reviewed the behavioral definitions, including definitions of positive and negative instances. If not, do so.

2. _____ Have you rechecked the "suggestions for observers" given in Section 3 of Chapter 2? If not, do so.

3. _____ Is the equipment needed for taking data (pencils, stopwatches, data sheets) available? (For both observers, if it's a reliability assessment.)

4. _____ Be sure your data sheets are dated and otherwise labeled. If this is a reliability check, also staple the two observers' data sheets together after you have completed your observations.

5. _____ If your reliability wasn't acceptable when last assessed, discuss your errors, and include another reliability assessment.

6. _____ Do you have enough data during this condition? Remember, if you plan to group your data (for example, plot them weekly rather than daily), the number of required daily observations is greater than if you do not group your data.

7. _____ Have you included a reliability check within the past five or six sessions or within the current design phase? If not, include another reliability assessment. If you have more than one target behavior, be certain to check the reliability of each one.

## Collecting Baseline Data

Formal data collection begins during the baseline condition. The record you obtain of the child's naturally occurring baseline rate of responding serves descriptive and predictive functions, and may also serve a hypothesis-generating function (e.g., Bloom & Fischer, 1982). The baseline data will describe the targeted characteristic, such as rate, of the child's responding. This rate will be compared with rates of the behavior during treatment and other subsequent conditions so that the degree of change can be determined and the variables responsible for this change can be identified. Finally, if the target behavior varies systematically during baseline, analysis of the factors associated with the variability might prove fruitful in planning a treatment program. For example, finding higher rates of the target behavior during the morning, or when dad is present, may suggest maintaining conditions that could be exploited in your treatment plan. You must attend to a number of issues in your baseline data to perform these three functions adequately.

## Length of Baseline Phase

Two factors (other than an inadequate treatment) that may prevent you from demonstrating a change in the target behavior in your study are marked performance instability or variability and pre-intervention shifts in the desired or therapeutic direction, e.g., losing weight before initiating a diet program. Ideally then, you should continue to collect baseline data until you obtain a stable rate of responding. Realistically, however, the length of baseline will depend not only on the variability and trend or direction of change in the target behavior, but also upon reality factors such as length of the school term in which you are to complete your project and upon ethical concerns, such as the length of time you can delay treatment without harming the child. The following section discusses some recurrent problems with baseline data and their potential solutions.

## Problems

1. Zero rate of a desirable target behavior.

*Solution*: This circumstance makes a formal and extended period of baseline observation virtually unnecessary. The baseline rate is, has been, and probably will remain at zero — e.g., the child has never made his bed, tied his shoe, or written his name. If so, you can commence with your behavior modification program. (See Section 2 of Chapter 4.)

2. Highly erratic rate of baseline responding. Sidman (1960) recommends that a baseline should not vary more than five percent. That is a reasonable value for a rat in a Skinner box, but unreasonable for a child in a complex and varying social environment. However, if your baseline data resemble those displayed in Figure 9-1, you may have difficulty demonstrating treatment-produced changes in the target behavior.

*Solution*: Attempt to identify the factors that produce variability. As we have previously suggested, doing so may help you to generate a successful treatment strategy and suggest how the baseline conditions might be modified so as to reduce highly variable responding. (The checklist given in Table 9-2 provides a number of factors to consider in trouble-shooting highly variable baseline data.) The experimental control of variability is one of the hallmarks of the experimental analysis of behavior (Johnston & Pennypacker, 1980; Sidman, 1960). While experimental control of variability may seem to be a luxury, some investigators would argue that it is a luxury we can ill afford

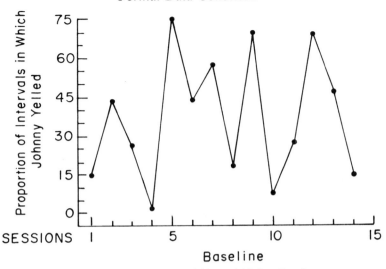

**Figure 9-1.** Graph showing highly variable baseline data.

to do without (e.g., Michael, 1974). Other investigators (e.g., Hartmann, 1977) suggest other strategies for dealing with variability that are more efficient of time, so that one doesn't "spend a lifetime" on the same study. One of these strategies is simply to gather more data, the assumption being that with variable performance, more data are required to confidently project into the future (Mann, 1976).

If your data are variable, you might use the following rule of thumb to decide how many baseline sessions to include: three, the minimum recommended by Hersen and Barlow (1976), plus one additional day for each 10%

**Table 9-2.** Trouble-shooting Variable Baseline Data

Does the target behavior vary as a function of:

1. _____ the observer gathering the data? If so, review the behavioral definitions, check the observational equipment, and include a reliability assessment to determine the source of observer inconsistency.

2. _____ the time of day? What factor(s) covary with time of day that might exert control over the child's responding? Fatigue, hunger, a favorite activity, or TV program? Can these factors be modified?

3. _____ the presence of particular people, such as a parent, sibling, or friend? Can these people either be consistently present or consistently absent during observation periods?

of variability — that is, Number of days of baseline = 3 + 10 [(Highest Rate – Lowest Rate)/Highest Rate]. For example, if the number of homework problems solved varies from 6 to 20 during the first three days of baseline, continue to take baseline data for seven additional days — 10[(20 − 6)/20] = 7. This rule of thumb for determining the length of baseline is for use when one's schedule is under the control of data — an admirable criterion, but one that we only infrequently can afford. It will probably be necessary for you to keep uppermost in mind the constraints imposed by academic scheduling. If too much time is spent collecting baseline data, it might then be necessary to skimp on either the treatment or other phases of your study, which in the long run might have greater importance.

Once the baseline data appear orderly, consult with your instructor before proceeding with the treatment program; your assessment of stability may be premature. The baseline data shown in Panel A of Figure 9-2 could be considered sufficiently stable to begin treatment; the mean number of room-cleaning items completed is 17, with scores ranging from 15–18.

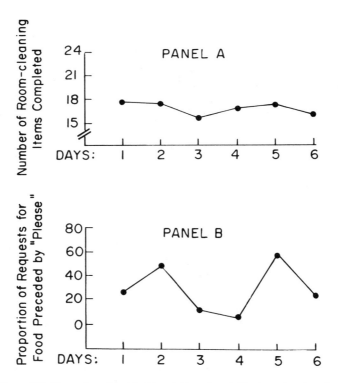

**Figure 9-2.** Examples of stable (Panel A) and variable (Panel B) baselines.

The baseline data presented in Panel B of Figure 9-2 are not sufficiently stable to begin modifying the behavior. The rate of food requests including "please" varies from 15% to 55% with a mean of 27%; an additional 6 or 7 days of baseline data should be obtained. At the end of that time, the data may become more stable, the factors that produce extensive variability may become apparent, or at least the future pattern of the behavior can be estimated.

A second strategy for reducing the variability in a set of data is to *group* the data across larger time intervals. Instead of plotting daily session totals, one could plot the average performance over a number of days, perhaps even a week. This procedure has much to recommend it as a method of producing apparent clarity where before there was only chaos. On the other hand, grouping data may disguise controlling factors that could be discerned with ungrouped data (Sidman, 1960), and also usually requires additional data. For example, if data were grouped or collapsed over 5-day averages, a minimum of 10 days of data would be required for 2 data points.[1]

As an aid to understanding your data, you may find it useful to construct one graph of daily session totals and a second graph of totals averaged over several days or some other convenient period of time.

3. Variable but patterned baseline rate. Data that are variable, but patterned demonstrate the difference between stability and predictability or regularity. For example, a child may show a high rate of refusal to eat each weekend, but a low rate during the week. A resulting graph of this response (refusing food) might show great regularity from week to week but little apparent stability from day to day. Cyclic data of this type are shown in Figure 9-3.

*Solution*: As the first step to arriving at a solution, be sure you have correctly identified the problem. Recognition of cyclic patterns requires a more extended observation period (usually twice as many observations as the length of the cycle) than is necessary when the rate is quite stable. If baseline data collection would have been terminated at Day 4 in Figure 9-3, no notion of the regularity of the data would have been obtained. Data with recurring cycles such as these are more often seen in weekly cycles — i.e., the rates of the behavior are discriminated on the day of the week, so that room-cleaning might be unlikely to occur on weekdays and more likely to occur on weekends. In order to clarify these weekly cycles, be sure to label the horizontal axis of your baseline graph with the day of the week on which each data point was obtained (see Figure 9-3).

---

[1]Note that the rule of thumb described above can be used to decide the number of data points to include when the data are averaged. If the data are to be averaged over 3-day periods, substitute in the rule-of-thumb formula "number of data points based on 3-day averages" for "number of days," and define highest and lowest rate based on 3-day averages.

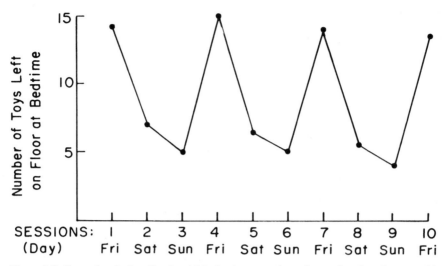

**Figure 9-3.** Example of a baseline in which the data vary from day to day, but show a stable weekly pattern.

Cyclic data, once identified, need not present a problem, particularly if certain precautions are taken during data analysis. These precautions may include grouping the data over the sessions involving a cycle (e.g., over the seven days that constitute a weekly cycle). If so, it may be necessary for you to gather additional data (see Problem No. 2 above). Alternatively, it may be sufficient merely for you to express performance during treatment as improvement over baseline performance during the equivalent days of the cycle. A similar solution is described in Problem No. 3 under "Collecting data during the first treatment phase" in Section 2 of this chapter.

4. Baseline rate is shifting progressively from day to day. It is acceptable to initiate a program when the direction of progressive shift or trend is opposite to the change direction desired. Panel A of Figure 9-4 shows a baseline appropriate for beginning a deceleration program. Although the rate of thumb-sucking is on the increase, continual increases will work against rather than in the direction of your program. As a result of beginning on the upswing, you will underestimate the potency of your program. (Part of the scientific tradition is that if you must err, do so conservatively. This is another example of scientists' reinforcement schedules being thinned by institutionalized practices.) You might not want to begin an acceleration program with the target behavior on the increase. If your baseline looked like the one for time spent interacting with peers (presented in Panel B of Figure 9-4), it would

be appropriate for you to begin an acceleration program but not a deceleration program.[2]

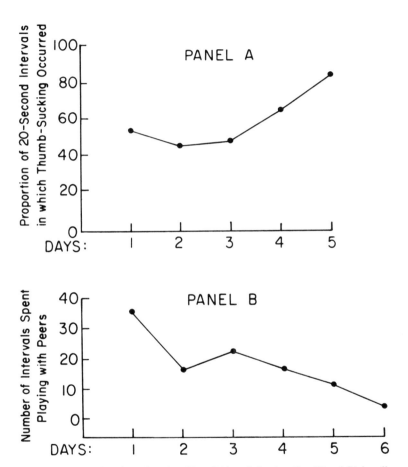

**Figure 9-4.** Example of accelerating (Panel A) and decelerating (Panel B) baselines.

---

[2]Kazdin (1982b) suggests that sometimes substantial baseline trends in the therapeutic direction can be tolerated by shifting to a design for which stable baseline responding is less critical,
e.g., the multiple treatment design.

When the trend of the data is in the desired direction, but very gradual, you may begin your modification program. The baseline rate of minutes crying before afternoon nap (shown in Figure 9-5) provides just such an example. Although the behavior is decreasing, it is doing so very slowly; if your program is successful, the behavior should decrease more rapidly. If you are able to do so, check into the factors that are responsible for the declining baseline rate; they may suggest a method of controlling the behavior. When the shift is dramatic and in the desired direction, a more serious problem is at hand.

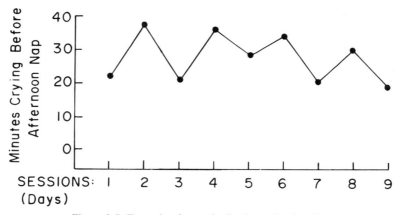

**Figure 9-5.** Example of a gradually decreasing baseline.

*Solution*: It may be unnecessary for you to add a separate therapeutic manipulation. Someone or something else is effectively modifying the behavior. You had best select another behavior for modification. Perhaps your observations are reactive — e.g., the teacher knows what behavior you are observing and she begins to respond differently to that behavior with a resulting impact on its rate, or the child realizes that his table manners are annoying others so he initiates some self-control procedures. Unanticipated changes of this sort are a boon to the child, but perhaps temporarily disappointing to you because of the time you have invested in the project. Perhaps all is not lost, however, if you select another target behavior for modification with the same child. Like adults, few children are perfect.

## Other Considerations

A number of other factors should be considered when conducting baseline assessments. For example, the length of the baseline phase, as well as of the succeeding phases of your study, will depend upon whether or not you intend to use a formal statistical analysis. If you do intend to subject your data to such an analysis (see Chapter 10), recommendations for the number of data points per condition vary from as few as seven for the celeration line approach (White, 1977), to as many as 100 for certain forms of interrupted time-series analysis (Hartmann, Gottman, Jones, Gardner, Kazdin, & Vaught, 1980).

For further discussions of baseline stability and related matters, see Bloom and Fischer (1982, Chapter 12), Kazdin (1982b, Chapter 11), and Mann (1976).

## *Generalization Probes*

If your study is one in which generalization probes would be useful (e.g., training occurs for a very limited portion of the day, and the behavior is relevant to a much wider variety of contexts), you should begin gathering baseline data in those situations in which you wish to test for generalization (see Section 3 of Chapter 3). Again, the rules regarding stability, etc., are applicable to evaluating the baseline data collected during generalization probes. However, if generalization is only a minor focus of your study, it may be acceptable to include weekly rather than daily generalization probes and bend the rules concerning stability. Check with your instructor.

## *Conclusions*

When you believe that you have collected sufficient baseline data — that is, when the data are predictable, reliable, and not changing in the treatment-aimed direction — check with your instructor to be certain that it is appropriate to begin the treatment manipulation.

*Note.* Periodically review Table 9-1, the Data Collection Checklist, and regularly (on a daily basis) summarize your data in a Data Summary Table (e.g., Table 8-4) and on a working graph.

## Probe Questions for Chapter 9, Section 1

1. *What are the advantages of maintaining a graph of your data throughout the study?*

2. *What important functions do baseline data perform?*

3. *Before moving from the baseline to the treatment phase of your study, what criteria regarding stability, trends, and grouping of data should be fulfilled?*

4. The baseline rate of food-throwing for a 2-year-old boy over the course of six consecutive days is as follows: 23%, 16%, 18%, 13%, and 10%. Comment on the advisability of beginning a deceleration program at this point.

5. Distinguish between a regular or predictable baseline and a stable baseline.

# Behavioral Objectives for Chapter 9, Section 2

*After studying this section, you should be able to:*

1. *State the criteria for terminating the treatment phase of your study.*

2. *Determine the length of each subsequent phase of your study.*

3. *Solve problems that commonly occur during the treatment and subsequent phases of your study.*

## SECTION 2: COLLECTING DATA DURING TREATMENT AND FOLLOW-UP

### *Collecting Data During the First Treatment Phase*

Continue to collect data throughout the treatment phase of your study. If you have included generalization probes, also collect generalization data during the treatment phase. If you are using a multiple baseline or alternating treatment design, continue to collect data on both the treated and untreated target behaviors.

### *Length of Treatment Manipulation*

Two formal criteria should be considered in determining the length of your treatment manipulation: the social relevance criterion and the scientific or experimental criterion (Risley, 1969). In addition, the matter of expediency and your (and the child's) academic requirements may help determine the length of your project's treatment phase.

*The social relevance or validity criterion.* Has the rate of the target behavior been changed sufficiently so that the child is no longer considered atypical when compared to his same-aged peers? Are the child and his caretakers satisfied with the change produced? For example, if the target behavior was thumb-sucking, the rate should be lowered sufficiently so that the behavior is no longer of concern to the child's caretakers. If, instead, you worked with an acceleration problem, such as taking out the garbage, the rate should be sufficiently high so that the child's caretakers would agree that the performance is now thoroughly acceptable. Although social validity is not the only criterion for determining length of treatment, it is certainly an important one; unless it is met, treatment should not be terminated without good reason (the end of the academic term often is a good reason).

*The scientific criterion.* Has the behavior been changed sufficiently so that any reasonable person examining a graph of the rate of the behavior would agree that the behavior has been changed? This criterion implies that, in comparison with the baseline rate, the treatment rate has *stabilized* at a discernibly different rate. While formal rules for determining change are presented in Chapter 10, it is well to be forewarned here of a common methodological error, that of terminating treatment before a clear pattern of responding emerges (Kazdin, 1982b). It is sometimes difficult to know when to terminate treatment phases, particularly for those designs in which interventions are sandwiched between other phases (i.e., the withdrawal, changing criterion and multiple treatment designs). A number of guidelines follow to aid you in deciding the length of treatment phases or conditions (also see Sections 2–4 of Chapter 4, and Kazdin, 1982b, Chapter 11).

If you have selected a withdrawal design, the first treatment phase may be terminated well before the desired rate of responding is reached.[3] In fact, maintaining the child's performance at the desired terminal rate during this phase may preclude a successful reversal (e.g., Bijou et al., 1969). So change conditions as soon as the pattern of responding during this first treatment condition is clear. If instead you chose a changing criterion design, continue each treatment subphase until performance stabilizes at or near the *criterion* for that subphase. Because of the limitations of academic scheduling, be careful not to choose too many small criterion changes. Numerous small criterion changes necessitate a greater number of treatment sessions.

Finally, if you selected a multiple treatment design, such as the alternating treatment design, terminate the comparative treatment phase when one intervention shows clear superiority over the other(s). A problem may occur when the two or more interventions pitted against one another all can be expected to produce the same eventual level of responding, but to do so at different rates. In this case, change phases as soon as one procedure clearly demonstrates improvement, *but before* all techniques produce maximum performance changes. Protracting the comparative treatment phase will seriously limit your opportunity to demonstrate further changes in the target behavior during the final treatment phase when the most effective intervention is applied under all baseline conditions.

Occasionally, the social relevance criterion is apparently met (i.e., the child's caretakers agree that the problem no longer exists), but the data fail to substantiate their claim. When this occurs, interview the caretakers and attempt to understand the basis of their judgment; also, continue treatment

---

[3]The same is true for all but the final behavior treated with a multiple baseline design. Remember that you will continue to treat, and presumably improve early treated behaviors while the intervention is applied to the later treated behaviors.

until the reports by caretakers and your data are congruent. If the data indicate changes in the target behavior, but the caretakers report no change,
check with your instructor as to how to proceed.

## Problems

Again there are a number of problems that might occur during the initial
treatment portion of your study. Some of these problems and their solutions
are given below.
1. The rate during treatment fails to stabilize.

*Solution*: If the rate has clearly changed in the desired directon, you need
only be concerned if you are using a changing criterion design. With members
of the other three design families, simply institute the next condition. With
the changing criterion design you may have to adjust the next criterion so
that it is substantially more difficult.

If the rate deteriorates after an initial improvement, it may be that the
behavior was being controlled by some extratherapeutic factor. Or perhaps
the child is satiating on whatever reinforcer is being used. Continue the treatment sessions a bit longer to see what will happen, and re-read Chapter 5
carefully for other suggestions.

2. Nonindependent behaviors or situations in a multiple baseline design.
If you look carefully at the multiple baseline data in Figure 9-6, you'll notice
something peculiar. When treatment was instituted for setting the lunch table,
the behavior improved — but so did setting the breakfast and the dinner
table. We might optimistically say that the treatment generalized to the other
conditions. Obviously then, the three stimulus situations were not independent. A skeptic might doubt that the treatment changed the behavior, and
the skeptic is, of course, correct. Some concomitant event not included in
the treatment program might just as well have been responsible for the
behavior change. Without further information, the two alternative interpretations may be equally compelling. Although the target behavior is undoubtedly
changed, we can't specify what is responsible for the change (see Kazdin &
Kopel, 1975).

*Solution*: If you find an upward drift in all behaviors following institution
of treatment for the first behavior in a multiple baseline design, you might
superimpose a reversal phase. If this does not seem to be a reasonable tactic,
check with your instructor.

3. Excessive variability in the comparative treatment phase of an alternating treatment design. The data on number of correct quiz responses in
Figure 9-7 are so variable that differences in treatment effectiveness are dif-

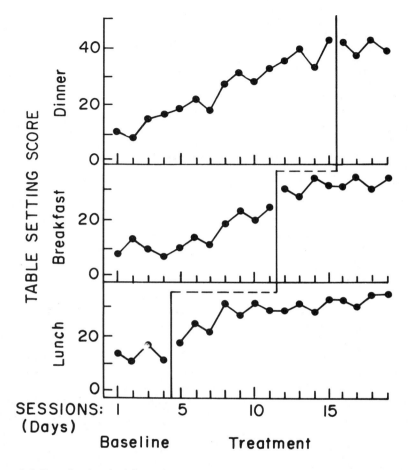

**Figure 9-6.** Data showing the failure of a multiple baseline design to demonstrate experimental control because of the nonindependence of the three behaviors.

ficult to detect. This problem could have been anticipated from examination of baseline performance. If detected early, variability might have been reduced by any of the techniques suggested in Chapter 4 such as gaining experimental control of the source or sources of variability, or gathering additional data and grouping observations for purposes of graphing. These solutions are not desirable when the project has advanced into the treatment phase, however.

*Solution*: The problem posed by variability due to class periods in these data has a relatively simple solution. Graph a function of the observed perform-

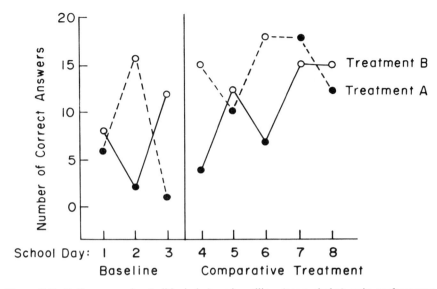

**Figure 9-7.** Daily geography (solid circles) and spelling (open circles) quiz performance demonstrating excess variability in an alternating treatment design.

ance, rather than the observed performance itself. This is perhaps most easily done by expressing each score as a deviation from the average performance during the baseline phase for the class in which the score was observed. So the treatment scores obtained during geography would be expressed as a deviation from 3.0 (average geography scores obtained during the baseline phase) and those obtained during spelling would be expressed as a deviation from 12.0 (average spelling scores obtained during the baseline phase). Using this approach, the first three Treatment A scores obtained during the Comparative Treatment condition correspond to deviation scores of 15 - 12 = 3, 10 - 3 = 7, and 18 - 12 = 6. The graph of these adjusted or transformed scores, shown in Figure 9-8, clearly shows the superiority of Treatment A over Treatment B during the Comparative Treatment phase.

4. On occasion, students — and professionals as well — simply cannot modify a behavior. Sometimes target behaviors are strongly under the control of variables that themselves are not readily amenable to change. At other times, a correct treatment technique is not employed until too late in the project. At still other times, no effective treatment is available. In all of these situations, the data look like a greatly extended baseline — no changes observed, no control over the behavior. In such situations, one can often say nothing with certainty except that the behavior was untreatable with the techniques used.

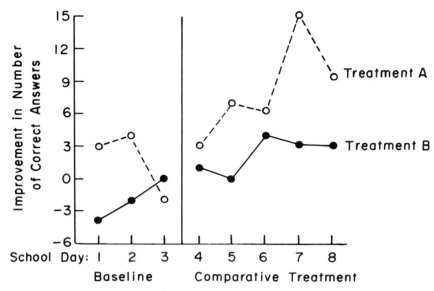

**Figure 9-8.** Daily quiz performance expressed as improvement over average geography and spelling performance during baseline (see Figure 9-7).

*Solution*: There is really no very acceptable solution for such a problem. If time allows, you may, of course, attempt other treatment techniques. If that is impossible, sometimes careful scrutiny of the data in comparison with a retrospective diary of concomitant changes in the child's life may produce some useful hypotheses that can be tested at a later time. Tukey (1977) suggests various methods that can be applied in exploratory data analysis.

While treatment failure is certainly less desirable than treatment success, students should be consoled by the observation that most often projects are graded on the care with which they were planned and conducted, rather than on the success which they achieved. Furthermore, even failure can have its advantages, because inadequacy of our present treatment techniques may spur the search for new and more effective ones.

## Conclusion

If careful inspection of your data and the report of the child's caretakers indicate that the target behavior has been successfully modified, go on to the next stage in your study after you have checked with your instructor.

## Collecting Data in the Remaining Phases of Your Study

The general rules for determining the length of each succeeding phase of your study are the same as those already described, with one exception: The

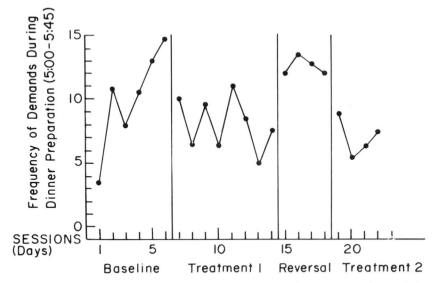

**Figure 9-9.** Data during baseline and reversal conditions were obtained by mother, and those during treatments 1 and 2 were obtained by daughter. Differences between conditions are thus confounded with differences between observers.

length of the reversal phase in an ABAB design is often abbreviated because of the inconvenience associated with returning a behavior to an undesirable rate. You should, however, have a sufficient number of data points during the reversal phase so that any reasonable person would agree that a real change in the rate has occurred, though the rate may not have stabilized. Again, the rules for determining change are described in Chapters 8 and 10.

*Note*: Be sure to continue your generalization probes. Also continue to review the Data Collection Checklist and to use the Data Summary Sheet and a daily graph.

## Problems

We again describe for you a number of problems that may first become apparent during the later phases of your study — and offer some suggestions for solving these problems.

1.Treatment-by-observer confounding. The data presented in Figure 9-9 illustrate a major flaw in an $N = 1$ study. The mother was the principal data gatherer during baseline and reversal conditions, while the daughter took data during the two treatment phases. When the reliability data were examined carefully, it was found that the mother had consistently higher rates, higher

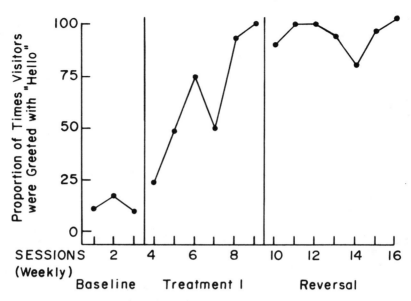

**Figure 9-10.** Graph showing the failure of a reversal condition to recapture baseline rates.

by 30% on the average. What seems to be a clear-cut treatment effect might instead be nothing but differences in the way the two observers code the target behavior.

*Solution*: Obviously the best solution for treatment-by-observer confounding is to avoid it by carefully noting any tendency of the observers to differ in their coding of the target behavior early in the study and either resolve the problem or use one observer as the primary data gatherer. If you have been inattentive to signs of observer bias early in the study and find yourself with data like those shown in Figure 9-9, you may still be able to save your project. If there is a fairly consistent trend for one observer to see more of the target behavior than the other, you might subtract that constant quantity from the higher observer's data when you prepare your final graph. Before taking such drastic action, check with your instructor. If your instructor approves of making adjustments to the data, be sure to note these adjustments on your graph, and provide your justification for manipulating the data in the text of your final report.

2. Inability to recapture baseline in an *ABAB design*. An examination of Figure 9-10 clearly indicates that the baseline rate could not be recaptured during the reversal phase. Consequently, there was no opportunity to demonstrate control by repeatedly turning the behavior on and off by introducing and removing the treatment variable. We might speculate that

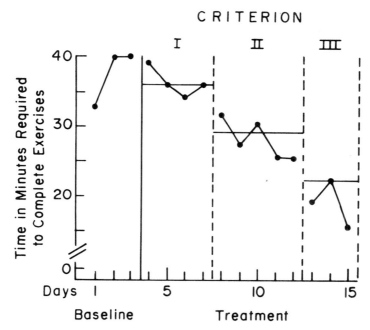

**Figure 9-11.** Graph showing lack of correspondence between criterion and performance in the later phases of a changing criterion design.

perhaps the child was obtaining generous social reinforcement for his new social skills outside of the home, and that this reinforcement was sufficient to maintain the behavior at home even when it was put on extinction.

*A solution*: If time enough remains, add a DRO condition (see Section 2 of Chapter 4 and Section 2 of Chapter 6), then remove the DRO when the behavior has decreased. If the rate of behavior remains low (stabilizes), reinstitute the treatment. If the behavior remains unaffected by either the DRO or other decelerating procedures, you may be able to add a second AB component by selecting another target behavior. The two temporally uncoordinated AB components then would constitute a multiple baseline-like design (see Hayes, 1981). Perhaps it would be best to discuss this problem with your instructor.

3. Failure of the target behavior to match criteria during the later phases of a *changing criterion design*. Inspection of the data shown in Figure 9-11 suggests that the investigator should have imposed more stringent (larger) criterion changes. Because performance changes do not closely parallel criterion changes, and, in fact, exceed the programmed criteria, demonstration of control is questionable.

*Solution*: Two potential solutions are worth considering here. The first involves imposing a substantially more stringent criterion in the next criterion change subphase. Perhaps a reduction of 10 minutes rather than of 6½ minutes would be more in keeping with the child-subject's apparent capacity to change. Remember, however, that changes become more difficult as performance approaches the minimum time to perform the task. For example, it may be easy to clip 5 minutes from the one-half hour a child requires to undress, but it may be impossible to do so when that time has already been reduced to 8 minutes.

An alternative solution may be to institute a brief reversal phase, as we suggested for errant changing criterion designs in Chapter 4, Section 5. Adopting this approach, the next criterion subphase might impose a criterion of 35 minutes, or perhaps no criterion — a veritable program holiday. Before choosing between these two alternatives, check with your instructor.

## Collecting Data During Follow-up

For most student projects that are squeezed into an already tight academic program, the project will be concluded, often prematurely, during the treatment phase. If you should happen to be one of those rare individuals who achieves treatment objectives before the project must be terminated, check the durability of the therapeutic changes by collecting follow-up data. Follow-up data preferably are collected in the same situation and in the same manner as were the data collected during the baseline and treatment phases of your project (see Chapter 8). If you are unable to match these ideal circumstances in collecting follow-up data, you will not be out of keeping with current clinical practice. A brief phone interview with a parent or a teacher or an informal observation of the child is often the best that a busy therapist can manage. Should your schedule afford more time for follow-up assessments, consult Hartmann, Roper, and Gelfand (1977) and Mash and Terdal (1977) for discussions on the host of factors that deserve consideration in planning the collection of formal follow-up data.

After you have completed data collection and tabulation during all phases of your study (possibly including generalization probes and a follow-up phase), you will be ready to analyze your data. The procedures to be followed are described in Chapter 10.

## Probe Questions for Chapter 9, Section 2

1. *What relevance do the social validity and scientific criteria have for deciding upon the length of a treatment phase?*

2. *Why might it be desirable to terminate the comparative treatment phase of an alternating treatment design before all of the interventions being compared achieve desired performance levels?*

3. *What are some of the data collection problems that might occur during the treatment phase of a study? How might these problems be solved?*

4. *Define treatment-by-observer confounding. Describe the potential remedies for this problem.*

5. *If the baseline rate of the target behavior cannot be recaptured in an ABAB design by reinstituting the conditions present during baseline, what procedures might be employed to demonstrate experimental control?*

6. *Think of a situation in which it might be better to employ a reversal, rather than vary the magnitude of criterion changes, in a defective changing criterion design?*

# Chapter 10
## ASSESSING THE EFFECTS OF YOUR TREATMENT PROGRAM

### Behavioral Objectives for Chapter 10, Section 1

*After studying Section 1 of this chapter, you should be able to:*

1. *Summarize your reliability data and determine the degree of observer bias.*

2. *Choose the best form of your data for analysis (e.g., graphing).*

3. *State the factors that should be considered in determining how and when to group your data.*

4. *Determine the number of graphs necessary to present your data clearly.*

5. *Construct graphs of your data so that the results of your study can be easily understood.*

## SECTION 1. SUMMARIZING RELIABILITY AND TARGET BEHAVIOR DATA AND CONSTRUCTING GRAPHS

By now you have completed the formal data-gathering requirements of your study and terminated or reduced your therapeutic contacts with the child and his caretakers. While your regular data collection procedures have provided you with continuous measures of the progress of your study, it is now time to summarize those data systematically. It is the purpose of this chapter, then, to describe useful techniques for summarizing, analyzing, and presenting the data you have collected on the target behavior throughout the study. We will also describe for you the process of preparing a final report summarizing your project.

## Summarizing Reliability Data

The directions for summarizing your reliability data have been described in Section 2 of the chapter on reliability (Chapter 8). For your report, indicate the number of reliability check sessions, the phases during your study in which they were conducted, and the mean and range of your reliability estimates (see Table 8-4). If you used more than one target behavior (i.e., a between-behavior multiple baseline design) or more than two observers, these values should be reported for each target behavior and for each *pair* of observers. Should the observer totals reported in Table 8-4 prove to be discrepant, report the extent of the discrepancy and whether changes in the child's behavior were confounded with observer differences (see Chapter 9, Section 2). Additional recommendations for summarizing and presenting reliability information can be found in Hartmann and Wood (1982) and in Morris and Rosen (1982).

## Graphing Your Data

The usual (though not necessarily the only) method of analyzing individual subject data is a careful visual examination of graphic displays. For this reason, correct graphic methods are vitally important.

Before constructing your final graphs, you must decide what form of the data should be graphed, if and how the data should be averaged, and how many graphs are needed to portray the data.

## Choice of Metric

Depending on which form of data you choose to collect, you could represent your data either in terms of:

1. absolute number (number of responses, intervals, or time),

2. relative number (proportion of intervals or time),

3. rate per unit of time, such as hits per minute, or

4. a difference measure, involving one of the above forms of data such as rate per unit of time during the treatment phase minus rate per unit of time during the baseline phase.

Although these methods seem equally acceptable, there are many occasions when they are not; in fact, absolute number is often troublesome, and in some cases the data will be unclear unless difference scores are used (see examples in Chapter 9). Consider the case in which data collection periods vary in length from day to day, and the absolute number method is used.

If the scores from irregular sessions were not prorated (see Section 1 of Chapter 9), daily "rate" changes might be interpreted as reflecting changes in the target behavior rather than as daily variation in the length of the observation period.

The absolute method also might prove deceptive when generalization probes are consistently different (usually briefer) than regular data collection sessions, and it is desirable to compare the data from the two sources. It may not be apparent for example, that 27 responses in a 7-minute generalization probe are equivalent to 78 responses in a 20-minute regular data collection session — both equal 3.9 responses per minute.

In addition to making within-study comparisons easier, data expressed as rate per unit of time (either rate per minute for frequently occurring responses or rate per hour for infrequently occurring responses) also has the advantage of facilitating badly needed cross-study comparisons (Hartmann, 1972). Therefore, avoid the absolute method and use the rate per unit of time method if possible. For examples of data graphed in terms of rate per unit of time, see Figures 10-3 and 10-4.

The more complex data form described in (4) may be necessary if you selected an alternating treatment design and data were gathered in conditions having substantially different rates (see Chapter 9, Section 2 for an illustration).[1]

## Averaging Your Data

Most, if not all, data are averaged over some period of time. The problem, then, is not usually whether to average but rather over what period of time to average the data. The most obvious answer to that question for most student projects is to graph daily session totals. Although minute-by-minute fluctuations within a session are lost by representing an entire session by a single number, these fluctuations are of little importance in evaluating your entire study (although they may be useful in suggesting variables that control the child's behavior). At other times, as we have previously suggested in Chapter 9, it may be useful to group your data over two, three, or even more sessions. If grouping over sessions seems desirable because of excessive variability in your data, you must decide upon the number of sessions over which scores should be grouped. One major and a number of minor factors should be considered in making this decision.

---

[1]Complex data transformations might also be required if a statistical analysis is applied to multiple baseline design data (i.e., Revusky, 1967).

*Fairness.* The major factor you should consider is fairness — that is, to portray your data in a manner that fairly represents what actually occurred. The temptation is great to try a variety of different grouping procedures and then select the one that portrays the data in the most favorable light. This is not unlike the questionable practice of some group-design experimenters who try every conceivable statistical analysis on their data and then report the results of the particular analysis that are most favorable to the experimenter's favorite theory. In both cases, the experimenters have exploited chance variations in their data and have obviously violated the fairness criterion.

*Number of trials included in each session total.* You should aggregate your data if the target behavior has relatively few opportunities to occur each day, as would be the case for responses such as kissing mother when she returns from work or brushing teeth after each meal. Compare the ungrouped data portrayed in Figure 10-1 with the grouped data portrayed in Figure 10-2. In the former figure (the graph of daily occurrence-nonoccurrence of feeding the family pets) it is difficult to distinguish trends due to intervention.

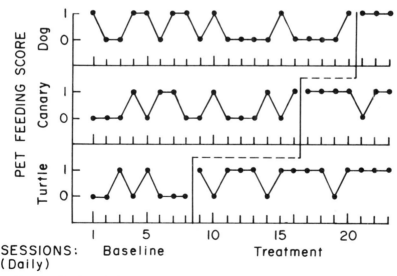

**Figure 10-1.** Application of reinforcement procedures in a multiple baseline design to increase feeding of the family pets. Daily data are not collapsed.

When these same data are grouped over 4-day sessions, treatment effects are clear and easily distinguished (see Figure 10-2).

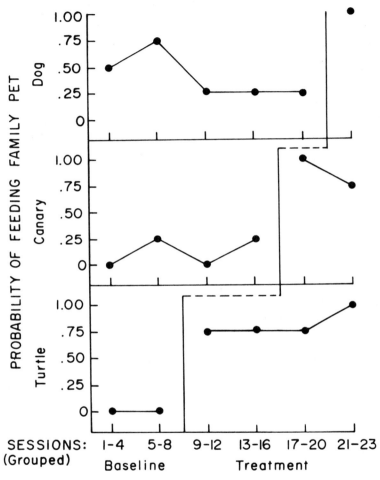

**Figure 10-2.** Application of reinforcement procedures in a multiple baseline design to increase feeding of the family pets. Data are collapsed over 4-day periods, except for the last data point for each behavior, which is based on three days of data.

*Number of sessions included in each condition.* Ordinarily, you will need more data collection sessions within each phase of your study if you group your data. For example, compare the treatment phase of Figures 10-1 and 10-2 for the target behavior, feeding the dog. Before averaging over 4-day periods (Figure 10-1), this condition contained three data points; after averaging, it contained only a single (prorated) data point. The latter case does not provide sufficient data to examine trends in the data across time.

If, early in your study, you are able to anticipate the number of sessions over which your data will be grouped, try to use some multiple of that number for the number of sessions within each condition. For example, if you expect to group over 4 sessions, use 8, 12, or 16 sessions in each condition, so that you will have more than a single data point within each phase and so that you can avoid having to prorate your data.

If you are grouping data over, say, 4-day intervals, and if the number of sessions in one or more condition is not divisible by four, you must prorate your data. For example, if the totals for the three sessions of reversal were 14, 22, and 18, the average is 18 and the number you should graph is either 18, if you are plotting averages, or 72 (18 × 4), if you are plotting totals. Be sure to indicate in the figure legend when you have prorated your data.

*Are your data cyclic?* If your data indicate the presence of cyclic trends (see Figure 9-3), it is generally advisable to group your data over the length of the cycle as we previously suggested. That is, for 4-day cycles, use a 4-day grouping interval. The reason for this is simple: Your treatment effects, which have been superimposed on the cyclic trend, will be more easily discerned with the grouped data, as contrasted with the ungrouped data.

A final warning: If you group your data, be certain that you don't misrepresent them. The line between fudging your data and honestly representing them is sometimes a thin one, so take care that you don't fool your readers as well as yourself with misleading data manipulations. If you think that grouping might in fact result in misrepresentation, you should include graphs of both the grouped and the ungrouped data. Readers can then reach their own conclusions.

## Number of Graphs

There are at least three situations when two or more graphs should be used to display your data. If you have used a multiple baseline design, it is generally best to use the "piggyback" format shown in Figures 10-1 and 10-2. You should also use this format if your treatment involved a combined acceleration-deceleration technique and you tabulated both the behavior to be increased and the behavior to be decreased. And, finally, use two or more graphs if you included generalization probes in your study and collected generalization data each day (or each day a training session was conducted). A sample graph of generalization data of this kind is presented in Figure 10-3.

If you have included generalization probes only occasionally, indicate the generalization data on the same graph as is used for your regular data. Be sure, however, that both sources of data are expressed in the same rate

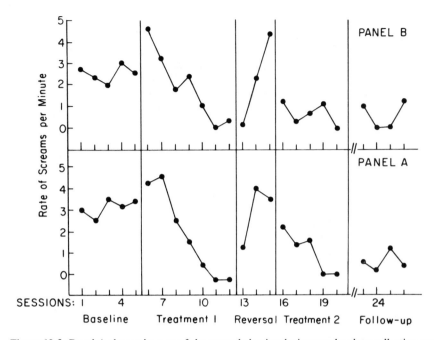

**Figure 10-3.** Panel A shows the rate of the target behavior during regular data collection sessions. Panel B shows the rate of the target behavior during generalization probes. Follow-up began two weeks after the termination of treatment.

measure and that a unique symbol is used for each source of data (see the example shown in Figure 10-4).

## Constructing the Graphs

The graphs presented in this monograph provide models for you to follow in graphing your data. Additional information on graphing can be found in the American Psychological Association's *Publication Manual*, 3rd ed. (1983), and in Parsonson and Baer (1978). After you have experimented with various graphic displays, be certain that your final graphs are neatly constructed and easy to interpret. To help you achieve this result, follow these rules:

1. Use a height-to-width ratio that is aesthetically pleasing: Do *not* allow the graph itself to completely fill the page on which it occurs, as you must leave room for the figure legend, etc.

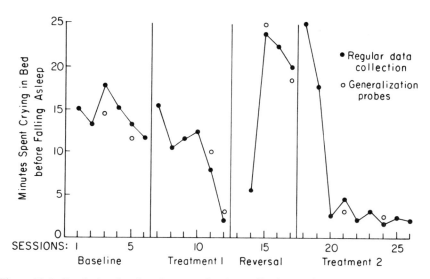

**Figure 10-4.** Graph showing data from regular data collection sessions (afternoon nap) and periodic generalization probes (evening bedtime). (Note, however, that it would have been preferable to begin treatment when the baseline was *not* descending.)

2. Clearly label both the horizontal and vertical axes. Begin the zero point above the horizontal baseline of the graph if you have zero entries. Failure to do so makes it difficult to discriminate the data line from the graph's horizontal baseline or abscissa (compare Panel A of Figure 10-5 with Panel B).

3. Use a solid vertical line to separate conditions (except the subphases of a changing criterion design, in which case use a broken vertical line). Break the data line (the line that connects the data points) between conditions. Do not connect the first data point to zero on the vertical axis.

4. Use a curved hatched line to indicate breaks in the vertical or horizontal axis (see Figure 10-3, horizontal axis of follow-up condition).

5. Make the data points sufficiently large so that they are not obliterated by the connecting line. (Compare Panel B of Figure 10-5 with Panel A of the same figure.)

6. Prepare a figure legend that describes the content of the figure. This legend goes *below* the figure. If your graph needs qualifying — e.g., that some data points were prorated or that some sessions were interrupted and produced atypical responding — indicate that in the figure legend. (The graph together with its legend should be understandable without reference to the text material.)

7. If you have more than one graph, number them consecutively.

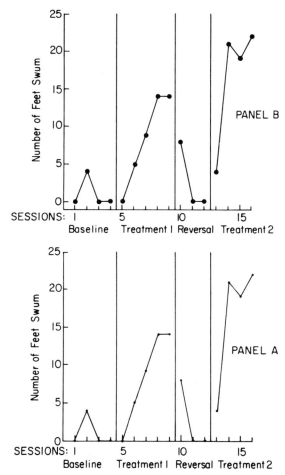

**Figure 10-5.** Two graphs of the same data. In Panel A data points indicating zero rate lie on the abscissa or horizontal axis; in Panel B data points indicating zero rate lie above the abscissa.

# Probe Questions for Chapter 10, Section 1

1. What reliability information should be included in your final report?

2. What are the advantages and limitations of presenting data in terms of absolute number, relative number, rate per unit of time, and as a difference score?

3. How might an experimenter misrepresent his or her data by grouping them?

4. *What factors should be given serious consideration when deciding whether to group and how to group data?*

5. *The figure given below violates which of the recommendations given in Section 1 of Chapter 10. How could the figure be improved?*

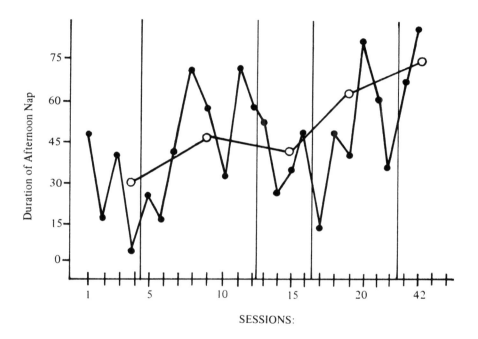

SESSIONS:

## Behavioral Objectives for Chapter 10, Section 2

*After studying Section 2 of this chapter, you should be able to:*

1. *Calculate the descriptive statistics that aid in the interpretation of individual subject data.*

2. *Determine whether your data require statistical analysis.*

3. *Identify the statistical test appropriate for your data, if indeed one is appropriate.*


## SECTION 2.
## ASSESSING CHANGES IN THE TARGET BEHAVIOR

Now that you have summarized the data on your target behavior in one or more graphs, you are ready to analyze these data and decide whether treatment produced changes in the target behavior (see the discussion of social and experimental change criteria in Section 2 of Chapter 9). Analysis of individual subject data typically involves careful visual inspection of graphic displays. These "binocular tests" may be supplemented by examining various descriptive statistics calculated on the data. We describe the most common of these in the section that follows.

Some investigators check or verify decisions made in this manner with formal tests of statistical significance, though this approach is controversial. In latter sections we describe the bases for this controversy, the conditions under which a test of statistical significance might be a useful decision aid, and the kinds of statistical tests that might be conducted on your data.

### Calculating Descriptive Statistics

Four descriptive statistics may aid you in understanding your target behavior data. Two of these, the mean $(X)$ and standard deviation $(SD)$, will be familiar to you. Two other descriptive statistics, level and slope or trend line, may be less familiar to you. However, these latter two are particularly relevant when interpreting the kind of temporally ordered (time-series) data you gathered, and so deserve at least brief consideration. We will apply these four descriptive statistics to the Treatment A data shown in Figure 9-8; the calculations are summarized in Table 10-1.

The mean describes the average performance. The mean calculated for the baseline phase data for Treatment A is $1.7 = \Sigma X/N$ (where $\Sigma X$ signifies the sum of the scores and $N$ indicates the number of scores). The mean of Treatment A scores during the intervention phase is 8.0. Comparing these two values indicates that average quiz difference scores clearly improved from

**Table 10-1.** Calculation of Descriptive Statistics for the Treatment A Data Shown in Figure 9-8

|  | Baseline Phase | Intervention Phase |
|---|---|---|
| $\bar{X} = \Sigma X/N$ |  |  |
| $\Sigma X =$ | $[3 + 4 + (-2)]$ | $[3 + 7 + 6 + 15 + 9]$ |
| $=$ | 5 | 40 |
| $N =$ | 3 | 5 |
| $\bar{X} =$ | 1.67 (rounded to 1.7) | 8.0 |
| $SD = [\Sigma(X - \bar{X})^2/N]^{1/2}$ |  |  |
| $\Sigma(X - \bar{X})^2 =$ | $(3-1.7)^2 + (4-1.7)^2 + (-2-1.7)^2$ | $(3-8)^2 + (7-8)^2 + (6-8)^2 + (15-8)^2 + (9-8)^2$ |
| $=$ | 20.6 | 80.0 |
| $N =$ | 3 | 5 |
| $SD =$ | 2.62 | 4.0 |
| Slope $= b = r(SD_x/SD_y)*$ | $-2.5$ | $+2.0$ |
| Level (estimated level) | $-2.0 \, (-.83)**$ | $+3.0 \, (4.0)**$ |

\* $r$ is the correlation between the day on which data are collected (e.g., 1, 2, and 3) and performance score. The sign of $r$ indicates whether scores are increasing (positive $r$) or decreasing (negative $r$) with advancing days. The correlations are $-.77$ and $.81$ for the baseline and intervention phases, respectively. $SD_x$ is the standard deviation of performance scores, and $SD_y$ is the standard deviation of days.

\*\* Estimated from the formula $X' = bY + A$ where $b =$ slope and $A =$ the value of $X$ on day zero (the $x$ intercept). $A = 6.67$ and $-4.0$ for baseline and intervention phases, respectively.

baseline to intervention, a conclusion that also is apparent from examining Figure 9-8.

While the mean indicates the average or central tendency of scores, the standard deviation describes the variability of scores; it is given by the formula $SD = [\Sigma[X - X)^2/N]^{1/2}$. For the Treatment A scores, the $SD$s are 2.62 and 4.0 for baseline and intervention phase (see Table 10-1) respectively. Thus, the increase in average performance during the intervention phase is associated with a corresponding increase in variability — again a performance characteristic discernible from the graphic display shown in Figure 9-8.

The *slope* or trend (symbolized $b$) for time-series data indicates any tendency of the scores to drift upward or downward with time. Data drifting downward, as do the baseline data in Figure 9-8, have a negative slope. The slope of –2.5 for these data indicates that the performance score *decreases* an average of 2.5 points each day.[2]

Data drifting upward, as do the intervention phase data in Figure 9-8, have a positive slope. The slope of 2.0 for these data indicates that the performance scores *increase* an average of 2.0 points each day. The calculated

---

[2]Despite the relatively formidable appearance of the slope formula given in Table 10-1, the calculations require less than a minute when conducted with a simple hand calculator.

slope values are clearly in agreement with the results of a visual inspection of the data in Figure 9-8; the negative trend during the baseline phase is reversed during the intervention phase.

The *level* of a time series is the score obtained immediately preceding or following a change in conditions or phases. For the Treatment A data shown in Figure 9-8, the levels at the end of the baseline phase and beginning of the intervention phase are −2.0 and +3.0, respectively.[3] Changes in level indicate whether the time series changed abruptly or not when condition changes were implemented. For the data in Figure 9-8, it would appear that performance did change quite dramatically as a result of the intervention.

To summarize, Figure 9-8 in conjunction with the statistics shown in Table 10-1 indicate that performance increased in level and changed in slope from negative to positive following the introduction of treatment. In comparison, the mean and standard deviation were less adequate measures of performance during either the baseline or intervention phase. In general, the mean and standard deviation will be of limited value when calculated on time-series data displaying substantial trends. For additional information on evaluating your data based on the approach described here, see Bloom and Fischer (1982, Chapter 20), Jones, Vaught, and Weinrott (1977), Kazdin (1982b, Chapter 10), and Parsonson and Baer (1978).

After you have calculated the descriptive statistics that seem useful for your project and interpreted them in conjunction with your graphs, you also may want to apply another decision aid to your data, an inferential statistic test. A discussion of the necessity for doing so follows.

## Is a Statistical Analysis Required?

In certain circumstances, graphic decision aids may produce uncertain or even misleading conclusions about the results of your study. Difficulties in interpretation are most likely to arise if your intervention produced small effects or if baseline trend or variability was pronounced. Problems in interpretation also may arise if your data are strongly serially dependent (Jones, Weinrott, & Vaught, 1978). The presence of serial dependency in a time series means that scores occurring later in the series are predictable from scores occurring earlier in the series (see Hartmann, Gottman, Jones, Gardner, Kazdin, & Vaught, 1980). Issues concerning serial dependency are complex, controversial, and generally beyond the scope of this book.

Briefly, controversy exists regarding whether or not serial dependency is a common property of individual subject behavioral data (cf. Gottman & Glass, 1978; and Huitema, in press), and whether statistical techniques proposed to deal with the problems caused by serial dependency are useful for

---

[3]An improved estimate of the level for a condition — one that takes into account all the scores within the condition — is given by the least squares approach. See, for example, Parsonson and Baer (1978, p. 131), and Table 10-1 (note b).

the brief time series typically obtained by behavior therapists (e.g., Hartmann et al., 1980). There is agreement, however, regarding how to detect serial dependency in time-series data; and fortunately, the method is not difficult. Serial dependency is detected by calculating a correlation coefficient called the autocorrelation coefficient. If you have ever calculated an ordinary correlation between two variables, for example, between the target behavior scores obtained by two observers over a number of sessions (see Section 2 of Chapter 8), you will find it easy to calculate an autocorrelation. The only important differences between the two types of correlations are in forming pairs of scores for an autocorrelation. For example, in the intervention time series for Treatment A shown in Figure 9-8, the pairs of scores used in calculating the autocorrelation that would be used to predict adjacent scores are (3,7), (7,6), (6,15), and (15,9). Thus, with the exception of the first and last scores (3 and 9), each score enters into two score pairs, once as the second member of a pair, and then as the first member of a pair. For the pairs of scores given above, $r_1$ (called the lag one autocorrelation coefficient) is essentially zero (−.03). This autocorrelation indicates that the value of a score cannot be predicted from knowledge of the immediately prior score, and strongly suggests that the data are *not* serially dependent. More information on assessing serial dependency is given in Bloom and Fischer (1982), in Hartmann et al. (1980), and in Wallace and Elder (1980). More technically complex discussions are given in Gottman (1981) and in McCleary and Hay (1980). If the meaning of your data is unclear because your treatment produced a weak effect, because of excess baseline variability or trend, or because of substantial serial dependency, you may want to conduct a formal test of statistical significance.

## The Controversy Over Statistical Tests

It may come as a surprise to you to learn that scientists disagree over whether or not it is *ever* appropriate to apply formal statistical tests to individual subject data. But be assured, they do disagree on just that question. Proponents argue that statistical testing is an objective and replicable alternative to the subjectivity and unreliability of visual appraisals, and that statistical tests may be particularly critical when it is important to detect small changes, or when the data are problematic for any of the reasons previously described, such as serial dependency. More extensive presentations of the pro-statistical position can be found in Hartmann et al. (1980), Kazdin (1982b, Chapter 10) and in Kratochwill and Brody (1978).

Opponents argue that the insensitivity of visual analysis is a blessing, as it rightly focuses our attention on effective interventions that produce socially important changes (Baer, 1977). Other opponents allege that statistical tests interfere with investigators' contact with their data, result in inflexibility or otherwise inconveniently designed studies, and promote undesirable data aggregation (see summary by Kazdin, 1982b). These points are argued forcefully in detail, and with some eloquence, by Johnston and Pennypacker (1980), by Michael (1974), and by Sidman (1960).

## Selection of a Statistical Test

If, after examining your data and considering the pros and cons of statistical testing you believe that a formal statistical test should be applied to your data, read this section. We will not describe how to conduct such a test, but we will (a) familiarize you with the general statistical testing procedures available, (b) help you select an appropriate technique from among those available, and (c) direct you to key references that will show you how to apply the procedure that you select.

There are some six different statistical approaches from which to choose. These approaches vary along a number of dimensions, including (a) the designs for which they are applicable, (b) whether and how they are affected by trends and serial dependency in the data, (c) their data and random assignment requirements, and (d) the difficulty of their calculations. Table 10-2 summarizes the tests' ratings on these dimensions and also provides key references for each technique. Ironically, the less complex techniques are likely to be inappropriate for just the kinds of data that require statistical analysis (e.g., data with baseline trends and serial dependency). A partial exception is the split-middle or celeration line technique. This technique is simple, relatively unaffected by trends and serial dependency, and is applicable to a wide range of designs. It has the added advantage of being illustrated in a number of general references, including Bloom and Fischer (1982) and Kazdin (1982b). The split-middle technique may serve you well if your data require statistical analysis.

If you think a statistical approach is suitable for your study, examine the techniques described in Table 10-2. Narrow your choices to the two techniques most appropriate for your study. Read one or more of the key references for each technique and tentatively select the technique that seems best suited to your unique problems. Before making a final decision, check with your instructor. *Note:* If you conduct a formal statistical analysis, be careful not to equate statistical significance with social importance or validity (see Section 2 of Chapter 9).

**Table 10-2.** Selected Statistical Techniques for Evaluating Individual Subject Data

| Technique | Especially Suited for | Special Requirements | Difficulty | Key References |
|---|---|---|---|---|
| Comparison of overlap (Stewart Charts) | Detecting changes between adjacent phases even with few unstable baseline data points | Absence of baseline trend and serial dependency | Easy | Darlington (1973); Gottman & Leiblum (1974) |
| Split-middle (Celeration line) | Detecting changes between adjacent phases | Absence of extreme baseline trends; may also be affected by some forms of serial dependency | Easy | Gingerick & Feyerharm (1979); White (1977) |
| Revusky $R_n$ test | Multiple baseline designs | Four or more independent baselines; treatment assigned to baselines in random order | Easy | Revusky (1967); Wolery & Billingsley (1982) |
| $t$ and $F$ tests | Detecting changes between two or more phases | Absence of baseline trends and serial dependency | Moderate | Hartmann (1974); Shine (1977) |
| Randomization tests | Multiple treatments designs, even in the presence of trend and serial dependency | Treatment conditions randomly assigned to conditions of administration | Moderate | Edington (1982); Kratochwill & Levin (1980) |
| Box-Jenkins (Time-series analysis) | Detecting changes between adjacent phases, even in the presence of trend and serial dependency | Multiple data points, particularly in the baseline phase | Difficult | Gottman (1981); McCleary & Hay (1980) |

*Note:* Based in part on Kazdin (1982b, Table 10-1.)

## Probe Questions for Chapter 10, Section 2

1. Name two descriptive statistics that are particularly useful in interpreting time-series data.

2. Graph a target behavior that shows the following changes from baseline to treatment: (a) a change in level from +4 to +8, and (b) a change in slope from −3 to +3.

3. What is serial dependency? How can you tell if time-series data are serially dependent?

4. On what basis should the decision be made to omit formal statistical analysis of the target behavior?

5. Describe the advantages and disadvantages of using statistical tests with individual subject data.

6. What six classes of statistical analysis may be appropriate for individual subject data? Which one(s) can be used by someone with a modest degree of sophistication in statistics? Which one(s) are relatively unaffected by serially dependent data?

# Behavioral Objectives for Chapter 10, Section 3

*This section will help you to prepare a written report of your treatment project, and will offer suggestions for terminating your therapeutic relationships on a positive note.*

## SECTION 3. WRITING A FINAL REPORT AND PROMOTING GOOD WILL

### *Writing a Report*

Now that you have collected, graphed, and analyzed the data on treatment-related changes in your child-client's behavior, you are ready to communicate your results to other people. You will want to do so with some detail and precision. Because it is preferable to have a permanent record of the behavior management program and its results, you will probably wish to write a final report. This report may meet an academic requirement or may simply be submitted as a courtesy to the school or agency in which your child-client is enrolled. Agency staff members or volunteers may decide to carry on the treatment effort you initiated. Therefore, a copy of your procedures, sample data sheets, and results and suggestions will prove helpful to them. This concluding section presents a format to use in preparing a final report and suggests some actions you might take to leave your clients and your instructor with a positive impression of your work.

The completed report should consist of the following sections:

*Introduction*, including an anecdotal description of the child-client and his or her behavioral deficits or excesses and a brief description of other published behavior modification programs dealing with the same target behavior.

*Method*, precisely describing the target behavior and the goals of your treatment program. The Method section also should include the assessment and treatment procedures you employed and the experimental design used (e.g., reversal or changing criterion design). Also include plans for collecting follow-up data.

*Results*, describing the rate or other measure of the target behavior during the various phases of the project. The Results section should also describe the reliability of your data and the method used to determine reliability.

*Discussion*, summarizing the results obtained, the probable reasons for successes and failures, and suggested treatment program improvements.

*References*, listing in alphabetical order by first author surname each work cited in the report. Table 10-3 illustrates the sequence and content of the various sections of a report. Appendix C contains a sample report submitted by two of our students who used the first edition of *Child Behavior Analysis and Therapy* as the text in a course on child behavior change.

**Table 10-3.** The Behavior Modification Program Report

I. *Introduction*

    A. Anecdotal description of the child (to protect his or her privacy, use a disguised name for the child in your classroom report).

        1. Child's age and gender, general physical description.

        2. Child's family, siblings, the family's socioeconomic status, and anything remarkable about them or their situation (as long as this does not violate their anonymity).

        3. Child's reported behavior deficits or excesses.

        4. Who referred the child for help; their description of the problem.

        5. Previous attempts to modify this child's behavior and how they fared.

    B. Description of published behavior modification treatment programs dealing with the same or similar target behaviors. Cite each reference by author's surname and the date of publication — e.g., (Brown, 1969).

    C. Brief explanation of the intervention tactic employed and the reasons for using this rather than another technique — e.g., "Because Kara had never dressed herself, we devised a modification program for her which included modeling, verbal instructions, and shaping procedures."

II. *Method*

    A. The design used to demonstrate the effectiveness of the treatment program — e.g., "A multiple baseline design was used with separate baselines for socks, pants, shirt, and shoes. Throughout the project Kara's success at putting on her shirt, pants, socks, and shoes was observed each morning. Following a week of baseline observations, treatment was implemented for one item of clothing each week in the order described."

    B. Precise and complete definitions of the target behavior, including behavioral descriptions of instances and of noninstances of target behavior.

    C. The recording and scoring procedures used. Include a sample data sheet.

    D. Procedures followed in tracking the target behavior. Include the setting, time of day, and weekly schedule of data collection.

    E. Treatment procedures employed. This description should be sufficiently detailed to allow a reader to replicate your program. Include samples of training materials used if possible.

    F. Plans for Future Treatment sessions or for collection of Follow-up data.

III. *Results*

    A. Interobserver reliability values obtained. Describe how and when reliability checks were made. Explain reasons for low interobserver reliabilities, if necessary.

    B. Explain, if necessary, how statements regarding treatment effectiveness must be qualified.

    C. Respective rates of target performance during program phases, and results of your data analysis. Present the data in graphic form and accompany them with a description of the changes observed. Also point out unusual circumstances, such as the child's being ill, that accompanied any remarkable fluctuations in behavior.

    D. Supplementary data, such as follow-up or generalization data, or the results of caretaker interviews, if available.

IV. *Discussion*

    A. Summary of results obtained.

    B. Probable reasons for the relative success or failure of the treatment program.

    C. Suggestions for increasing the program's effectiveness.

    D. Suggestions for caretakers. How can they maintain a child's improved behavior and teach him or her additional desirable behaviors? (Remember to offer only realistic advice; impractical solutions only discourage caretakers.)

    E. Your plans, if any, for additional future work with this child.

V. *References*

    Include here citations to all papers to which you have referred in the body of your report. The most frequently used citation style used is that recommended by the American Psychological Association's *Publication Manual*, 3rd ed. (1983), and complete instructions for preparation of reference lists appear in that manual. A sample (fictitious) reference is as follows:

    Brown, G. D. (1972). Treatment of a child's fear of dogs using an extinction procedure. *Journal of Experimental Child Behavior Analysis*, **43**, 101-113.

    In this format the periodical's volume number is underlined to indicate boldface type, and the inclusive page numbers are presented last in the citation. The references are not numbered, and appear alphabetically by the first author's surname.

---

If you have followed this manual's instructions faithfully, you will already have written a complete description of the target behavior and of the data-recording procedures you used, as well as of the procedures followed during the baseline and treatment phases of the project. This is nearly all the information you need for the Method section of your report.

You also will have calculated interobserver reliabilities and completed one or more graphs displaying the course of the target behavior during all phases of the program. Consequently, a large part of your Results section is ready. You need only write a short Introduction, perhaps edit your Method section, calculate descriptive statistics and describe the results as concisely as possible, discuss the merits and limitations of your program, and your report is completed. Published models for behavioral modification treatment reports can be found in the *Journal of Applied Behavior Analysis* and *Behavior Therapy*.

## Thank You and Goodbye

When you converse with the persons involved in your program for the very last time, be sure that you give them a complete description of the results of the program (also supply them with your written report, if that is available) and that you express your appreciation for their cooperation. If the child is able to understand, you will probably want to explain the treatment results to her also and to show her the improvements she has made. As we pointed out initially, every treatment program involves costs as well as benefits, and the client and caretakers have borne some of those costs. Show them that you recognize this fact and are grateful. It is very important to treat school personnel and members of the community in such a way that they will be willing to work with your successors — the students who will conduct behavior modification projects in the future.

Just one more word on closing shop. Please be sure that any equipment you used is returned, repaired if necessary, and cleaned and ready for use by the next generation of students. Whether or not your department will remember you with pleasure will depend in part upon how you handled the program termination.

## Epilogue

Now at last we come to the end of the lengthy process of child behavior therapy. If you have just completed your first such project, you will have realized that much additional supervised experience will be required before you can function independently as a professional therapist. You will have learned, perhaps to your surprise, that a great number and diversity of skills are necessary. Well-prepared therapists must have compassion and concern for their clients, must make sometimes painful and far-reaching decisions regarding the lives of others, and must acquire the human relations skills necessary to the success of any intervention program. Therapists must know the relevant state and federal statutes and regulations governing treatment, and must be aware of the ethical guidelines for their profession. In addition, therapists must be scholars — readers of the therapy research literature — so that they can devise the most powerful treatment method available to help their clients. They must be able to assess problems accurately, observe reliably, and determine whether or not their treatments have had the desired effects. Furthermore, each therapist must upon occasion become a writer able to describe his or her procedures and results clearly for the instruction and information of readers. Scholar, humane practitioner, scientist, and writer — the behavior therapist must be all of these. We hope that this book has helped the reader progress at least a little way toward these ambitious goals.

## Probe Questions for Chapter 10, Section 3

1. *Describe the various sections of a written treatment program report and the information each section should contain.*

2. *What steps can you take to insure that the child, his teachers and family, and your sponsoring department will all remember you fondly?*

# APPENDIX A
# Initial Interview of Caretaker

The interview consists both of the culturally prescribed social behavior greeting (polite interaction, and farewell) and of questions aimed to detect and explore behavior problems. The interviewee must be made at ease and helped to feel comfortable when discussing problematic situations, and must be encouraged to provide all of the relevant information possible. The interviewer must convince the interviewee of his or her sympathetic interest in the welfare of both the child and the adult caretakers. Social skills are a necessity for an effective interviewer. The following description of interview components has been adapted, with permission, from Iwata, Wong, Riordan, Dorsey, and Lau (1982).

1. Clinician greets the client and chats briefly to make the client feel at ease. If necessary, the clinician should introduce herself and explain that she is a student, which program she is in, and what educational institution she attends.

2. Asks for needed biographical information regarding the child, such as age, grade in school, name of school, siblings, marital status of parents, etc.

3. Asks interviewee to describe the child's major behavioral problems, and inquires about other types of problems with academic work, social behavior at home and at school, relations with adults, relations with siblings, classmates and other peers, health problems, habit problems regarding sleep, eating, or elimination, speech problems, and any others volunteered by the interviewee.

4. Requests interviewee to rank the major problems in priority.

5. Asks interviewee to provide an examplar of the problem in behavioral terms.

6. Asks for additional specific instances and noninstances of the problem.

7. Summarizes interviewee's description as a particular, observable, and quantifiable behavior, and asks for feedback on accuracy of description.

8. Determines possible origins and frequency and concomitants of the target behavior. When and where did interviewee first notice the problem? What other events or responses appear to covary with the target behavior? What times, places, events, or persons are associated with occurrence of the problem?

9. Identifies current consequences. What happens after the behavior occurs or not, and who provides these consequences?

10. Asks for description of any prior attempts to deal with the problem. How successful were they?

11. Summarizes discussion of the problem, requests confirmation, and asks for additions, if any.

12. Asks interviewee to specify criteria for successful problem solution in order to determine the treatment goal.

13. Asks for description of child's strengths and skills, and for potential reinforcers (see Appendix B for a reinforcer checklist).

14. If feasible, conducts direct observation of child and interviewee interacting in order to help confirm target behavior and treatment goal selection.

15. Describes potential treatment program and solicits interviewee reactions and suggestions.

16. Describes referral possibilities in the community, if appropriate, and alternative sources of help for the child.

17. Schedules next appointment for review of treatment plan and possibly for further information from interviewee.

18. Thanks interviewee for her time, escorts her from the room, and bids her farewell.

Finally, a word of caution: Don't become too formal and mechanical in an effort to perform super-professionally as an interviewer. Remember these suggestions by Holland (1970, p. 71): "(This) guide does not suggest the use of a mechanical gathering of information devoid of the rhythm and pace found in the counseling experience. The points covered in the guide are logical in nature and are not intended to place artificial constraints on the counselor or the (interviewee). Neither are they intended as substitutes for the more traditional skills of a sensitive ear or a judicious tongue."

# APPENDIX B

Please indicate (child's name)'s favorite foods and activities on the checklist below. Make a checkmark opposite each item that is this child's particular favorite, then circle the three items you think he likes best of all.

1. *Foods*

_____ brownies
_____ cake: what kind(s)? _____
_____ candy: what kind(s)? _____
_____ chewing gum: what brand(s)? _____
_____ cookies: what kind(s)? _____
_____ fruit: what kind(s)? _____
_____ nuts: what kind(s)? _____
_____ popcorn
_____ popsicles: what flavor(s)? _____
_____ sugar-coated cereals: what brand(s)? _____
_____ other favorite foods (please specify) _____
_____

2. *Drinks*

_____ flavored milk: which flavor(s)? _____
_____ Koolaid®: what flavor(s)? _____
_____ milk
_____ milkshakes: what flavor(s)? _____
_____ soft drinks: what kind(s)? _____

Are there any foods or drinks this child is allergic to or any others he should NOT be given? If so, please specify:
_____

3. *Playing Games and Sports*

_____ boxing
_____ camping
_____ fishing
_____ hide and seek
_____ hiking
_____ hopscotch
_____ hunting
_____ judo
_____ jump rope
_____ playground equipment (swings, climbing equipment, tether ball, seesaws) _____
        favorite(s)?_____
_____ playing baseball or softball
_____ playing football
_____ playing house
_____ playing pool
_____ playing in wading pool
_____ riding in wagon
_____ riding trike or bike
_____ skiing
_____ sledding or tubing
_____ snorkeling
_____ swimming
_____ shooting basketballs
_____ table tennis
_____ tag
_____ watching any of the above sport (please indicate which):_____

Does any physical illness or handicap prevent this child from full participation in sports or games? If so, please specify: _____

4. *Toys*

_____ checkers
_____ chess
_____ constructing models: what kind(s)? _____
_____ construction toys (e.g., Tinker toys™, Lego™): what kind(s)? _____

_____ doing artwork: what kind(s)? _____
_____ playing board games or card games: what kind(s)? _____

_____ playing with cars or trucks
_____ playing with dolls: what kind(s)? _____
_____ operating noise-making or moving toys: what kind(s)? _____
_____ other favorite toys (please specify): _____

5. *Books*

_____ books: favorite types? _____
_____ comics: favorites? _____
_____ magazines: favorites? _____
_____ visit to library

6. *Opportunities to be with Others*

_____ boys
    _____ younger     _____ same age     _____ older
_____ girls
    _____ younger     _____ same age     _____ older
_____ babies
_____ adults
    _____ men     _____ women
_____ Boy or Girl Scouts, Campfire Girls
_____ attending parties
_____ holding parties
favorite companions: _____

7. *Play with or Care for Animals*

_____ birds
_____ cats
_____ dogs
_____ farm animals: what kind(s)? _____
_____ fish
_____ horses
_____ insects: what kind(s)? _____
_____ reptiles
_____ turtles

8. *Travel*

_____ amusement park
_____ aviary
_____ city parks
_____ harbors
_____ lakes and streams

_____ mountains
_____ museums and observatories
_____ store
_____ zoo
_____ other local attractions: what kind(s)? e.g., dairies, mines _____

9. *Music and Dancing*

_____ dancing: what kind(s)? _____
_____ phonograph records or tapes: favorites? _____
_____ playing a musical instrument: type(s)? _____
_____ singing: alone or with others? _____

10. *Hobbies*

_____ collecting: specify _____
_____ gardening
_____ insect, bird, animal, plant identification (specify type): _____

_____ other hobbies (specify): _____

11. _____ watching television: favorite programs? _____

12. _____ attending movies: favorite types of films? _____

13. _____ attending other types of meetings or performances: favorite types?

14. _____ having a room of one's own
    _____ being left alone, quiet

15. _____ helping mother, father, siblings around the house (circle the ones that apply)
    _____ playing with construction tools
    _____ playing with garden equipment
    _____ playing with mother's makeup
    _____ playing with pots and pans

Please remember to circle the three items this child likes best of all.

Thank you for your cooperation. This information will be most helpful in our constructing a program for this child.

# APPENDIX C
## Sample Student Report[1]

## INTRODUCTION

For our study we tried to answer the question, "What are the effects of a running program on disruptive behaviors?" The study was conducted at the Children's Behavior Therapy Unit (henceforth referred to as CBTU) which is a behaviorally oriented treatment facility. The Elementary Unit of CBTU consists of 15 children, 13 boys and 2 girls, ages 9 to 13. They have been referred for a variety of reasons including learning disabilities, behavioral problems, borderline mental retardation, and childhood schizophrenia. The unit we worked in used a token point system, with point cards.

The Winter 1980 copy of *Teaching Exceptional Children* magazine had a description of a program that was run in California with a population very similar to ours both in age and behavioral problems. In the study, the children jogged for 10 minutes before class. Several behaviors were tracked and the frequency was compared with a baseline taken before the running program was started. The behaviors tracked were: hitting/bothering others, name calling/throwing things, yelling/talking out of turn, moving or sitting inappropriately, and refusing to participate or cooperate. The study reported that in a class of 12 boys, the daily mean of disruptive behaviors during baseline was 63.0 as compared with 31.8 on days when the boys had run for 10 minutes before class. The study also reported that the fewest disruptive behaviors occurred the first hour after the 10-minute jog.

As we searched through the literature we could not find any other study that duplicated this one so we decided to try a similar program at CBTU.

---

[1]This appendix contains a lightly edited version of a student project paper entitled, "The effects of running on disruptive behaviors." The paper was submitted by David Malyn and RaMona Hayward as part of the requirements for a course entitled "Child Behavior Change," University of Utah, Spring 1980.

We first selected five children from the Elementary Unit at CBTU on which to take data. The five included one girl and four boys ranging in age from 9 to 12 years old. One was diagnosed childhood schizophrenic, three with learning disabilities, and all had behavioral problems. We did not tell any of the five teachers who the five children were. We decided that since the behaviors "talking out," "not following directions," and "not paying attention" were already being tracked on the (token) point cards, we would use these as the disruptive behaviors to be tracked for our study rather than use the five behaviors tracked in the published study.

We had the class run between 11:20 and 11:30 a.m., right after recess. After running, the children went inside for a general knowledge session using discrete trial learning. Some of the areas covered during the session include geography, logic, calendar skills, anatomy, analogies, and synonyms. The teachers continued to mark point cards as usual; however, we gave each of them a red pen and told them to mark points with it during the general knowledge sessions. We also took several random samples of four target behaviors on each of the five target children. During these observations, we used an interval recording system, each interval being 15 seconds long and the sample lasting 5 minutes. A 5-minute sample was done on each target child each day that the random samples were taken.

## METHOD

### Design

For this project, a reversal design was used. Five children were targeted and their behavior tracked for the study but the entire class participated in the running program. Baseline lasted for 10 days and the children did not run during this time.

For the first phase of treatment, a running program was started. The children were required to run or walk around the outdoor track for the full 10 minutes, and data were recorded on the number of laps completed (see Table 1). There was an indoor track available if the weather would not permit outdoor running so that the program could continue uninterrupted. The running session started daily at 11:20 a.m., Monday through Friday. Following the 10 minute run, the children returned to their classroom at 11:30 a.m.

During reversal, the children went back to baseline conditions — no running before class. After four days of reversal, the second treatment phase was begun. This second treatment phase followed the same procedures as the first treatment phase.

The children were asked to wear comfortable clothes, and sneakers or running shoes. A note was also sent home to the parents to inform them of the program and to obtain their consent (see Table 2). Social reinforcement for

**Table 1.** Data Sheet Used to Keep Track of the Number of Laps Completed Daily by Each of the Children.

| Subject | Laps | HR* | Subject | Laps | HR* |
|---|---|---|---|---|---|
| Carl | | | Carl | | |
| Junior | | | Junior | | |
| Gus | | | Gus | | |
| Sandon | | | Sandon | | |
| Jennifer | | | Jennifer | | |
| Matt | | | Matt | | |
| Brice | | | Brice | | |
| Scott Z | | | Scott Z | | |
| Darin | | | Darin | | |
| Scott H | | | Scott H | | |
| Rob | | | Rob | | |
| Dawna | | | Dawna | | |
| DeWane | | | DeWane | | |
| Steve | | | Steve | | |
| Shawn | | | Shawn | | |
| | | | | | |

*It was our intention to record a daily heart rate for each child after the 10 minute jog. This was not done after we were told by a doctor that the jogging was not enough physical exertion to be concerned with.

running came from the children's peer group as the result of a chart that was placed in the classroom. Each child's name was listed on the chart, and next to each name was recorded the distance (cumulative) in miles that the child had run. Reinforcement was also given in the form of awards the children could earn for completion of 10, 25, and 50 miles. Each child could earn one of these awards.

## Measurement

Target behaviors were tracked during the general knowledge class which was conducted immediately after the run (11:30 a.m.). Talking out, not following directions, and not paying attention were the behaviors tracked by the teachers. They recorded these and other disruptive behaviors with a red pen. The teachers were not informed who the children were that were being tracked for the study, nor which of the disruptive behaviors would be used in the data analysis. They did know about the program and what we were attempting to show.

Three data takers did random checks of attending behavior. This was done using a data collection sheet (see Table 3) and a stop-watch. Attending, nonat-

**Table 2.** Letter Sent Home to Obtain Permission for the Program from the Parents.

Dear Parents,

We would like your permission for your child to take part in a running program, here at CBTU. Your child will need a pair of sneakers which he/she can either wear or bring to school.

We will be running every day starting Monday, April 21, 1980.

Name: _____

Date: _____

If you have any questions, please feel free to call.

---

tending, out of seat, and delay were the behaviors recorded on an interval recording method. These data takers reached 85% reliability during interobserver reliability checks before their data were used for the study.

Following are the operational definitions for the four observer tracked behaviors (1-4) and the three teacher-tracked behaviors (5-7) that were recorded.

1. *Attending*: Physical manipulation or eye direction toward work objects or teacher or speaker in an adaptive and specified manner for greater than or equal to 10 consecutive seconds per 15 second interval.

2. *Nonattending*: Physical manipulation of or eye direction toward objects or teacher as per attending definition for less than 9.99 consecutive seconds per 15 second interval.

3. *Out of Seat*:[2] Neither buttock on the seat of the chair, either foot above the level of the desk or in the desk, head below the level of the desk or on the desk top, and/or the chair more than one foot away from the desk.

4. *Delay*:[2] Waiting for help that involves raising hand for at least 30 seconds (or two intervals) while being quiet and appropriate.

5. *Talking Out*: Speaking without permission during sessions. Talking to friend when working in workbooks.

6. *Not Paying Attention*: Eyes oriented toward other than assigned material or stimulus.

7. *Not Following Directions*: Not starting a task within 10 seconds of their presentation and/or not continuing to perform in an adaptive and specified manner once the 10 second limit has been given.

---

[2]These data in Numbers 3 and 4 were not used in the remaining part of the study.

**Table 3.** Data Sheet Used During Five Minute Interval Data Collection by the Observers.

REL _____

DATE _____    ROOM ___    OBSERVER _____    TIME START _____

TIME END _____

SETTING: INDIV. OR GP ACTIVITY:   ANN.   TRANS.   READ.   MATH.
        COMM.   ACAD.   OTHER

CODE: A = ATTENDING   N = NONATTENDING
      + + DELAY   O.S. = OUT OF SEAT   √ = REINFORCEMENT

ATTENDING DATA IS TAKEN ON INSEAT CHILDREN. SCORE O.S. WHEN CHILD IS NOT
IN SEAT. MARK THE DESIGNATED CODE AT THE END OF THE INTERVAL FOR THE
EXHIBITED BEHAVIOR(S).

| Name 0 | | | 1 | | | 2 | | | 3 | | | 4 | | |
|---|---|---|---|---|---|---|---|---|---|---|---|---|---|---|---|
| | | | | | | | | | | | | | | | |
| | | | | | | | | | | | | | | | |
| | | | | | | | | | | | | | | | |
| | | | | | | | | | | | | | | | |
| | | | | | | | | | | | | | | | |
| | | | | | | | | | | | | | | | |
| | | | | | | | | | | | | | | | |
| | | | | | | | | | | | | | | | |
| | | | | | | | | | | | | | | | |
| | | | | | | | | | | | | | | | |
| | | | | | | | | | | | | | | | |
| | | | | | | | | | | | | | | | |
| | | | | | | | | | | | | | | | |
| | | | | | | | | | | | | | | | |
| | | | | | | | | | | | | | | | |

# RESULTS

We began taking baseline data on teacher-tracked behaviors on April 4 and this phase lasted 10 sessions until April 17. Our first treatment lasted 10 sessions, the reversal 4 sessions, and our second treatment phase lasted four days.

Teacher-collected data on Not Paying Attention, Not Following Directions, and Talking Out do show a change during the study. (See Figure C-1.) Following is a list of the average number of disruptive behaviors per day, for all five target children, that occurred during each phase of our study: Baseline, $X = 8.1$; Treatment 1, $X = 5.8$; Reversal, $X = 9.5$; and Treatment 2, $X = 4.0$.

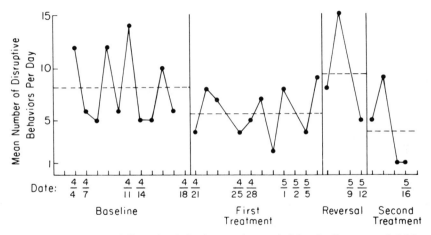

**Figure C-1.** Mean rate of disruption behavior per class period for the five targeted children. Dashed lines indicate condition means.

Before we began to take observer data we were trained to 85% reliability, using percentage agreement, by the CBTU Data Taker, Jane Kesler. We began observer data collection on April 14 and we took random samples of attending throughout the study. We also got data on attending behavior from Ms. Kesler when she did random probes.

Our data show no change in attending behavior during the first three phases of our study. The fourth phase (the second treatment phase) did show a change but it was not in the desired direction. Below is the mean of the attending samples across the five target children, during each phase of the study: Baseline, $X = 68.6\%$; Treatment 1, $X = 68.5\%$; Reversal, $X = 69.0\%$; Treatment 2, $X = 51.2\%$.

At the completion of our study we asked the three permanent teachers in the classroom if they had noticed any change in the behavior of the class while the treatment was in effect. Two of the three teachers said they did not notice any change, and the third said she did notice a change but that it lasted only about an hour. The room supervisor said that she wanted to see the results of our study before she decided whether or not to continue the treatment program.

## DISCUSSION

During this treatment program we were able to effectively change the number of occurrences of disruptive behavior. Those behaviors were Talking Out, Not Paying Attention, and Not Following Directions. The means during baseline and reversal were 8.1 and 9.5, respectively; and during treatment the mean dropped to 5.8 for the first treatment phase and to 4.0 during the second treatment phase. The random observations, usually done three times each week, showed no change in attending behavior over time during the first three phases of our study. During the final treatment phase, attending behavior dropped. This drop may have been caused by a decreased interest in school on the part of the target children. We stopped taking data on May 16 and school was to end on May 23 for a one-week vacation. This ending of school could have had a confounding effect on the attending behavior.

The effectiveness of the treatment in reducing the disruptive behaviors might have been due to the children being tired out from the physical activity of running. The effects of the treatment program seemed to last about one hour according to both the magazine article on which our study was based and one of the teachers at CBTU. This effect lasting only about one hour may be about the length of time needed for a child's energy level to come back up to his normal level. Once this normal level is regained, then disruptive behaviors go back up.

If this treatment program were run again, several changes might make this program more effective and might allow certain treatment effects to be more visible. Instead of tracking behaviors on only five members of the class, the entire group should be tracked. In this way, the treatment may show to be more effective for certain types of behavior problems. The five children that were chosen for the project consisted of three different behavior types: a diagnosed childhood schizophrenic with very low attending behavior, three children with behavior problems who also have very low attending behavior, and one child with behavior problems but with very high attending behavior. This sample was too small to show any significant differences between the three types. Also, if the entire class had been tracked for disruptive behaviors, there might not have been so much variability in the data. This would have made it easier to determine if the running program is more effective for a particular behavior problem.

A final change would require the tracking of behaviors not only during the class immediately following the 10 minute run, but also during class periods throughout the day to see if changes in behavior occurs after the run that do not occur during the rest of the day. This would also help to determine how long the possible effects will last after the group runs for 10 minutes.

If this program is continued, a determination should be made of the class that requires the greatest degree of attention from the children. The running program should then be implemented just before this class period. If the child can attend better, with less disruptions, he might get reinforcement because of better understanding of the subject material being studied.

## BIBLIOGRAPHY

Allen, J. I. Jogging can modify disruptive behaviors. *Teaching Exceptional Children*, Winter 1980.

# REFERENCES

Addison, R.M., & Homme, L. The reinforcing event (RE) menu. *NSPI Journal*, 1966 **1**, 8–9.

Alexander, J.F., Barton, C., Schievo, R.S., & Parsons, B.V. Systems-behavioral intervention with families of delinquents: Therapist characteristics, family behavior, and outcome. *Journal of Consulting and Clinical Psychology*, 1976, **44**, 656–664.

Alexander, R., Corbett, T., & Smigel, J. The effects of individual and group consequences on school attendance and curfew violations with predelinquent adolescents. *Journal of Applied Behavior Analysis*, 1976, **9**, 221–226.

American Psychological Association. *Standards for providers of psychological services*. Washington, DC: American Psychological Association, 1974.

American Psychological Association. *Ethical standards of psychologists*. Washington, DC: American Psychological Association, 1979.

American Psychological Association. *Publication manual of the American Psychological Association* (3rd ed.). Washington, DC: American Psychological Association, 1983.

Anastasi, A. *Psychological testing* (4th ed.). New York: Macmillan, 1976.

Apolito, P.M., & Sulzer-Azaroff, B. *Lemon-juice therapy: The control of chronic rumination in a twelve-year-old profoundly retarded female*. Unpublished manuscript, University of Massachusetts, 1981.

Aragona, J., Cassady, J., & Drabman, R.S. Treating overweight children through parental training and contingency contracting. *Journal of Applied Behavior Analysis*, 1975, **8**, 269–278.

Arnold, S.C., & Forehand, R. A comparison of cognitive training and response cost in modifying cognitive styles of impulsive children. *Cognitive Therapy and Research*, 1978, **2**, 183–187.

Arrington, R.E. Time-sampling studies of child behavior. *Psychological Monographs*, 1939, **51**(2).

Arrington, R.E. Time sampling in studies of social behavior: A critical review of techniques and results with research suggestions. *Psychological Bulletin*, 1943, **40**, 81–124.

Association for Advancement of Behavior Therapy. *Ethical issues in human services*. Author, 1977.

Atkeson, B.M., & Forehand, R. Parent behavioral training: An examination of studies using multiple outcome measures. *Journal of Abnormal Child Psychology*, 1978, **6**, 449–460.

Atthowe, J.M., Jr., & Krasner, L. Preliminary report on the application of contingent reinforcement procedures: Token economy on a "chronic" psychiatric ward. *Journal of Abnormal Psychology*, 1968, **73**, 37–43.

Axelrod, S. Comparison of individual and group contingencies in two special classes. *Behavior Therapy*, 1973, **4**, 83–90.

Azrin, N.H., & Besalel, V.A. *How to use overcorrection*. Lawrence, KS: H & H Enterprises, 1980.

Azrin, N.H., & Foxx, R.M. *Toilet training in less than a day*. New York: Simon & Schuster, 1974.

Azrin, N.H., Gottlieb, L., Highart, L., Wesolowski, M.D., & Rehn, T. Eliminating self-injurious behavior by educative procedures. *Behavior Research and Therapy*, 1975, **13**, 101–111.

Bacon-Prue, A., Blount, R., Hosey, C., & Drabman, R.S. The public posting of photographs as a reinforcer for bedmaking in an institutional setting. Unpublished manuscript, University of Mississippi Medical Center, 1981.

Baer, D.M. A technique of social reinforcement for the study of child behavior: Behavior avoiding reinforcement withdrawal. *Child Development*, 1962, **33**, 847–858.

Baer, D.M. Some remedial uses of the reinforcement contingency. In J.M. Shlien (Ed.), *Research in psychotherapy* (Vol. 3, pp.3–20). Washington, DC: American Psychological Association, 1968.

Baer, D.M. Reviewer's comment: Just because its reliable doesn't mean that you can use it. *Journal of Applied Behavior Analysis*, 1977, **10**, 117–119.

Baer, D.M. How to plan for generalization. Lawrence, KS: H & H Enterprises, 1981.

Baer, D.M., & Wolf, M.M. The entry into natural communities of reinforcement. Paper presented at the meetings of the American Psychological Association, Washington, D.C., September 1967.

Baer, D.M., & Wolf, M.M. Recent examples of behavior modification in preschool settings. In C. Neuringer & J.L. Michael (Eds.), *Behavior modification in clinical psychology* (pp. 10–25). New York: Appleton-Century-Crofts, 1970.

Baer, D.M., Wolf, M.M., & Risley, T.R. Some current dimensions of applied behavior analysis. *Journal of Applied Behavior Analysis*, 1968, **1**, 91–97.

Baer, D.M., Rowbury, T.G., & Goetz, E.M. Behavioral traps in the preschool: A proposal for research. In A.D. Pick (Ed.), *Minnesota symposia on child psychology* (Vol. 10, pp. 3–27). Minneapolis: University of Minnesota Press, 1976.

Bailey, J., & Meyerson, L. Vibration as a reinforcer with a profoundly retarded child. *Journal of Applied Behavior Analysis*, 1969, **2**, 135–137.

Ballard, K.D., & Glynn, T. Behavioral self-management in story writing with elementary school children. *Journal of Applied Behavior Analysis*, 1975, **8**, 387–398.

Bandura, A. *Principles of behavior modification*. New York: Holt, Rinehart & Winston, 1969.

Bandura, A. *Social learning theory*. Englewood Cliffs, NJ: Prentice-Hall, 1977.

Bandura, A., Grusec, J., & Menlove, F.L. Vicarious extinction of avoidance behavior. *Journal of Personality and Social Psychology*, 1967, **5**, 16–23.

Barlow, D.H., & Hayes, S.C. Alternating treatments design: One strategy for comparing the effects of two treatments in a single subject. *Journal of Applied Behavior Analysis*, 1979, **12**, 199–210.

Barton, E.S., Guess, D.G., Garcia, E., & Baer, D.M. Improvement of retardates' mealtime behaviors by time-out procedures using multiple baseline techniques. *Journal of Applied Behavior Analysis*, 1970, **3**, 77–84.

Barrish, H., Saunders, M., & Wolf, M. Good behavior game: Effects of individual contingencies for group consequences on disruptive behavior in the classroom. *Journal of Applied Behavior Analysis*, 1969, **2**, 110–124.

Bassett, J.E., & Blanchard, E.B. The effect of the absence of close supervision on the use of response cost in a prison token economy. *Journal of Applied Behavior Analysis*, 1977, **10**, 375–379.

Baum, C.G., Forehand, R., & Zegiob, L.E. A review of observer reactivity in adult-child interactions. *Journal of Behavioral Assessment*, 1979, **1**, 167–178.

Beck, A.T. The development of depression: A cognitive model. In R. Friedman & M. Katz (Eds.), *The psychology of depression: Contemporary theory and research*. Washington, DC: V.H. Winston, 1974.

Berk, R.A. Generalizability of behavioral observations: A clarification of interobserver agreement and interobserver reliability. *American Journal of Mental Deficiency*, 1979, **83**, 460-472.

Bernal, M.E., Williams, D.E., Miller, W.H., & Reagor, P.A. The use of videotape feedback and operant learning principles in management of deviant children. In R. Rubin, H. Feinsterheim, J. Henderson, & L. Ullmann (Eds.), *Advances in behavior therapy*. New York: Academic Press, 1972.

Bijou, S.W., & Baer, D.M. *Child development: A systematic and empirical theory* (Vol. 1). New York: Appleton-Century-Crofts, 1961.

Bijou, S.W., & Baer, D.M. Operant methods in child behavior and development. In W.K. Honig (Ed.), *Operant behavior: Areas of research and application*. New York: Appleton-Century-Crofts, 1966.

Bijou, S.W., Peterson, R.F., & Ault, M.H. A method to integrate descriptive and experimental field studies at the level of data and empirical concepts. *Journal of Applied Behavior Analysis*, 1968, **1**, 175-191.

Bijou, S.W., Peterson, R.F., Harris, F.R., Allen, K.E., & Johnston, M.S. Methodology for experimental studies of young children in natural settings. *Psychological Record*, 1969, **19**, 177-210.

Bitgood, S.C., Crowe, M.J., Suarez, Y., & Peters, R.D. Immobilization: Effects and side effects on stereotyped behavior in children. *Behavior Modification*, 1980, **4**, 187-208.

Blanchard, E.B. Relative contributions of modeling, informational influences and physical contact in the extinction of phobic behavior. *Journal of Abnormal Psychology*, 1970, **76**, 55-61.

Blechman, E.A. Family problem-solving training. *American Journal of Family Therapy*, 1980, **8**, 3-21.

Bloom, M., & Fischer, J. *Evaluating practice: Guidelines for the accountable professional*. Englewood Cliffs, NJ: Prentice-Hall, 1982.

Boer, A.P. Application of a single recording system to the analysis of free-play behavior in autistic children. *Journal of Applied Behavior Analysis*, 1968, **1**, 335-340.

Bostow, D.E., & Bailey, J.B. Modification of severe disruptive and aggressive behavior using brief time-out and reinforcement procedures. *Journal of the Experimental Analysis of Behavior*, 1969, **2**, 31-37.

Boykin, R.A., & Nelson, R.O. The effects of instructions and calculation procedures on observers' accuracy, agreement, and calculation correctness. *Journal of Applied Behavior Analysis*, 1981, **14**, 479-489.

Brennan, R.L. *Elements of generalizability theory*. Iowa City: ACT Publications, 1983.

Broden, M. *Notes on recording and on conducting a basic study*. Unpublished manuscript, University of Kansas, undated.

Broden, M., Bruce, C., Mitchell, M.A., Carter, V., & Hall, R.V. Effects of teacher attention on attending behavior of two boys at adjacent desks. *Journal of Applied Behavior Analysis*, 1970, **3**, 205-211.

Brown, P., & Elliott, R. Control of aggression in a nursery school class. *Journal of Experimental Child Psychology*, 1965, **2**, 103-107.

Brownell, K.D., Colletti, G., Ersner-Hershfield, R., Hershfield, S.M., & Wilson, G.T. Self-control in school children: Stringency and leniency in self-determined and externally imposed performance standards. *Behavior Therapy*, 1977, **8**, 442-455.

Browning, R.A. A same-subject design for simultaneous comparison of these reinforcement contingencies. *Behavior Research and Therapy*, 1967, **5**, 237-243.

Burchard, J.D., & Barrera, F. An analysis of timeout and response cost in a programmed environment. *Journal of Applied Behavior Analysis*, 1972, **5**, 271-282.

Calhoun, K.S., & Lima, P.P. Effects of varying schedules of timeout on high- and low-rate behaviors. *Journal of Behavior Therapy and Experimental Psychiatry*, 1977, **8**, 189-194.

Campbell, D.T., & Fiske, D. Convergent and discriminant validation by the multi-trait, multi-method matrix. *Psychological Bulletin*, 1959, **56**, 81-105.

Campbell, D.T., & Stanley, J.C. *Experimental and quasi-experimental designs for research*. Chicago: Rand McNally, 1963.

Cantor, N.L. *A multi-component training program to teach children social and problem-solving skills*. Unpublished doctoral dissertation, University of Utah, 1980.

Carter, D.B., Patterson, C.J., & Quasebarth, S.J. Development of children's use of plans for self-control. *Cognitive Research and Therapy*, 1979, **3**, 169-177.

Cautela, J.R., & Kostenbaum, R. A reinforcement survey schedule for use in therapy, training, and research. *Psychological Reports*, 1967, **20**, 1115-1130.

Chaplin, J.P. *Dictionary of psychology* (rev. ed.). New York: Dell, 1975.

Christy, P.R. Does use of tangible rewards with individual children affect peer observers? *Journal of Applied Behavior Analysis*, 1975, **8**, 187-198.

Clark, H.B., Greene, B.F., Macrae, J.W., McNees, M.P., Davis, J.L., & Risley, T.R. A parent advice package for family shopping trips: Development and evaluation. *Journal of Applied Behavior Analysis*, 1977, **10**, 605-624.

Clark, H.B., Rowbury, T., Baer, A.M., & Baer, D.M. Time-out as a punishing stimulus in continuous and intermittent schedules. *Journal of Applied Behavior Analysis*, 1973, **6**, 443-455.

Clement, P.W., & Richard, R.C. Identifying reinforcers for children. In E.J. Mash & L.G. Terdal (Eds.), *Behavior therapy assessment* (pp. 207-216). New York: Springer, 1976.

Cohen, E.A., Gelfand, D.M., Dodd, D.K., Jensen, J., & Turner, C. Self-control practices associated with weight loss maintenance in children and adolescents. *Behavior Therapy*, 1980, **11**, 26-37.

Cohen, E.A., Gelfand, D.M., & Hartmann, D.P. Causal reasoning on a function of behavioral consequences. *Child Development*, 1981, **52**, 514-522.

Cohen, H.L. Educational therapy: The design of learning environments. In J.M. Shlien (Ed.), *Research in psychotherapy* (Vol. 3, pp. 21-53). Washington, DC: American Psychological Association, 1968.

Cohen, J. A coefficient of agreement for nominal scales. *Educational and Psychological Measurement*, 1960, **20**, 37-46.

Cole, P.M., & Kazdin, A.E. Critical issues in self instruction training with children. *Child Behavior Therapy*, 1980, **2**, 1-23.

Combs, M.L. & Lahey, B.B. A cognitive social skills training program. *Behavior Modification*, 1981, **5**, 39-60.

Cone, J.D. Psychometric considerations. In M. Hersen & A.S. Bellack (Eds.), *Behavioral assessment* (2nd ed., pp. 38-68). New York: Pergamon Press, 1981.

Cone, J.D. Validity of direct observational assessment. In D.P. Hartmann (Ed.), *Using observers to study behaviors* (pp. 67-79). San Francisco: Jossey-Bass, 1982.

Cone, J.D., & Foster, S.L. Direct observation in clinical psychology. In P.C. Kendall & J.N. Butcher (Eds.), *Handbook of research methods in clinical psychology* (pp. 311-354). New York: John Wiley, 1982.

Cone, J.D., & Sloop, E.W. Parents as agents of change. In W.W. Spradlin & A. Jacobs (Eds.), *The group as agent of change*. New York: Behavioral Publications, 1974.

Cook, T.D., & Campbell, D.T. The design and conduct of quasi-experiments and true experiments in field settings. In M.D. Dunnette (Ed.), *Handbook of industrial and organizational research.* Chicago: Rand McNally, 1976.

Cook, T.D., & Campbell, D.T. (Eds.), *Quasi-experimentation: Design and analysis issues for field settings.* Chicago: Rand McNally, 1979.

Copeland, A.P. Individual difference factors in children's self-management: Toward individualized treatments. In P. Karoly & F.H. Kanfer (Eds.), *Self-management and behavior change: From theory to practice.* New York: Pergamon Press, 1982.

Costello, J., & Ferrer, J. Punishment contingencies for the reduction of incorrect responses during articulation instruction. *Journal of Communication Disorders,* 1976, **9,** 43-61.

Cronbach, L.J., Gleser, G.C., Nanda, H., & Rajaratnam, N. *The dependability of behavioral measurements: Theory of generalizability for scores and profiles.* New York: Wiley, 1972.

Cuvo, A.J. Multiple-baseline design in instructional research: Pitfalls of measurement and procedural advantages. *American Journal of Mental Deficiency,* 1979, **84,** 219-228.

Darlington, R.B. Comparing two groups by simple graphs. *Psychological Bulletin,* 1973, **79,** 110-116.

Davis, A.F., Rosenthal, T.L., & Kelley, J.E. Actual fear cues, prompt therapy, and rationale enhance participant modeling with adolescents. *Behavior Therapy,* 1981, **12,** 536-542.

Deci, E. *Intrinsic motivation.* New York: Plenum, 1975.

Deitz, S.M. An analysis of programming DRL schedules in educational settings. *Behavior Research and Therapy,* 1977, **15,** 103-111.

Deitz, S.M., Slack, D.J., Schwarzmueller, E.B., Wilander, A.P., Weatherly, T.J., & Hilliard, G. Reducing inappropriate behavior in special classrooms by reinforcing average interresponse times: Interval DRL. *Behavior Therapy,* 1978, **9,** 37-46.

Denney, D.R. The effects of exemplary and cognitive models and self-rehearsal in children's interrogative strategies. *Journal of Experimental Psychology,* 1975, **19,** 476-488.

Dineen, J.P., Clark, H.B., & Risley, T.R. Peer tutoring among elementary students: Educational benefits to the tutor. *Journal of Applied Behavior Analysis,* 1977, **10,** 231-238.

Doleys, D.M., Wells, K.C., Hobbs, S.A., Roberts, M.W., & Cartelli, L.M. The effects of social punishment on noncompliance: A comparison with time-out and positive practice. *Journal of Applied Behavior Analysis,* 1976, **9,** 471-482.

Drabman, R.S., & Creedon, D.L. Marking time-out. *Child Behavior Therapy,* 1979, **1,** 99-101.

Drabman, R.S., Hammer, D., & Rosenbaum, R.S. Assessing generalization in behavior modification with children: The generalization map. *Behavioral Assessment,* 1979, **1,** 203-219.

Edgar, R., & Clement, P.W. Teacher-controlled and self-controlled reinforcement with under-achieving, black children. *Child Behavior Therapy,* 1980, **2,** 33-56.

Edgington, E.S. Random assignment and statistical tests for one-subject experiments. *Behavioral Assessment,* 1980, **2,** 19-28.

Edgington, E.S. Nonparametric tests for single-subject multiple schedule experiments. *Behavioral Assessment,* 1982, **4,** 83-91.

Etzel, B.C., & LeBlanc, J.M. The simplest treatment alternative: The law of parsimony applied to choosing appropriate instructional control and errorless-learning procedures for the difficult-to-teach child. *Journal of Autism and Developmental Disorders,* 1979, **9,** 361-382.

Etzel, B.C., LeBlanc, J.M., Schilmoeller, K.J., & Stella, M.E. Stimulus control procedures in the education of young children. In S.W. Bijou & R. Ruez (Eds.), *Contributions of behavior modification to education*. Hillsdale, NJ: Erlbaum, 1981.

Evans, I.M., & Nelson, R.O. Assessment of child behavior problem. In A.R. Ciminero, K.S. Calhoun, & H.E. Adams (Eds.), *Handbook of Behavioral Assessment*. New York: Wiley, 1977.

Eysenck, H.J. Learning theory and behavior therapy, *Journal of Mental Science*, 1959, **195**, 61–75.

Fantuzzo, J.W., & Clement, P.W. Generalizations of the effects of teacher- and self-administered token reinforcers to nontreated students. *Journal of Applied Behavior Analysis*, 1981, **14**, 435–448.

Ferguson, B.F. Preparing young children for hospitalization: A comparison of two methods. *Pediatrics*, 1979, **64**, 656–664.

Ferster, C.B., & Perrott, M.C. *Behavior principles*. New York: Appleton-Century-Crofts, 1968.

Fishbein, J.E., & Wasik, B.H. Effect of the good behavior game on disruptive library behavior. *Journal of Applied Behavior Analysis*, 1981, **14**, 89–93.

Fiske, D.W. *Strategies for personality research*. San Francisco: Jossey-Bass, 1978.

Fleiss, J.L. Measuring nominal scale agreement among many raters. *Psychological Bulletin*, 1971, **76**, 378–382.

Fleiss, J.L. Measuring agreement between two judges on the presence or absence of a trait. *Biometrics*, 1975, **31**, 651–659.

Forehand, R.L., & McMahon, R.J. *Helping the noncompliant child: A clinician's guide to parent training*. New York: Guilford, 1981.

Fowler, S.A., & Baer, D.M. "Do I have to be good all day?" The timing of delayed reinforcement as a factor in generalization. *Journal of Applied Behavior Analysis*, 1981, **14**, 13–24.

Fox, J.E., & Houston, B.K. Efficacy of self-instructional training for reducing children's anxiety in an evaluative situation. *Behavior Research and Therapy*, 1981, **19**, 509–551.

Foxx, R.M., & Azrin, N.H. Restitution: A method of eliminating aggressive disruptive behavior of retarded and brain damaged patients. *Behavior Research and Therapy*, 1972, **10**, 15–27.

Foxx, R.M., & Azrin, N.H. The elimination of autistic self-stimulatory behavior by overcorrection. *Journal of Applied Behavior Analysis*, 1973, **6**, 1–14.

Foxx, R.M., & Shapiro, S.T. The timeout ribbon: A nonexclusionary timeout procedure. *Journal of Applied Behavior Analysis*, 1978, **11**, 125–136.

Frankel, F., Moss, D., Schofield, S., & Simmons, J.Q. Case study: Use of differential reinforcement to suppress self-injurious and aggressive behavior. *Psychological Reports*, 1976, **39**, 843–849.

Freeman, B.J., Moss, D., Somerset, T., & Ritvo, E.R. Thumbsucking in an autistic child overcome by overcorrection. *Journal of Behavior Therapy and Experimental Psychiatry*, 1977, **8**, 211–212.

Friedling, C., & O'Leary, S.G. Effects of self-instructional training on second- and third-grade hyperactive children: A failure to replicate. *Journal of Applied Behavior Analysis*, 1979, **12**, 211–219.

Furman, W., & Drabman, R.S. Methodological issues in child behavior therapy. In M. Hersen, R.M. Eisler, & P.M. Miller (Eds.), *Progress in behavior modification* (Vol. 1). New York: Academic Press, 1981.

Gast, D.L., & Nelson, C.M. Legal and ethical considerations for the use of timeout in special education settings. *The Journal of Special Education*, 1977, **11**, 457–467.

Gelfand, D.M. Social withdrawal and negative emotional states: Behavioral treatment. In B.B. Wolman, J. Egan, & A.E. Ross (Eds.) *Handbook of treatment of mental disorders in childhood and adolescence*. Englewood Cliffs, NJ: Prentice-Hall, 1978.

Gelfand, D.M., & Hartmann, D.P. Behavior therapy with children: A review and evaluation of research methodology. *Psychological Bulletin*, 1968, **69**, 204-215.

Gelfand, D.M., & Hartmann, D.P. *Child behavior analysis and therapy*. New York: Pergamon Press, 1975.

Gelfand, D.M., Hartmann, D.P., Lamb, A.K., Smith, C.L., Mahan, M.A., & Paul, S.C. Effects of adult models and described alternatives on children's choice of behavior management techniques. *Child Development*, 1974, **45**, 585-593.

Gelfand, D.M., Jenson, W.R., & Drew, C.J. *Understanding child behavior disorders*. New York: Holt, Rinehart, & Winston, 1982.

Geller, E.S., Casali, J.G., & Johnson, R.P. Seat belt usage: A potential target for applied behavior analysis. *Journal of Applied Behavior Analysis*, 1980, **13**, 677-691.

Gelles, R.J. Violence toward children in the United States. *American Journal of Orthopsychiatry*, 1978, **48**, 580-592.

Gingerick, W., & Feyerharm, W. The celeration line technique for assessing client change. *Journal of Social Science Research*, 1979, 3(1), 99-113.

Goetz, E.M., & Baer, D.M. Social control of form diversity and the emergence of new forms in children's blockbuilding. *Journal of Applied Behavior Analysis*, 1973, **6**, 123-128.

Goetz, E.M., & Salmonson, M.M. The effect of general and descriptive reinforcement on "creativity in easel painting." In G. Semb (Ed.), *Behavior analysis and education* (pp. 53-61). Lawrence, KS: University of Lawrence, 1972.

Goldstein, D., Cooper, A.Y., Ruggles, T.R., & LeBlanc, J.M. A teaching package for increasing compliance in an oppositional child during preacademic activities. Paper presented at the Council for Exceptional Children, Dallas, Texas, April 1979.

Gordon, S.B., & Davidson, N. Behavioral parent training. In A. Gurman & D. Kniskern (Eds.), *Handbook of family therapy*. New York: Brunner/Mazel, 1981.

Gottman, J.M. *Time-series analysis: A comprehensive introduction for social scientists*. Cambridge, England: Cambridge University Press, 1981.

Gottman, J.M., & Glass, G.V. Analysis of interrupted time-series experiments. In T.R. Kratochwill (Ed.), *Single subject research: Strategies for evaluating change*. New York: Academic Press, 1978.

Gottman, J.M., & Leiblum, S.R. *How to do psychotherapy and how to evaluate it*. New York: Holt, Rinehart, & Winston, 1974.

Graziano, A.M. Parents as behavior therapists. In M. Hersen, R.M. Eisler, & P.M. Miller (Eds.), *Progress in behavior modification*. New York: Academic Press, 1977.

Greenwood, C.R., Hops, H., & Walker, H.M. The durability of student behavior change: A comparative analysis at follow-up. *Behavior Therapy*, 1977, **8**, 631-638.

Gross, A.M., & Drabman, R.S. Behavioral contrast and behavior therapy. *Behavior Therapy*, 1981, **12**, 231-246.

Gross, A.M., Thurman, C., & Drabman, R.S. The teaching reinforcer: Increasing phonics performance using contingent videotaping. Unpublished manuscript, University of Mississippi Medical Center, 1981.

Grusec, J.E., Kuczynski, L., Rushton, J.P., & Simutis, Z. Modeling, direct instruction, and attributions: Effects on altruism. *Developmental Psychology*, 1978, **14**, 51-57.

Guskin, S.L., Bartel, N.R., & MacMillan, D.L. Perspectives on the labeled child. In N. Hobbs (Ed.), *Issues in the classification of children*. San Francisco: Jossey-Bass, 1975.

Hall, R.V., Axelrod, S., Foundopoulos, M., Shellman, J., Campbell, R.A., & Cranston, S. The effective use of punishment to modify behavior in the classroom. *Educational Technology*, 1971, **11**, 24-26.

Hall, R.V., Axelrod, S., Tyler, L., Grief, E., Jones, F.C. & Robertson, R. Modification of behavior problems in the home with a parent as observer and experimenter. *Journal of Applied Behavior Analysis*, 1972, **5**, 53-64.

Hall, R.V., Cristler, C., Cranston, S.S., & Tucker, B. Teachers and parents as researchers using multiple baseline designs. *Journal of Applied Behavior Analysis*, 1970, **3**, 247-255.

Hall, R.V., & Fox, R.G. Changing-criterion designs: An alternate applied behavior analysis procedure. In B.C. Etzel, J.M. LeBlanc, & D.M. Baer (Eds.), *New developments in behavioral research: Theory, method, and application. In honor of Sidney W. Bijou*. Hillsdale, NJ: Erlbaum, 1977.

Hall, R.V., & Hall, M.C. *How to use time out*. Lawrence, KS: H & H Enterprises, 1980.

Hall, S.M. Self-management and therapeutic maintenance: Theory and research. In P. Karoly & J.J. Steffen (Eds.), *Improving the long-term effects of psychotherapy: Models of durable outcome*. New York: Gardner Press, 1980.

Halle, J.W., Baer, D.M., & Spradlin, J.E. Teachers' generalized use of delay as a stimulus control procedure to increase language use in handicapped children. *Journal of Applied Behavior Analysis*, 1981, **14**, 389-409.

Hammer, D., & Drabman, R.S. *Child discipline: What we know and what we can recommend*. Unpublished Manuscript, University of Mississippi Medical Center, Jackson, Mississippi, 1981.

Haney, J.I., & Jones, R.T. Programming maintenance as a major component of a community-centered preventive effort: Escape from fire. *Behavior Therapy*, 1982, **13**, 47-62.

Harris, S.L., & Ersner-Hershfield, R. Behavioral suppression of seriously disruptive behavior in psychotic and retarded patients: A review of punishment and its alternatives. *Psychological Bulletin*, 1978, **85**, 1352-1375.

Harris, S.L., & Romanczyk, R.G. Treating self-injurious behavior of a retarded child by overcorrection. *Behavior Therapy*, 1976, **7**, 235-239.

Harris, F.R., Wolf, M.M., & Baer, D.M. Effects of adult social reinforcement on child behavior. *Young Children*, 1964, **20**(1), 8-17.

Hart, B. Assessing spontaneous speech. *Behavioral Assessment*, 1983, **5**, 71-82.

Hart, B., & Risley, T. Incidental teaching of language in the preschool. *Journal of Applied Behavior Analysis*, 1975, **8**, 411-420.

Hartmann, D.P. Some neglected issues in behavior modification with children. Paper presented at the Sixth Annual Meeting of the American Association of Behavior Therapy, New York, October 1972.

Hartmann, D.P. Forcing square pegs into round holes: Some comments on "An analysis-of-variance model for the intrasubject replication design." *Journal of Applied Behavior Analysis*, 1974, **7**, 635-638.

Hartmann, D.P. Understanding the design and analysis of experiments. In D. M. Gelfand (Ed.), *Social learning in childhood: Readings in theory and application* (2nd ed.). Belmont, CA: Brooks/Cole, 1975.

Hartmann, D.P. Must the baby follow the bathwater? Psychometric principles — behavioral data. Paper presented at the symposium entitled "Behavioral assessment: The relevance of traditional psychometric procedures," American Psychological Association meetings. Washington, D.C., September 1976.

Hartmann, D.P. Considerations in the choice of interobserver reliability estimates. *Journal of Applied Behavior Analysis*, 1977, **10**, 103-116.

Hartmann, D.P. Assessing the dependability of observational data. In D.P. Hartmann (Ed.), *Using observers to study behavior: New directions for methodology of social and behavioral science* (pp. 51-65). San Francisco: Jossey-Bass, 1982. (a)

Hartmann, D.P. (Ed.). *Using observers to study behavior: New directions for methodology of social and behavioral science.* San Francisco: Jossey-Bass, 1982. (b)

Hartmann, D.P., Gelfand, D.M., Smith, C.L., Paul, S.C., Cromer, C.C., Page, B.C., & LaBenta, D.V. Factors affecting the acquisition and elimination of children's donating behavior. *Journal of Experimental Child Psychology*, 1976, **21**, 328-338.

Hartmann, D.P., Gottman, J.M., Jones, R.R., Gardner, W., Kazdin, A.E., & Vaught, R.S. Interrupted time-series analysis and its application to behavioral data. *Journal of Applied Behavior Analysis*, 1980, **13**, 543-559.

Hartmann, D.P., & Hall, R.V. The changing criterion design. *Journal of Applied Behavior Analysis*, 1976, **9**, 527-532.

Hartmann, D.P., Roper, B.L., & Bradford, D.C. Some relationships between behavioral and traditional assessment. *Journal of Behavioral Assessment*, 1979, **1**, 3-21.

Hartmann, D.P., Roper, B.L., & Gelfand, D.M. Evaluation of alternative modes of child psychotherapy. In B. Lahey & A. Kadin (Eds.), *Advances in child clinical psychology* (Vol. 1, pp. 1-46). New York: Plenum, 1977.

Hartmann, D.P., & Wood, D.D. Observational methods. In A.S. Pollack, M. Herson, & A.E. Kazdin (Eds.), *International handbook of behavior modification and therapy* (pp. 109-138). New York: Plenum, 1982.

Hathaway, S.R. Some considerations relative to nondirective counseling as therapy. *Journal of Clinical Psychology*, 1948, **4**, 226-231.

Hawkins, R.P. The function of assessment: Implications for selection and development of devices for assessing repertoires in clinical, educational, and other settings. *Journal of Applied Behavior Analysis*, 1979, **12**, 501-516.

Hawkins, R.P. Developing a behavior code. In D.P. Hartmann (Ed.), *Using observers to study behavior: New directions for methodology of social and behavioral science* (pp. 21-35). San Francisco: Jossey-Bass, 1982.

Hawkins, R.P., & Dobes, R.W. Behavioral definitions in applied behavior analysis: Explicit or implicit. In B.C. Etzel, J.M. LeBlanc, & D.M. Baer (Eds.), *New directions in behavioral research: Theory, methods, and applications. In honor of Sidney W. Bijou.* Hillsdale, NJ: Erlbaum, 1977.

Hayes, S.C. Single case experimental design and empirical clinical practice. *Journal of Consulting and Clinical Psychology*, 1981, **49**, 193-211.

Haynes, S.N. *Principles of behavioral assessment.* New York: Gardner Press, 1978.

Haynes, S.N., & Horn, W.F. Reactivity in behavioral observations: A methodological and conceptual critique. *Behavioral Assessment*, 1982, **4**, 369-385.

Haynes, S.N., & Wilson, C.C. *Behavioral assessment.* San Francisco: Jossey-Bass, 1979.

Herbert, E.W., Pinkston, E.M., Hayden, M.L., Sajwaj, T.E., Pinkston, S., Cordua, G., & Jackson, C. Adverse effects of differential parental attention. *Journal of Applied Behavior Analysis*, 1973, **6**, 15-30.

Hersen, M., & Barlow, D.H. *Single case experimental designs: Strategies for studying behavior change.* Oxford: Pergamon Press, 1976.

Hobbs, S., & Forehand, R. Important parameters in the use of time out with children: A re-examination. *Journal of Behavior Therapy and Experimental Psychiatry*, 1977, **8**, 365-370.

Hobbs, S.A., Forehand, R., & Murray, R.G. Effects of various durations of timeout on the noncompliant behavior of children. *Behavior Therapy*, 1978, **9**, 652-656.

Hobbs, S.A., & Goswick, R.A. Behavioral treatment of self-stimulation: An examination of alternatives to physical punishment. *Journal of Clinical Child Psychology*, 1977, **6**, 20-23.

Hobbs, S.A., Moquin, L.E., Tyroler, N., & Lahey, B.B. Cognitive-behavior therapy with children: Has clinical utility been demonstrated? *Psychological Bulletin*, 1980, **87**, 147-165.

Holland, C. J. An interview guide for behavioral counseling with parents. *Behavior Therapy*, 1970, **1**, 70-79.

Hollenbeck, A.R. Problems of reliability in observational research. In G.P. Sackett (Ed.), *Observing behavior: Data collection and analysis methods* (Vol. 3, pp. 79-98). Baltimore: University Park Press, 1978.

Holm, R.A. Techniques of recording observational data. In G.P. Sackett (Ed.), *Observing behavior: Data collection and analysis methods* (Vol. 2, pp. 99-108). Baltimore: University Park Press, 1978.

Homer, A.L., & Peterson, L. Differential reinforcement of other behavior: A preferred response elimination procedure. *Behavior Therapy*, 1980, **11**, 449-471.

Homme, L., Csanyi, A.P., Gonzales, M.A., & Rechs, J.R. *How to use contingency contracting in the classroom*. Champaign, IL: Research Press, 1970.

Hopkins, B.L., Schutte, R.C., & Garton, K.L. The effects of access to a playroom on the rate and quality of printing and writing of first and second grade students. *Journal of Applied Behavior Analysis*, 1971, **4**, 77-87.

Horner, R.D., & Baer, D.M. Multiple-probe technique: A variation of the multiple baseline. *Journal of Applied Behavior Analysis*, 1978, **11**, 189-196.

House, A.E., House, B.J., & Campbell, M.B. Measures of interobserver agreement: Calculation formulas and distribution effects. *Journal of Behavioral Assessment*, 1981, **3**, 37-57.

Huitema, B. Autocorrelation in behavior modification data: Wherefore art thou? *Behavioral Assessment*, in press.

Humphrey, L.L., Karoly, P., & Kirschenbaum, D.S. Self-management in the classroom: Self-imposed response cost versus self-reward. *Behavior Therapy*, 1978, **9**, 592-601.

Hundert, J. The effectiveness of reinforcement, response cost, and mixed programs on classroom behaviors. *Journal of Applied Behavior Analysis*, 1976, **9**, 107.

Hutt, S.J., & Hutt, C. *Direct observation and measurement of behavior*. Springfield, IL: Charles C. Thomas, 1970.

Iwata, B., & Bailey, J.S. Reward versus cost token systems: An analysis of the effects on students and teacher. *Journal of Applied Behavior Analysis*, 1974, **7**, 567-576.

Iwata, B. A., Wong, S. E., Riordan, M. M., Dorsey, M. F., & Lau, M. M. Assessment and training of classical interviewing skills: Analogue analysis and field replication. *Journal of Applied Behavior Analysis*, 1982, **15**, 191-203.

Jackson, D.A. A critical analysis of the multiple baseline design in applied behavior analysis. Unpublished manuscript, Department of Educational Research, University of Utah, Salt Lake City, Utah, 1973.

Jackson, J.L., & Calhoun, K.S. Effects of two variable-ratio schedules of timeout: Changes in target and non-target behavior. *Journal of Behavior Therapy and Experimental Psychiatry*, 1977, **8**, 195-199.

Jayaratne, S., & Levy, R.L. *Empirical clinical practice*. New York: Columbia University Press, 1979.

Jenson, W.R., & Sloane, H. Chart moves and grab bags: A simple contingency management system. *Journal of Applied Behavior Analysis*, 1979, **12**, 334.

Johnson, S.M., & Bolstad, O.D. Methodological issues in naturalistic observation: Some problems and solutions for field research. In L.A. Hamerlynck, L.C. Handy, & R.J. Mash (Eds.), *Behavior change: Methodology, concepts, and practice.* Champaign, IL: Research Press, 1973.

Johnston, J.M. Punishment of human behavior. *American Psychologist*, 1972, **27**, 1033–1054.

Johnston, J.M., & Pennypacker, H.S. *Strategies and tactics of human behavioral research.* Hillsdale, NJ: Erlbaum, 1980.

Johnston, M.K., & Harris, F.R. Observation and recording of verbal behavior in remedial speech work. In H. Sloan & B. MacAulay (Eds.), *Operant procedures in remedial speech and language training* (pp. 40–60). Boston: Houghton-Mifflin, 1968.

Jones, R.T., Kazdin, A.E., & Haney, J.E. Social validation and training of emergency fire safety skills for potential injury prevention and life saving. *Journal of Applied Behavior Analysis*, 1981, **14**, 249–260.

Jones, R.R., Vaught, R.S., & Weinrott, M. Time-series analysis in operant research. *Journal of Applied Behavior Analysis*, 1977, **10**, 151–166.

Jones, R.R., Weinrott, M.R., & Vaught, R.S. Effects of serial dependency on the agreement between visual and statistical inference. *Journal of Applied Behavior Analysis*, 1978, **11**, 277–283.

Kalish, H.I. *From behavioral science to behavior modification.* New York: McGraw-Hill, 1981.

Kanfer, F.H. Issues and ethics in behavior manipulation. *Psychological Reports*, 1965, **16**, 187–196.

Kanfer, F.H., & Karoly, P. Self-control: A behavioristic excursion into the lion's den. *Behavior Therapy*, 1972, **3**, 398–416.

Kanfer, F.H., & Saslow, G. Outline of interview information needed for a functional analysis. Addendum to: Behavioral analysis: An alternative to diagnostic classification. *Archives of General Psychiatry*, 1965, **12**, 529–538.

Kanfer, F.H., & Saslow, G. Behavioral diagnosis. In C.M. Franks (Ed.), *Behavior therapy: Appraisal and status.* New York: McGraw-Hill, 1969.

Kantor, J.R. *Interbehavioral psychology.* Bloomington, IN: Principia Press, 1958.

Karoly, P. Behavioral self-management in children: Concepts, methods, issues, and directions. In M. Hersen, R. Eisler, & P. Miller (Eds.), *Progress in behavior modification* (Vol. 5). New York: Academic Press, 1977.

Karoly, P. Self-management problems in children. In E. Mash & L. Terdal (Eds.), *Behavioral assessment of childhood disorders.* New York: Guilford Press, 1981.

Karoly, P. Perspectives on self-management and behavior change. In P. Karoly & F.H. Kanfer (Eds.), *Self-management and behavior change: From theory to practice.* New York: Pergamon Press, 1982.

Karoly, P., & Kanfer, F.H. *Self-management and behavior change: From theory to practice.* New York: Pergamon Press, 1982.

Kazdin, A.E. Characteristics and trends in applied behavior analysis. *Journal of Applied Behavior Analysis*, 1975, **8**, 332.

Kazdin, A.E. Artifact, bias, and complexity of assessment: The ABC's of reliability. *Journal of Applied Behavior Analysis*, 1977, **10**, 141–150. (a)

Kazdin, A.E. Assessing the clinical or applied importance of behavior change through social validation. *Behavior Modification*, 1977, **1**, 353–374. (b)

Kazdin, A.E. *History of behavior modification.* Baltimore, MD: University Park Press, 1978.

Kazdin, A.E. Advances in child behavior therapy: Applications and implications. *American Psychologist*, 1979, **34**, 981–987.

Kazdin, A.E. *Behavior modification in applied settings* (rev. ed.). Homewood, IL: Dorsey, 1980.

Kazdin, A.E. Behavioral observation. In M. Hersen & A.S. Bellack (Eds.), *Behavioral assessment: A practical handbook* (2nd ed.). New York: Pergamon Press, 1981. (a)

Kazdin, A.E. Behavior modification in education: Contributions and limitations. *Developmental Review*, 1981, **1**, 34–57. (b)

Kazdin, A.E. Observer effects: Reactivity of direct observation. In D.P. Hartmann (Ed.), *Using observers to study behavior: New directions for methodology of social and behavioral science* (pp. 5–19). San Francisco: Jossey-Bass, 1982. (a)

Kazdin, A.E. *Single-case research designs. Methods for clinical and applied settings.* New York: Oxford University Press, 1982. (b)

Kazdin, A.E., & Bootzin, R.R., The token economy: An evaluative review. *Journal of Applied Behavior Analysis*, 1972, **5**, 343–372.

Kazdin, A.E., & Cole, P.M. Attitudes and labeling biases toward behavior modification: The effects of labels, content, and jargon. *Behavior Therapy*, 1981, **12**, 56–68.

Kazdin, A.E., & Hartmann, D.P. The simultaneous treatment design. *Behavior Therapy*, 1978, **9**, 912–922.

Kazdin, A.E., & Kopel, S.A. On resolving ambiguities of the multiple-baseline design: Problems and recommendations. *Behavior Therapy*, 1975, **6**, 601–608.

Kazdin, A.E., & Marholin, D. II Program evaluation in clinical and community settings. In D. Marholin II (Ed.), *Child behavior therapy*. New York: Gardner Press, 1978.

Keller, F.S. A personal course in psychology. In R. Ulrich, T. Stachnik, & J. Mabry (Eds.), *The control of behavior* (pp. 91–93). Glenview, IL: Scott, Foresman, 1966.

Keller, F.S. "Good-bye-teacher..." *Journal of Applied Behavior Analysis*, 1968, **1**, 79–89.

Kelly, J.A., & Drabman, R.S. Generalizing response suppression of self-injurious behavior through an overcorrection punishment procedure: A case study. *Behavior Therapy*, 1977, **8**, 468–472.

Kelly, M.B. A review of the observational data-collection and reliability procedures reported in *The Journal of Applied Behavior Analysis*. *Journal of Applied Behavior Analysis*, 1977, **10**, 97–101.

Kendall, P.C. Cognitive-behavioral interventions with children. In B. Lahey & A. Kazdin (Eds.), *Advances in clinical psychology* (Vol. 4). New York: Plenum, 1981.

Kendall, P.C., & Finch, A.J. Developing nonimpulsive behavior in children's cognitive-behavioral strategies on self-control. In P.C. Kendall & S.D. Hollon (Eds.), *Cognitive-behavioral interventions: Theory, research, and procedures*. New York: Academic Press, 1979.

Kendall, P.C., & Hollon, S.D. *Cognitive-behavioral interventions: Theory, research, and procedures*. New York: Academic Press, 1979.

Kendall, P.C., Nay, W.R., & Jeffers, J. Timeout and contrast effects: A systematic evaluation of a successive treatments design. *Behavior Therapy*, 1975, **6**, 609–615.

Kendall, P.C., & Williams, C.L. Assessing the cognitive and behavioral components of children's self-management. In P. Karoly & F.H. Kanfer (Eds.), *Self-management and behavior change: From theory to practice*. New York: Pergamon Press, 1982.

Kent, R.N., & Foster, S.L. Direct observational procedures: Methodological issues in naturalistic settings. In A.R. Ciminero, K.S. Calhoun, & H.E. Adams (Eds.), *Handbook of behavioral assessment.* New York: Wiley, 1977.

Kiesler, C.A. Social psychological issues in studying consumer satisfaction. *Behavior Therapy,* 1983, **14**, 226-236.

Kircher, A.S., Pear, J.J., & Martin, G.L. Shock as punishment in a picture-naming task with retarded children. *Journal of Applied Behavior Analysis,* 1971, **4**, 227-233.

Kirkland, K.D., & Thelen, M.H. Uses of modeling in child treatment. In B. Lahey & A. Kazdin (Eds.), *Advances in clinical psychology* (Vol. 1). New York: Plenum, 1977.

Klorman, R., Hilpert, P., Michael, R., LaGana, C., & Sveen, O. Effects of coping and mastery modeling on experienced and inexperienced pedodontic patients' disruptiveness. *Behavior Therapy,* 1980, **11**, 156-168.

Kohlenberg, R.B. The punishment of persistent vomiting: A case study. *Journal of Applied Behavior Analysis,* 1970, **3**, 241-245.

Krasner, L. Behavior control and social responsibility. *American Psychologist,* 1964, **17**, 199-204.

Kratochwill, T.R. Foundations of time-series research. In T.R. Kratochwill (Ed.), *Single subject research: Strategies for evaluating change.* New York: Academic Press, 1978. (a)

Kratochwill, T.R. (Ed.) *Single subject research: Strategies for evaluating change.* New York: Academic Press, 1978. (b)

Kratochwill, T.R., & Brody, G.H. Single subject designs: A perspective on the controversy over employing statistical inference and implications for research and training in behavior modification. *Behavior Modification,* 1978, **2**, 291-307.

Kratochwill, T.R., & Levin, J.R. On the applicability to various data analysis procedures to the simultaneous and alternating treatment designs in behavior therapy research. *Behavioral Assessment,* 1980, **2**, 353-360.

Lahey, B.B., & Drabman, R.C. Behavior modification in the classroom. In W.E. Craighead, A.E. Kazdin, & M.J. Mahoney (Eds.), *Behavior modifications: Principles, issues, and applications.* Boston: Houghton-Mifflin, 1981.

Lang, P.J., & Melamed, B.C. Case report: Avoidance conditioning therapy of an infant with chronic ruminative vomiting. *Journal of Abnormal Psychology,* 1969, **74**, 1-8.

LeBlanc, J.M., Busby, K.H., & Thomson, C.L. The functions of timeout for changing the aggressive behaviors of a preschool child: A multiple baseline analysis. In R. Ulrich, T. Stachnik, & J. Mabry (Eds.), *Control of human behavior* (Vol. 3). Glenview, IL: Scott, Foresman, 1974.

Leitenberg, H. The use of single case methodology in psychotherapy research. *Journal of Abnormal Psychology,* 1973, **82**, 87-101.

Lepper, M.R. Intrinsic and extrinsic motivation in children: Detrimental effects of superfluous social controls. In W.A. Collins (Ed.), *Minnesota symposium on child psychology* (Vol. 14). Hillsdale, NJ: Erlbaum, 1981.

Lepper, M.R., Greene, D, & Nisbett, R.E. Undermining children's intrinsic interest with extrinsic rewards: A test of the "overjustification" hypothesis. *Journal of Personality and Social Psychology,* 1973, **28**, 129-137.

Lewis, S. A comparison of behavior therapy techniques in the reduction of fearful avoidance behavior. *Behavior Therapy,* 1974, **5**, 648-655.

Libet, A.Q., & Forehand, R. A component analysis of positive practice overcorrection: An examination of re-educative effects. *Psychological Record,* 1979, **29**, 219-229.

Lovaas, O.I., & Simmons, J.Q., MD. Manipulation of self-destruction in three retarded children. *Journal of Applied Behavior Analysis*, 1969, **2**, 143-157.

Lovitt, T.C., & Curtiss, K.S. Effects of manipulating an antecedent event on mathematics response rate. *Journal of Applied Behavior Analysis*, 1968, *1*, 329-333.

Luce, S.C., Delquadri, J., & Hall, R.V. Contingent exercise: A mild but powerful procedure for suppressing inappropriate verbal and aggressive behavior. *Journal of Applied Behavior Analysis*, 1980, **13**, 583-594.

Luiselli, J. Programming overcorrection with children: What do the data indicate? *Journal of Clinical Child Psychology*, 1980, **9**, 224-228.

Luiselli, J.K., Colozzi, G.A., & O'Toole, K.M. Programming response maintenance of differential reinforcement effects. *Child Behavior Therapy*, 1980, **2**, 65-73.

Luiselli, J.K., Helfen, C.S., Colozzi, G., Donellon, S., & Pemberton, B. Controlling self-inflicted biting of a retarded child by the differential reinforcement of other behavior. *Psychological Reports*, 1978, **42**, 435-438.

Luiselli, J.K., Helfen, C.S., Pemberton, B.W., & Reisman, J. The elimination of a child's in-class masturbation by overcorrection and reinforcement. *Journal of Behavior Therapy and Experimental Psychiatry*, 1977, **8**, 201-204.

Luiselli, J.K., & Krause, S.J. Reducing stereotypic behavior through a combination of DRO, cuing, and reinforcer isolation procedures. *The Behavior Therapist*, 1981, **4**, 2-3.

Lytton, H. Observational studies of parent-child interactions: A methodological review. *Child Development*, 1971, **42**, 651-684.

Madsen, C.H. Jr., Becker, W.C., Thomas, D.R., Koser, L., & Plager, E. An analysis of the reinforcing function of "sit-down" commands. In R.K. Parker (Ed.), *Readings in educational psychology*. Boston: Allyn & Bacon, 1968.

Madsen, C.K., & Madsen, C.H., Jr. *Parents/children discipline: A positive approach*. Boston: Allyn & Bacon, 1972.

Mann, J., & Rosenthal, T.L. Vicarious and direct counterconditioning of test anxiety through individual and group desensitization. *Behavioral Research and Therapy*, 1969, **7**, 359-367.

Mann, R.A. Assessment of behavioral excesses in children. In M. Hersen & A.S. Bellack (Ed.), *Behavioral assessment*. New York: Pergamon Press, 1976.

Mansdorf, I.J. Reinforcer isolation: An alternative to subject isolation in time out from positive reinforcement. *Journal of Behavior Therapy and Experimental Psychiatry*, 1977, **8**, 391-393.

Marholin, D., II., Luiselli, J.K., & Townsend, N.M. Overcorrection: An examination of its rationale and treatment effectiveness. In M. Hersen, R.M. Eisler, & P.M. Miller (Eds.), *Progress in behavior modification* (Vol. 9). New York: Academic Press, 1980.

Marholin, D., II., & Siegel, L.J. Beyond the law of effect: Programming for the maintenance of behavior change. In D. Marholin II (Ed.), *Child behavior therapy*. New York: Gardner Press, 1978.

Martin, G., & Pear, J. *Behavior modification: What it is and how to do it*. Englewood Cliffs, NJ: Prentice-Hall, 1978.

Mash, E.J. & Terdal, L.G. Behavior therapy assessment: Diagnosis, design, and evaluation. In E.J. Mash & L.G. Terdal (Eds.), *Behavior therapy assessment*. New York: Springer, 1976.

Mash, E.J., & Terdal, L.G. After the dance is over: Some issues and suggestions for follow-up assessment in behavior therapy. *Psychological Reports*, 1977, *41*, 1287-1308.

Mash, E.J., & Terdal, L.G. Follow-up assessments in behavior therapy. In P. Karoly & J.J. Steffen (Eds.), *The long range effects of psychotherapy: Models of durable outcome.* New York: Gardner Press, 1980.

Mash, E.J., & Terdal, L.G. (Eds.), *Behavioral assessment of childhood disorders.* New York: Guilford Press, 1981.

Matson, J., Horne, A., Ollendick, D., & Ollendick, T. Overcorrection: A further evaluation of restitution and positive practice. *Journal of Behavior Therapy and Experimental Psychiatry*, 1979, **10**, 295-298.

Matson, J.L., & Ollendick, T.H. Issues in toilet training. *Behavior Therapy*, 1977, **8**, 549-553.

Matson, J.L., & Ollendick, T.H. The random stimulus design. *Child Behavior Therapy*, 1981, **3**(4), 69-75.

McCleary, R., & Hay, R.A. *Applied time series analysis for the social sciences.* Beverly Hills, CA: Sage, 1980.

McLaughlin, T., & Malaby, J. Reducing and measuring inappropriate verbalizations in a token classroom. *Journal of Applied Behavior Analysis*, 1972, **5**, 329-333.

McSweeney, A.J. Effects of response cost on the behavior of a million persons: Charging for directory assistance in Cincinnati. *Journal of Applied Behavior Analysis*, 1978, **11**, 47-51.

Measel, C.J., & Alfieri, P.A. Treatment of self-injurious behavior by a combination of reinforcement for incompatible behavior and overcorrection. *American Journal of Mental Deficiency*, 1976, **81**, 147-153.

Medley, D.M., & Mitzel, H.E. Measuring classroom behavior by stimatic observation. In. N.L. Gage (Ed.), *Handbook of research on teaching* (pp. 247-328). Chicago: Rand McNally, 1963.

Meichenbaum, D. *Cognitive-behavior modification: An integrative approach.* New York: Plenum, 1977.

Meichenbaum, D. Teaching children self-control. In B. Lahey & A. Kazdin (Eds.), *Advances in clinical child psychology* (Vol. 2). New York: Plenum, 1979.

Meichenbaum, D., & Goodman, J. Training impulsive children to talk to themselves: A means of developing self-control. *Journal of Abnormal Psychology*, 1971, **77**, 115-126.

Melamed, B.G., Klingman, A., & Siegel, L.J. Childhood stress and anxiety: Individualizing cognitive behavioral strategies in the reduction of medical and dental stress. In A. Meyers & N.E. Craighead (Eds.), *Cognitive behavior therapy with children.* New York: Plenum, 1982.

Melamed, B.G., & Siegel, L.J. Reduction of anxiety in children facing hospitalization and surgery by use of filmed modeling. *Journal of Consulting and Clinical Psychology*, 1973, **43**, 511-521.

Mercatoris, M., & Craighead, W.E. Effects of nonparticipant observation on teacher and pupil classroom behavior. *Journal of Educational Psychology*, 1974, **66**, 512-519.

Michael, J. Statistical inference for individual organism research: Mixed blessing or curse? *Journal of Applied Behavior Analysis*, 1974, **7**, 647-653.

Morris, E.K., & Rosen, H.S. The role of interobserver reliability in the evaluation of graphed data. *Behavioral Assessment*, 1982, **4**, 387-399.

Myers, D.V. Extinction, DRO, and response-cost procedures for eliminating self-injurious behavior: A case study. *Behavior Research and Therapy*, 1975, **13**, 189-191.

Nay, W.R. *Multimethod clinical assessment.* New York: Gardner Press, 1979.

Nelson, R.O. Methodological issues in assessment via self-monitoring. In J.D. Cone & R.P. Hawkins (Eds.), *Behavioral assessment: New directions in clinical psychology.* New York: Brunner/Mazel, 1977.

Nunnally, J. *Psychometric theory* (2nd ed.). New York: McGraw-Hill, 1978.

O'Brien, F., Azrin, N.H., & Bugle, C. Training profoundly retarded children to stop crawling. *Journal of Applied Behavior Analysis*, 1972, **5**, 131-137.

O'Connor, R.D. Modification of social withdrawal through symbolic modeling. *Journal of Applied Behavior Analysis*, 1969, **2**, 15-22.

O'Leary, K.D. The assessment of psychopathology in children. In H.C. Quay & J.S. Werry (Eds.), *Psychopathological disorders of childhood*. New York: Wiley, 1972.

O'Leary, K.D., Becker, W.C., Evans, M.B., & Saudargas, R.A. A token reinforcement program in a public school: A replication and systematic analysis. *Journal of Applied Behavior Analysis*, 1969, **2**, 3-13.

O'Leary, K.D., & Carr, E.G. Behavior therapy for children: Outcome and evaluation. In G.T. Wilson & C.M. Franks (Eds.), *Contemporary behavior therapy: Conceptual foundations of clinical practice*. New York: Guilford, 1982.

O'Leary, K.D., Kauffman, K.F., Kass, R.E., & Drabman, R.S. The effects of loud and soft reprimands on the behavior of disruptive students. *Exceptional Children*, 1970, **37**, 145-155.

O'Leary, K.D., & Kent, R.N. Behavior modification for social action: Research tactics and problems. In L.A. Hammerlynck, P.O. Davidson, L.E. Acker (Eds.), *Critical issues in research and practice*. Champaign, IL: Research Press, 1973.

O'Leary, S.G., & Dubey, D.R. Applications of self-control procedures by children: A review. *Journal of Applied Behavior Analysis*, 1979, **12**, 449-465.

Ollendick, T.H., & Cerny, J.A. *Clinical behavior therapy with children*. New York: Plenum, 1981.

Ollendick, T.H., & Matson, J.L. An initial investigation into the parameters of overcorrection. *Psychological Reports*, 1976, **39**, 1139-1142.

Ollendick, T.H., & Matson, J.L. Overcorrection: An overview. *Behavior Therapy*, 1978, **9**, 830-842.

Panyan, M. *How to use shaping*. Lawrence, KS: H & H Enterprises, 1980.

Parke, R.D. Punishment in children: Effects, side-effects, and alternative strategies. In H.L. Horn, Jr., & P.A. Robinson (Eds.), *Psychological processes in early education*. New York: Academic Press, 1977.

Parsonson, B.S., & Baer, D.M. The analysis and presentation of graphic data. In T.R. Kratochwill (Ed.), *Single subject research: Strategies for evaluating change*. New York: Academic Press, 1978.

Patterson, G.R. *A social learning approach (Vol. 3): Coercive family process*. Eugene, OR: Castalia, 1982.

Patterson, G.R., & Harris, A. Some methodological considerations for observation procedures. Paper presented at the meeting of the American Psychological Association, San Francisco, 1968.

Patterson, G.R., Reid, J.B., Jones, R.R., & Conger, R.E. *A social learning approach to family intervention* (Vol. 1). Eugene, OR: Castalia, 1975.

Paul, G.L. New assessment systems for residential treatment, management, research and evaluation: A symposium. *Journal of Behavioral Assessment*, 1979, **1**, 181-184.

Pawlicki, R. Behavior-therapy research with children: A critical review. *Canadian Journal of Behavioral Science/Revue Canadienne Des Sciences Du Comportement*, 1970, **2**, 163-173.

Perri, M.G., & Richards, C.S. An investigation of naturally occurring episodes of self-controlled behaviors. *Journal of Counseling Psychology*, 1977, **24**, 178-183.

Peterson, L., & Shigetomi, C.C. The use of coping techniques to minimize anxiety in hospitalized children. *Behavior Therapy*, 1981, **12**, 1-14.

Phillips, E.L., Phillips, E.A., Fixsen, D.L., & Wolf, M.M. Achievement Place: Modification of the behaviors of pre-delinquent boys within a token economy. *Journal of Applied Behavior Analysis*, 1971, **4**, 45-59.

Pinkston, E.M., Reese, N.M., LeBlanc, J.M., & Baer, D.M. Independent control of a preschool child's aggression and peer interaction by contingent teacher attention. *Journal of Applied Behavior Analysis*, 1973, **6**, 115-124.

Plummer, S., Baer, D.M., & LeBlanc, J.M. Functional considerations in the use of procedural time-out and an effective alternative. *Journal of Applied Behavior Analysis*, 1977, **6**, 115-124.

Pocke, C., Brower, R., & Swearingen, M. Teaching self-protection to young children. *Journal of Applied Behavior Analysis*, 1981, **14**, 131-140.

Porterfield, J.K., Herbert-Jackson, E., & Risley, T.R. Contingent observation: An effective and acceptable procedure for reducing disruptive behavior of young children in a group setting. *Journal of Applied Behavior Analysis*, 1976, **9**, 55-64.

Power, C.T. The time-sample behavioral checklist: Observational assessment of patient functioning. *Journal of Behavioral Assessment*, 1979, **1**, 199-210.

Premack, D. Toward empirical behavior laws: I. Positive reinforcement. *Psychological Review*, 1959, **66**, 219-233.

Rainwater, N., & Ayllon, T. Increasing academic performance by using a timer as antecedent stimulus: A study of four cases. *Behavior Therapy*, 1976, **7**, 672-677.

Rapport, M.D., Murphy, A., & Bailey, J.S. The effects of a response cost treatment tactic on hyperactive children. *Journal of School Psychology*, 1978, **18**, 98-110.

Redd, W.H., & Sleator, W.S. The theoretical foundations of behavior modification: In D. Marholin II (Ed.), *Child behavior therapy*. New York: Gardner Press, 1978.

Redfield, J.P., & Paul, G.L. Bias in behavioral observation as a function of observer familiarity with subjects and typicality of behavior. *Journal of Consulting and Clinical Psychology*, 1976, **44**, 156.

Reese, M. Helping human rights committees and clients balance intrusiveness and effectiveness: A challenge for research and therapy. *The Behavior Therapist*, 1982, **5**(1), 95-98.

Reid, J.B. Reliability assessment of observational data: A possible methodological problem. *Child Development*, 1970, **41**, 1143-1150.

Reiss, S., & Sushinsky, L.W. Overjustification, competing responses, and the acquisition of intrinsic interest. *Journal of Personality and Social Psychology*, 1975, **31**, 1116-1125.

Revusky, S.H. Some statistical treatments compatible with individual organism methodology. *Journal of Experimental Analysis of Behavior*, 1967, **10**, 319-330.

Rincover, A. Sensory extinction: A procedure for eliminating self-stimulatory behavior in psychotic children. *Journal of Abnormal Child Psychology*, 1978, **6**, 299-310.

Rincover, A., Cook, R., Peoples, A., & Packard, D. Sensory extinction and sensory reinforcement principles for programming multiple adaptive behavior change. *Journal of Applied Behavior Analysis*, 1979, **12**, 221-233.

Risley, T.R. The effects and side effects of punishing the autistic behaviors of a deviant child. *Journal of Applied Behavior Analysis*, 1968, **1**, 21-34.

Risley, T.R. Behavior modification: An experimental-therapeutic endeavor. In L.A. Hamerlynck, P.O. Davidson, & L.E. Acker (Eds.), *Behavior modification and ideal mental health services* (pp. 283-329). Calgary: University of Calgary Press, 1969.

Risley, T.R., & Baer, D.M. Operant behavior modification: The deliberate development of behavior. In B. Caldwell & H. Ricciuti (Eds.), *Review of child development research: Social influence and social action* (Vol. 3, pp. 283–329). Chicago: University of Chicago Press, 1973.

Ritter, B. The group treatment of children's snake phobias using vicarious and contact desensitization procedures. *Behavior Research and Therapy*, 1968, **6**, 1–6.

Ritter, B. Treatment of acrophobia with contact desensitization. *Behavior Research and Therapy*, 1969, **7**, 41–45.

Roberts, M.W., Hatzenbuehler, L.C., & Bean, A.W. The effects of differential attention and time out on child noncompliance. *Behavior Therapy*, 1981, **12**, 93–99.

Robertson, S.J., DeReus, D.M., & Drabman, R.S. Peer and college-student tutoring as reinforcement in a token economy. *Journal of Applied Behavior Analysis*, 1976, **9**, 169–177.

Rogers, C.R., & Skinner, B.F. Some issues concerning the control of human behavior: A symposium. *Science*, 1956, **124**, 1057–1066.

Rosenbaum, M.S., Creedon, D.L., & Drabman, R.S. Training preschool children to identify emergency situations and make emergency phone calls. *Behavior Therapy*, 1981, **12**, 425–435.

Rosenthal, R. *Experimenter effects in behavior research.* New York: Appleton-Century-Crofts, 1966.

Rosenthal, R., & Rosnow, R.L. (Eds.). *Artifact in behavioral research.* New York: Academic Press, 1969.

Rosenthal, T.B., & Zimmerman, B.J. *Social learning and cognition.* New York: Academic Press, 1978.

Rosenthal, T.L. Modeling therapies. In M. Hersen, R.M. Eisler, & P.M. Miller (Eds.), *Progress in behavior modification* (Vol. 2). New York: Academic Press, 1974.

Rosenthal, T., & Bandura, A. Psychological modeling: Theory and practice. In S.L. Garfield & A.E. Bergin (Eds.), *Handbook of psychotherapy and behavior change: An empirical analysis* (Vol. 2). New York: Wiley, 1978.

Ross, A.O. Behavior therapy with children. In S. Garfield & A. Bergin (Eds.), *Handbook of psychotherap*

Ross, A.O. Behavior therapy with children. In S. Garfield & A. Bergin (Eds.), *Handbook of psychotherapy and behavior change* (2nd ed.). New York: Wiley, 1978.

Ross, A.O. *Psychological disorders of children* (2nd ed.). New York: McGraw-Hill, 1980.

Ross, A.O. *Child behavior therapy: Principles, procedures, and empirical basis.* New York: Wiley, 1981.

Ross, M. The self-perception of intrinsic motivation. In J.H. Harvey, W.J. Ickes, & R. Kidd (Eds.), *New directions in attribution research.* Hillsdale, NJ: Erlbaum, 1976.

Sachs, D.A. The efficacy of time-out procedures in a variety of behavior problems. *Journal of Behavior Therapy and Experimental Psychiatry*, 1973, **4**, 237–242.

Sajwaj, T., Libet, J., & Agras, S. Lemon-juice therapy: The control of life-threatening ruminating in a six-month-old infant. *Journal of Applied Behavior Analysis*, 1974, **7**, 557–563.

Sajwaj, T., Twardosz, S., & Burke, M. Side effects of extinction procedures in a remedial preschool. *Journal of Applied Behavior Analysis*, 1972, **5**, 163–175.

Salzberg, B.H., Wheeler, A.A., Devar, L.T., & Hopkins, B.L. The effect of intermittent feedback and intermittent contingent access to play on printing of kindergarten children. *Journal of Applied Behavior Analysis*, 1971, **4**, 163–171.

Santogrossi, D.A., O'Leary, K.D., Romanczyk, R.G., & Kaufman, K.F. Self-evaluation by adolescents in a psychiatric hospital school token program. *Journal of Applied Behavior Analysis*, 1973, **6**, 277–287.

Saunders, J.T., & Reppucci, N.D. The social identity of behavior modification. In. M. Hersen, R. Eisler, & P. Miller (Eds.), *Progress in behavior modification* (Vol. 6). New York: Academic Press, 1978.

Scarboro, M.E., & Forehand, R. Effects of two types of response-contingent time-out on compliance and oppositional behavior of children. *Journal of Experimental Child Psychology*, 1975, **19**, 252–264.

Sechrest, L. (Ed.), *Unobtrusive measurement today: New direction for methodology of behavioral science.* San Francisco: Jossey-Bass, 1979.

Shapiro, E.S., Kazdin, A.E., & McGonigle, J.J. Multiple-treatment interference in the simultaneous- or alternating-treatments design. *Behavioral Assessment*, 1982, **4**, 105–115.

Sharp, K.C. Impact of interpersonal problem-solving on preschooler's social competency. *Journal of Applied Developmental Psychology*, 1981, **2**, 129–163.

Shine, L.C. Removing the restriction of an even number of trials for the Shine-Bower single-subject ANOVA. *Educational and Psychological Measurement*, 1977, **37**, 873–875.

Sidman, M. *Tactics of scientific research.* New York: Basic Books, 1960.

Simpson, M.J.A. Problems of recording behavioral data by keyboard. In M.E. Lamb, S.J. Suomi, & G.R. Stephenson (Eds.), *Social interaction analysis: Methodological issues.* Madison, WI: University of Wisconsin Press, 1979.

Skinner, B.F. *Science and human behavior.* New York: Macmillan, 1953. (a)

Skinner, B.F. Some contributions of an experimental analysis of behavior to psychology as a whole. *American Psychologist*, 1953, **8**, 69–78. (b)

Skinner, B.F. What is the experimental analysis of behavior? *Journal of the Experimental Analysis of Behavior*, 1966, **9**, 213–218.

Smith, C.L., Gelfand, D.M., Hartmann, D.P., & Partlow, M.E.P. Children's casual attributions regarding help giving. *Child Development*, 1979, **50**, 203–210.

Snyder, J.J., & White, M.J. The use of cognitve self-instruction in the treatment of behaviorally disturbed adolescents. *Behavior Therapy*, 1979, **10**, 227–235.

Solnick, J.V., Rincover, A., & Peterson, C.R. Some determinants of the reinforcing and punishing effects of timeout. *Journal of Applied Behavior Analysis*, 1977, **10**, 415–424.

Spitalnick, R., & Drabman, R. A classroom timeout procedure for retarded children. *Journal of Behavior Therapy and Experimental Psychiatry*, 1976, **7**, 17–21.

Stokes, T.F., & Baer, D.M. An implicit technology of generalization. *Journal of Applied Behavior Analysis*, 1977, **10**, 349–367.

Stolz, S.B. Evaluation of therapeutic efficacy of behavior modification in a community setting. *Behavior Research and Therapy*, 1976, **14**, 479–481.

Strain, P.S., & Shores, R.E. Additional comments on multiple-baseline designs in instructional research. *American Journal of Mental Deficiency*, 1979, **84**, 229–234.

Stuart, R.B. Behavior contracting within the families of delinquents. *Journal of Behavioral Therapy and Experimental Psychology*, 1971, **2**, 1–11.

Sulzbacher, S., & Houser, J.E. A tactic to eliminate disruptive behaviors in the classroom: Group contingent consequences. *American Journal of Mental Deficiency*, 1968, **73**, 88–90.

Sulzer-Azaroff, B., & Mayer, G.R. *Applying behavior-analysis procedures with children and youth.* New York: Holt, Rinehart & Winston, 1977.

Swan, G.E., & MacDonald, M.L. Behavior therapy in practice: A national survey of behavior therapists. *Behavior Therapy*, 1978, **9**, 799–807.

Tate, B.G., & Baroff, G.S. Aversive control of self-injurious behavior in a psychotic boy. *Behavior Research and Therapy*, 1966, **4**, 281–287.

Tavormina, J.B. Basic models of parent counseling: A critical issue. *Psychological Bulletin*, 1974, **81**, 827–835.

Tharp, R.G., & Wetzel, R.J. *Behavior modification in the natural environment*. New York: Academic Press, 1969.

Tukey, J.W. *Exploratory data analysis*. Reading, MA: Addison-Wesley, 1977.

Ulman, J.D., & Sulzer-Azaroff, B. Multielement baseline design in educational research. In E. Ramp & G. Semb (Eds.), *Behavior Analysis: Areas of research and applications*. Englewood Cliffs, NJ: Prentice-Hall, 1975.

Urbain, E.S., & Kendall, P.C. Review of social-cognitive problem-solving intervention with children. *Psychological Bulletin*, 1980, **88**, 109–143.

Van Houten, R., Hill, S., & Parsons, M. An analysis of a performance feedback system: The effects of timing and feedback, public posting, and praise upon academic performance and peer interaction. *Journal of Applied Behavior Analysis*, 1975, **8**, 449–457.

Wade, T.C., Baker, T.B., & Hartmann, D.P. The practice of behavior therapy. *The Behavior Therapist*, 1979, **2**, 3–6.

Wahler, R.G. Setting generality: Some specific and general effects of child behavior therapy. *Journal of Applied Behavior Analysis*, 1969, **2**, 239–246.

Wahler, R.G. The insular mother: Her problems in parent-child treatment. *Journal of Applied Behavior Analysis*, 1980, **13**, 207–219.

Wahler, R.G., Breland, R.M., & Coe, T.D. Generalization processes in child behavior change. In B. Lahey & A. Kazdin (Eds.), *Advances in clinical child psychology* (Vol. 2). New York: Plenum, 1979.

Wahler, R.G., Breland, R.M., Coe, T.D., & Leske, G. Social systems analysis: Implementing an alternative behavioral model. In A. Rogers-Warren & S.F. Warren (Eds.), *Ecological perspectives in behavior analysis*. Baltimore: University Park Press, 1977.

Wahler, R.G., & Fox, J.J. Setting events in applied behavior analysis: Toward a conceptual and methodological expansion. *Journal of Applied Behavior Analysis*, 1981, **14**, 327–338.

Walker, H.M., & Hops, H. Group and individual reinforcment contingencies in the modification of social withdrawal. In L.A. Hamerlynck, L. Handy, & E. Mash, (Eds.), *Behavior change: Methodology, concepts and practice*. Champaign, IL: Research Press, 1973.

Wallace, C.J., & Elder, J.P. Statistics to evaluate measurement accuracy and treatment effects in single-subject research designs. In M. Hersen, R.M. Eisler, & P.M. Miller (Eds.), *Progress in behavior modification* (Vol. 10). New York: Academic Press, 1980.

Wasik, B.H. The application of Premack's generalization on reinforcement to the management of classroom behavior. *Journal of Experimental Child Psychology*, 1970, **10**, 33–43.

Wasik, B.H., & Loven, M.D. Classroom observational data: Sources of inaccuracy and proposed solutions. *Behavioral Assessment*, 1980, **2**, 211–227.

Webb, E.J., Campbell, D.T., Schwartz, R.D., & Sechrest, L. *Unobtrusive measures: Nonreactive research in the social sciences*. Chicago: Rand McNally, 1966.

Webb, E.J., Campbell, D.T., Schwartz, R.D., Sechrest, L., & Grove, J.B. *Nonreactive measures in the social sciences* (2nd ed.). Boston: Houghton-Mifflin, 1981.

Webster, D.R., & Azrin, N.H. Required relaxation: A method of inhibiting agitative-disruptive behavior of retardates. *Behavior Research and Therapy*, 1973, **11**, 67–78.

Weick, K.E. Systematic observational methods. In G. Lindzey & E. Aronson (Eds.), *The handbook of social psychology* (Vol. 2, 2nd ed.). Menlo Park, CA: Addison-Wesley, 1968.

Weinrott, M.R., Reid, J.B., Bauske, B.W., & Brummett, B. Supplementing naturalistic observations with observer impressions. *Behavioral Assessment*, 1981, **3**, 151–159.

Wells, K.C., McMahon, R.J., Forehand, R., & Griest, D.L. Effect of a reliability observer on the frequency of positive parent behavior recorded during naturalistic parent-child instructions. *Journal of Behavioral Assessment*, 1980, **2**, 65–69.

Wexler, D.B. Token and taboo: Behavior modification, token economics, and the law. *California Law Review*, 1973, **61**, 81–109.

Whelan, P. *Reliability of human observers.* Unpublished doctoral dissertation, University of Utah, 1974.

White, G.D., Nielsen, G., & Johnson, S.M. Timeout duration and the suppression of deviant behavior in children. *Journal of Applied Behavior Analysis*, 1972, **5**, 111–120.

White, O.R. Data-based instruction: Evaluating educational progress. In J.D. Cone & R.P. Hawkins (Eds.), *Behavioral assessment: New directions in clinical psychology.* New York: Brunner/Mazel, 1977.

Wiggins, J.S. *Personality and prediction: Principles of personality assessment.* Reading, MA: Addison-Wesley, 1973.

Wildman, B.G., & Erickson, M.T. Methodological problems in behavioral observation. In J.D. Cone & R.P. Hawkins (Eds.), *Behavioral assessment: New directions in clinical psychology.* New York: Brunner/Mazel, 1977.

Williams, C.D. The elimination of tantrum behavior by extinction procedures. *Journal of Abnormal and Social Psychology*, 1959, **59**, 269.

Wilson, F.E., & Evans, I.M. The reliability of target-behavior selection in behavioral assessment. *Behavioral Assessment*, 1983, **5**, 15–32.

Wilson, G.T., & Evans, I.M. The therapist-client relationship in behavior therapy. In A.S. Gurman & A.M. Razin (Eds.), *The therapist's contribution to effective psychotherapy: An empirical approach.* New York: Pergamon Press, 1978.

Winett, R.A., & Winkler, R.C. Current behavior modification in the classroom: Be still, be quiet, be docile. *Journal of Applied Behavior Analysis*, 1972, **5**, 499–504.

Wolery, M., & Billingsley, F.F. The application of Revusky's $R_n$ test to slope and level changes. *Behavioral Assessment*, 1982, **4**, 93–103.

Wolf, M.M. Social validity: The case for subjective measurement or how applied behavior analysis is finding its heart. *Journal of Applied Behavior Analysis*, 1978, **11**, 203–214.

Woolfolk, R.L., & Woolfolk, A.E. Modifying the effects of the behavior modification label. *Behavior Therapy*, 1979, **10**, 575–578.

Woolfolk, A.E., Woolfolk, R.L., & Wilson, G.T. A rose by any other name: Labeling bias and attitudes toward behavior modification. *Journal of Consulting and Clinical Psychology*, 1977, **45**, 184–191.

Wright, H.F. Observational child study. In P. Mussen (Ed.), *Handbook of research methods in child development.* New York: Wiley, 1960.

Wright, H.F. *Recording and analyzing child behavior.* New York: Harper & Row, 1967.

Yarrow, M.R., Campbell, J.B., & Burton, R.V. *Child rearing.* San Francisco: Jossey-Bass, 1968.

Zegiob, L.E., Jenkins, J., Becker, J., & Bristow, A. Facial screening: Effects on appropriate and inappropriate behaviors. *Journal of Behavior Therapy and Experimental Psychiatry*, 1976, **7**, 355–-357.

# AUTHOR INDEX

# SUBJECT INDEX

# ABOUT THE AUTHORS

**Donna M. Gelfand** (Ph.D. Stanford University) is Professor of Psychology and Adjunct Professor of Family and Consumer Studies at the University of Utah. Her scholarly interests include the prevention of child behavior disorders, the development of prosocial behavior, and the interaction between child clinical and developmental psychology. She has served on the editorial boards of numerous journals including the *Journal of Consulting and Clinical Psychology*, the *Journal of Applied Behavior Analysis*, *Behavior Therapy*, and *Child Development*. Her previous books include the first edition of this volume, *Understanding Child Behavior Disorders* (with W. R. Jenson and C. J. Drew), and she edited two editions of *Social Learning in Childhood*.

**Donald P. Hartmann** (Ph.D. Stanford University) is Professor of Psychology and Adjunct Professor of Family and Consumer Studies at the University of Utah. His scholarly interests include child behavior therapy and assessment, the development of prosocial behavior, and design-statistics-methodology. He is editor of *Behavioral Assessment*, and has served as associate editor of *Behavior Therapy* and the *Journal of Applied Behavior Analysis*. His previous books include the first edition of this volume and *Using Observers to Study Behavior* (edited).